# OUR LOVE IS TOO GOOD
# TO FEEL SO BAD

**Also by Mira Kirshenbaum**

. . . . . . . . . . . . . . .

Too Good to Leave, Too Bad to Stay

Parent/Teen Breakthrough:
The Relationship Approach

# OUR LOVE IS TOO
# · GOOD ·
# TO FEEL SO BAD

A Step-by-Step Guide to
Identifying and Eliminating the
Love Killers in Your Relationship

## *Mira Kirshenbaum*

AVON BOOKS ◆ NEW YORK

AVON BOOKS
A division of
The Hearst Corporation
1350 Avenue of the Americas
New York, New York 10019

Copyright © 1998 by Mira Kirshenbaum
Interior design by Kellan Peck
Visit our website at **http://www.AvonBooks.com**
ISBN: 0-380-97608-0

Library of Congress Cataloging in Publication Data:

Kirshenbaum, Mira.
    Our love is too good to feel so bad : a step-by-step guide to identifying and eliminating
the love killers in your relationship / Mira Kirshenbaum.
        p.      cm.
        1. Man-woman relationships. 2. Interpersonal communication.
I. Title.
HQ801.K567   1998                                                        97-36407
646.7'8—dc21                                                                  CIP

First Avon Books Printing: April 1998

FIRST EDITION

QPM   10   9   8   7   6   5   4   3   2   1

To you, my reader. You have put your whole heart into trying to keep your love alive and healthy. And you have struggled so hard to try to understand *why* there are problems between you and your partner in spite of all the love you bring to your relationship. You deserve the best. I wrote this book to help you get it. It's caring like yours that keeps this world going.

# Acknowledgments

It's been a wonderful experience, researching and writing this book that answers the ultimate mystery of why love between two people gets sick and what can be done to bring it back to health. Like all wonderful experiences, this one has been the happy child of many, many fathers and mothers. There are so many people to thank that I almost don't know where to begin.

The first people to thank are the men and women, either patients or people whose lives I've followed, who've brought their lives and loves to me and let themselves be seen emotionally naked. They have known that sharing their lives would help other people, and for their courage, commitment, and honesty . . . well, it's not just me who will be eternally grateful. Everyone who will benefit from the revolutionary new understanding contained in this book also owes a tremendous debt of gratitude to the men and women whose relationships served as the laboratory that produced the new answers here.

Then I have to thank my constant collaborator, Dr. Charles Foster. Everything we do belongs to both of us and comes out of our joint efforts. It should be understood that Charles is as much the author of this book as I am. This book is a journey we've made together into the depth of love's truths, and it's wonderful to be able to say that with Charles this journey has been a labor of love.

I have a huge debt of gratitude to express to some of the best and brightest and most committed people in publishing in America today, the men and women at Avon. The support and understanding I've gotten there has been monumental. Let me begin by thanking Lou Aronica, who had the vision to take on this project in the first place and then has stayed on board doing everything possible to bring this book safely and triumphantly through the publishing process and into its final safe harbor: your hands.

Thanks to Mike Greenstein for his enthusiasm, savvy, and support, plus for being as nice to me as someone in his position could possibly be.

Thanks to Peter Schneider for being a true visionary, for knowing what's important, for knowing how to make things happen, and for being such a true-blue, long-time supporter. Thanks also to Joan Schulhafer, for her passion and energy, for knowing how to bring this book to the attention of absolutely everyone.

Chris Condry is as knowing and responsive as an editor could possibly be. I thank her for being someone who understands deeply what I'm trying to do with this book and why it's so important. Chris is someone I know I can rely on and look forward to relying on in the future.

Some fantastic publishing people at Avon I must also thank by name are Bill Wright, Tom Egner, Robin Davis-Gomez, Darlene DeLillo, Anne Marie Spagnuolo, Tom Dupree, Bruce Brill, Mary-Margaret Callahan, Constance Martin, Debby Tobias, Mark Maxwell, Lisa Rasmussen, and Saralyn Smith. And a special thanks to Christine Zika.

Howard Morhaim is just the best agent I could have. But I particularly have to thank him for making this book happen. Every book has one irreplaceable catalyst, and Howard's been that for this book. I couldn't be happier with him. And thanks to terrific Kate Hengerer for her all-important work.

This book would not have happened if it had not been for the incredible support I've gotten from people in the media for my previous book, *Too Good to Leave, Too Bad to Stay*. Radio and television talk-show hosts and producers, interviewers, journalists, and publicists—in America and throughout the world—

have been fantastically kind and generous, and I'm thankful for all the new friends I've made.

It's amazing what a debt of gratitude I owe my daughters, Rachel and Hannah. The sense of responsibility and caring we have for each other have been a powerful motivator for me. I've written this book for the whole world, but I've never forgotten for a moment that I've also written it for these two young women who mean the world to me, to help my own children save their love if it should ever be threatened.

There's no way I could have enough room to adequately name and thank all the colleagues and fellow professionals who have added a piece of knowledge and support to me and my work, and without whom this work would not have been possible. But some people I must thank by name here are Peter Breggin, Mihaly Csikszentmihalyi, Roger Fisher, Susan Greenfield, Rabbi Harold Kushner, Chloe Madanes, Pepper Schwartz, Robert Sternberg, Richard Stuart, and Paul Watzlawick.

If I roam around the depths of my feelings and try to figure out where I feel my gratitude most strongly, I'd have to focus on you, my readers, whose help and support have made this book possible. I thank you for your intelligent feedback and helpful comments, for the amazing stories you've given me, for your sincere desire to learn and grow, for your enthusiasm for what I'm trying to do, for the connection between us. You are the beginning and end of everything I do.

# Contents

# To My Reader

## If You Believe Your Love Is Too Good to Feel So Bad

It's one of the worst parts of having problems in your relationship, isn't it? The gut sense that love shouldn't be like this. The struggle that comes from trying to reconcile the depth of your love with the kinds of problems you've been having. Your world is upside down.

The feelings this churns up in you are intense. You're furious with your partner, and perhaps with yourself too. You're incredibly sad and disappointed. Most of all you're afraid, because we all know these days how the problems that spring up in relationships can easily kill love. Even when you're sure that yours is a love that would never die.

I'm here because I know it's realistic for you to feel hopeful, no matter how much time you've already spent working on your relationship. It's not love or good intentions that have been missing. What you've needed are answers. That's what this book provides. *It's not too late.* You may feel stuck now, but you're only one really good idea away from success. Once you discover exactly what's been causing your problems, your sense of confusion and helplessness will go away, and the love you've always known is there will come into full bloom again in all its health and strength and beauty.

# OUR LOVE IS TOO GOOD
# TO FEEL SO BAD

# Stop! In the Name of Love

## A Personal Introduction

It's time to put an end to feeling confused by what's going on with love in your life. What if there *are* problems in your relationship? Okay. Instead of feeling overwhelmed, let's find out exactly what's causing your problems, fix it, and get on with the business of being happy in love again. That's what we all want. That's what you'll get here.

I wrote this book because when your relationship is in trouble, you want to know why. Now, finally, you will know.

We're used to the idea of diagnosing the diseases that make our bodies feel bad, because that's the only way to know exactly what to do to make our bodies feel good again. In fact, you insist on a personalized diagnosis when you go to the doctor. Most of us would like custom-tailoring in every part of our lives—from our clothing to our kitchen cabinets to our financial plans. Don't you crave and deserve a personalized diagnosis and prescription when it comes to the problems that involve the love of your life?

This is the first book that will make it possible for you to diagnose the relationship diseases that are actually threatening the health and viability of your love. Now, finally, you will know exactly how to bring your relationship back to full health.

# Two Thousand Love Lessons

For twenty-five years now I've worked as a couples therapist, fighting alongside you in your battle to save your relationship. And I care about love now more than ever. I believe that at the end of the day, love is what matters most. No talent is more important than being able to love with your whole heart and all your smarts. No defeat is more gut wrenching than the loss of love. No accomplishment is more satisfying than keeping your love alive.

Sometimes, though, things go wrong with love. You're sure your relationship is too good to feel so bad, but somehow it gets sick anyway. It feels bad and functions poorly. And sometimes a relationship gets so sick it dies. Let's face it. It's easy for relationships to get sick these days, as you'll see, if only from the parts of our lives that stress us as individuals—overwork, worry, pressure, fatigue, and so on.

But if your relationship gets sick, what are the diseases it can come down with, and how do we cure them?

## Help at Last

It was people like you who helped me answer this. It can take one person a lifetime to learn just one true lesson about love. I've been lucky. I've intimately gotten to know and significantly touched the lives of over a thousand couples. That's two thousand people of every age, race, sexual orientation, and social and economic background. I've had this privilege because in addition to all the years I've devoted to helping people directly as a therapist, I've also spent the last fourteen years doing the research that led to this book.

I'll talk about this research later, but the essence of it is that we were trying to understand why some relationships live and others die. One thing I've learned is that there's nothing about who we are as people—not gender, not personal history, *nothing*—that dooms relationships to fall apart. You and I may be imperfect, but a lifetime of love is the way we humans mate—it's as natural to us as any form of mating is to any of God's creatures.

That's why it's so important to discover just what the potentially fatal relationship diseases really are, and over the years *men and women just like you have shown them to me.* Most important, you've shown me what works best to eliminate them, based on the hard-earned evidence of your own lives.

## What This Book Means for You

Whenever there's real trouble in your relationship, you just want to know what's causing it and how to make the trouble go away. Here's how one woman put it:

> NANCY: *"We just don't know how to make each other happy anymore. But I don't know what this unhappiness is about or where it's come from. It's like there's this lake of misery we've fallen into that we can't swim out of, even though we used to know how to swim. Why is this happening to us? Why?"*

Even though Nancy's racked her brains, ultimately it's a mystery to her where the problems in her relationship come from. Most of us are in the same boat.

Based on what everyday men and women report, here are the top ten relationship problems people find most mysterious:

### THE TOP TEN LOVE MYSTERIES

**1. Why can't we talk without fighting?** "I wish we could have one conversation that didn't end in an explosion. But if something's bothering me, or if I just want to know how Mike's day was, I say something, then he says something, and the next thing you know we're having a big fight.''

**2. Why can't we have more fun?** ''Jeez, we really used to have fun together, you know, go out and enjoy ourselves, or even just stay home. Well, I'd like us to have fun together again like that.''

**3. Why can't we feel closer?** ''When we were first together I felt Lisa and I were soulmates—we knew what the other was thinking. Now we're both so businesslike and busy I don't feel close to her at all.''

**4. Why can't we have more good sex?** ''Sex used to be okay, you know? Then it got lousy. You don't suddenly forget how to make scrambled eggs—why would we forget how to make love? We work at it, but it's become, like, a project. Now it never feels right.''

**5. Why can't we get our needs met?** ''He's always complaining, why can't I do this for him and why can't I be like that, and the fact is there are things *I* need I've given up on. We've both got to get more of what we want.''

**6. Why can't we feel appreciated?** '' 'You suck.' That's the message I get from morning until night. I don't need for her to kiss my ass or think I'm Superman, but I'd like to get a little of that gee-you're-terrific stuff I used to get all the time when we were first together.''

**7. Why can't we understand what makes the other tick?** ''This happens all the time. Yesterday he was happy, and the day before, but today we get up and it's a nice Saturday and suddenly I can't do anything right. And he says *he* can't figure *me* out.''

**8. Why doesn't it feel like love?** ''When we got married we promised we'd get a divorce if we ever stopped loving each other. But it's not that simple. I think we still love each other, but the way things are now we don't act like people who love each other. How did we go from *we love each other and it's easy* to *it's so hard for us to feel like we love each other?*"

**9. Why can't we stop hurting each other?** "I'm going to be honest with you. I don't want to hurt him, but I think he wants to hurt me. The thing is that either way, we say and do things that hurt each other, and we can't stop doing them. Why do we keep treating each other like crap?"

**10. Why can't we put the past behind us?** "Okay, I screwed up, I admit it. It's not like she hasn't done a lot of lousy things too. So are we going to fight about my 'crimes' forever?"

Now, finally, with *Our Love Is Too Good to Feel So Bad* you'll be able to solve these mysteries and put your finger on what the real problem is in your relationship. You'll be able to zero in on the one thing—not a million things—you need to do to eliminate the threat to your love. By pinpointing your real problem and the correct solution, here's what you'll get:

- You'll know how to counteract all the forces, from boredom to stress, that destroy respect and affection.
- You'll protect your love from the hassles and pressures of daily life.
- You'll be able to talk to each other like best friends again and feel as close to each other as you did when your relationship was at its best.
- You'll eliminate all the junk from the past that might have been polluting your relationship.
- You'll lose that awful sense that you just can't get your needs met.
- You'll be having sex again, or more sex, or better sex.
- You'll work out your differences.
- You'll know exactly what to do to make your love feel more alive.

And you'll be able to do all this without spending much more of the precious time that's in such short supply for most of us these days. Most of all, you'll be able to get help that fits your individual situation, based on your answers to carefully designed questions. Isn't it time you felt someone was really listening to you?

## Getting Help in Time

It's because we all believe in love that at least 40 percent of the 150 million American men and women currently in a relationship—that's 60 million people—say that they're trying to "work on" their relationship. But there's something wrong with all this "work": the divorce rate stays the same.

There's no shortage of wise friends or talented couples therapists in this country. What's been missing up until now is the ability to figure out what the real problem is and identify what works to solve it before it's too late. The evidence is that the divorce rate could be cut by four fifths if the diagnoses and prescriptions contained in this book were made available to everyone at the earliest possible moment. Instead of a 50 percent divorce rate, we'd have a 10 percent rate. And what a revolution that would create in our personal lives and in the social fabric of this country.

## Getting Back What Once Was Yours

So it's time you stopped feeling badly about your relationship. If it's worth saving at all—if indeed your love is too good to feel so bad—then *it was once healthy*. It was as healthy in relationship terms as the average twenty-year-old body is in physical terms. Not perfect, but quite healthy. You and your partner talked and laughed and listened. You did things with each other and for each other. You believed in each other and in your love.

Well, I have good news. Love *never* has to grow old, and it never has to die. All that happens to relationships is that they get sick as the latent germs of problems that might always have been there explode into a full-scale state of love trouble. It might start with a case of the love sniffles—the weekend where you felt there was some distance between you. Or you might first become aware of it when your relationship has the equivalent of a heart attack—a huge fight that comes out of nowhere and ends with one of you walking out of the house. But it's still just a disease that can be cured. And your relationship can become healthy again and can stay healthy for as long as you're alive.

I wasn't always so sure about this. In a sense I've spent my entire life looking for solutions to the problem of troubled love. As you'll see, this book celebrates the end of a long, fruitful journey for me. I hope it does for you too.

# A Love Story

Why do we care so much about love? We all care for the same reason: you need healthy love to have a healthy life. But each of us also has personal reasons for caring based on the lives we've led. You're entitled to know mine.

Let me tell you where my journey began.

My mother and father met when they were both trying to flee from the Nazis. I was born in Uzbekistan, in central Asia, at the end of World War II, after my parents had fled about as far east as they could go, almost to China. My parents had managed to survive the Holocaust and my father had managed to survive one of Stalin's Siberian labor camps as well.

After the war my parents smuggled us all, hidden in a hay wagon, back across Europe to an American Displaced Persons Camp in Germany. At every border crossing they'd had to hide in the straw and clasp a hand over my mouth to prevent my cries from being heard and risking all our lives.

For all their struggles and for what they accomplished just to keep their family alive, my parents were heroes. But it's not easy being heroes. The incredible stresses they went through broke the spirit of their love, and that's a way their story is connected to all of our life stories. One of the themes of this book is that a relationship is a living thing, as magical as, but no more magical than, any other living thing. And no living thing is so strong that it can't be killed by the real-life forces around it, if nothing is done to save it.

## A New Beginning

So my parents divorced. My father went to Israel with my half sister; my mother emigrated to America with me and my half brother, the child of her first marriage. She was safe, but her heart had been trampled on. Seeing the damage real life had done to my parents' ability to have love in their lives stamped into me forever the sense that love was something we need to take very seriously. I remember how I felt on the boat that took me to America. I was a little girl but I'd lost my father as so many people around me on that boat had lost loved ones and I remember feeling deeply struck by the sense that everyone deserves love. We're so hungry for it. Everyone deserves the help and understanding required to make love work in their lives.

We arrived in New York on October 1, 1949, as penniless immigrants. As the sole survivor of her family of nine brothers and sisters, my mother ended up on the Lower East Side of New York with no one to help her but some distant relatives. She worked incredibly hard in a dress factory to make a life for us. If you've ever been in a downtown factory district when the garment shops are letting out, and all the poor, mostly immigrant women are leaving after a day in the sweatshops, these women are my mother.

I was left alone while she worked, the way so many kids are today, and I had to take care of my brother when I still needed someone to take care of me. There are millions of us who've had this experience, and it does nothing to reduce our hunger for love. Under pressure the way so many of us are, there's just not enough time and energy for us to feel cared for.

## A Marriage of Necessity

Always practical like most women who are peasants, refugees, and immigrants, my mother's main goal had been to find a husband and a father for her two small children. Hitler and Stalin had destroyed every relationship she'd known and every one of her romantic illusions. I was almost seven when my mother married my stepfather. So like many of us, I had an experience that's sort of weird when you think about it: I saw my mother and her new husband fall into something that looked like love, get married, and then systematically, step by step, fall into hate.

I know she had plenty of reasons to stay married to my stepfather, but all I can remember now was their constant fighting. The way they were always screaming at each other. The Yiddish curses they used. It was an atmosphere of passionate, dramatic hatred. Paradoxically, they were able to work together to make their business a success, which put them ahead of a lot of marriages and made it hard for my mother to leave.

And there I was surviving their love troubles the way abuse victims survive, distancing myself from their fights by pretending it was theater, as if they were actors on a stage and I was in the audience watching their play. I wasn't abused myself, but I had to find a way to cope with their constant fighting.

## *Looking for Answers*

I coped the way we all cope with the difficulties of child-hood. I grew up. I promised myself I'd do better in my own life. I got married at nineteen, and I'm still married to the same guy, thirty-two years so far (and I'll tell you about some of the struggles we've gone through later).

I also promised myself I'd help others do better with love in their lives. Now you know why I became a couples therapist. I know from the inside how much help we need when it comes to love. It drives us crazy when things aren't going well in our relationship. It's bad enough that we're not getting along with our partner. It's even worse to feel that we're smart, loving people who can give good advice to friends, and yet we can't figure out why our own relationship hurts or how to make it better.

For twenty-five years I've been searching for answers to the mystery of what time and life and the complexities of the human personality do to love. I've been searching for a way to keep love alive and bring it back to full health. Now finally I've uncovered the real culprits. Once you know exactly what's been threatening your relationship, you'll know exactly what to do to save it. It's really a dream both of us have had, isn't it—finding a way to keep love alive. Now there's a way to make sure our dream comes true. I've written this book to show you how.

It would be wonderful if you would e-mail me at mirakirsh @aol.com to tell me how you used the prescriptions in this book to bring your relationship back to full health.

# How Deep Is Your Love?

## Why You Need to Diagnose
## the Potential Love Killer in Your Relationship

Here you are, a smart, savvy person who's worked hard to have a good relationship. What's scarier than finding that your hard work isn't paying off? Especially when you've put your whole heart into trying to make things better.

Well, you're not a fool. I believe that what you suspect is true: all the good stuff there ever was between you is still there. Buried, perhaps. Bruised, possibly. But it's alive and well. *You will get it back*, and the way to get it back is to diagnose exactly what's been causing all the trouble.

But make no mistake about it. Being baffled about what's wrong between you doesn't just feel bad—it can seriously damage your relationship.

### How Not Knowing What's Wrong Can Make Things Worse

When problems appear in our relationships, first we ignore them, then we try all the obvious solutions, from "talking things out'' to going on a romantic vacation. But we quickly run out of answers. Here's what three people have said to me recently:

- "My partner's been finding more and more fault with everything I do. I don't know why she's this way now—she used to be so nice to me. I try to do as much as I can, but nothing I do is good enough."
- "We used to like the same things but now we're on completely different wavelengths. We're polite about it but there's this huge angry gap between us. Now whenever anything comes up I *expect* we'll disagree, and I don't know where all this comes from or how to stop it."
- "How could it be that something went wrong with a love that once felt so right? He used to be my best friend; now we rarely get along. It just doesn't make any sense."

And when we run out of answers, we start believing our problems must be incredibly deep and complex. It's a basic psychological principle: When you don't know what's wrong, it seems as though *everything* is wrong. When my car has problems, I don't know why and so with every glitch I think, "That's it— the car's no good." If you feel sick and you don't know why, it's easy to think you've got something major wrong with you.

It works the same way with love. When you can't put your finger on precisely what's wrong, you think there's something wrong in every part of your relationship. And you know what happens to people who look for trouble? They find it. Soon it feels as though everything between you needs fixing. And if everything needs fixing . . . well, that's discouraging as hell.

## Hitting Bottom

Here's a story of two people like many of us. In an attempt to deal with the problems in their relationship they ended up so confused that it nearly destroyed their marriage.

## ⊃ *Helen and Phil*

The problem that first sent them looking for help was common and incredibly baffling: fights that seemed to come out of nowhere kept ruining their time together. Helen and Phil decided to go for help. In the two years before I saw them, a variety of therapists, books, and workshops had gotten them completely confused.

Take Helen. From saying something clear like "I wish we could stop fighting," Helen had reached the point where she was saying things like:

> HELEN: *"We have so many problems, I don't know where to begin. We speak different languages, which is why we can't talk to each other anymore. But even if we spoke the same language, we still can't negotiate. Phil really wants me to be his mother. But the thing is that every time he says no to me he reminds me of my father and of all my deprivation issues. In a weird way trying to grapple with Phil is a way I try to feed myself love, but the more we tangle with each other the hungrier I get for love. Phil represents power to me, the power I feel I lack, so in a way I must be collaborating in Phil's not giving me what I want. But that just enhances his power and makes Phil even more attractive because I have issues around disempowerment, and so I have a deep need to affiliate myself with a powerful person even if his power just ends up disempowering me."*

Whew. What a lot of . . . words. But aren't you *impressed?* Doesn't Helen sound *smart?* Look at all the *deep complicated issues* she talks about.

Let's get real. How smart are you really if slinging the bull does nothing to pinpoint your problem or help you solve it, but instead only digs you deeper into despair? Ultimately the trap people like Helen and Phil fall into is believing they can't solve problem A until they solve problem B, but they can't solve B until they solve C, and the thing is that they can't solve C because what about D, and on and on through endless alphabets of problems.

And so they start giving up. Why be nice to your partner when nothing good is going to happen anyway? Why risk telling the truth when things can't get better? Why not act selfish when you can't get what you need from your partner anymore? Because you don't know what's wrong, you end up feeling like your relationship is a piece of junk. And you know what we all do with junk. We start thinking of how to throw it away.

### Shooting the Rapids

So with all this confusion, we live in our relationship like people swept up in a raging torrent. There you are, whirled and tossed and spun, banged around, dunked, and threatened with drowning at every moment. And what do you do? What else *can* you do? You paddle like crazy. It's called working on the relationship. But if working on the relationship was what it took to heal love, we'd all be living in bliss.

Here are the facts. Of course no one's really average, but if you did fit the statistical average, I'd say that so far you've spent 163 hours working on your relationship with your partner, 194 hours talking about your relationship to friends, and 34 hours reading books and magazine articles about your relationship. And if you've sought professional help, you've put in *at least* 10 hours for about $100 a pop. Has all this work paid off for you?

### The Greatest Love of All

If you've lost something, why spend hours searching in the darkness if you could take a moment to turn on a light and see what's really there? When it comes to love, wouldn't you say that instead of working harder we all need to find a way to work smarter? I've now come to see that this is the greatest love of all: loving as a whole person, not just with your heart but with your head too, with all your knowledge and intelligence.

That's why blindly working on your relationship is not the answer. I know you're used to people in my position upholding the virtue of working on the relationship, the way dentists uphold the virtue of flossing after every meal. Work, work, work. Look, I know you can't ignore problems. But I know from my personal experience that at some point when you've spent too much time working and struggling and dealing without getting results, it's not just that you don't get anywhere, *it's that it doesn't feel like love.*

Well, enough of endless unproductive working on your relationship. You've already earned your A for effort. Now it's time for results.

## Using Your Head to Save Your Heart

What's been missing up until now is a way to zero in on the exact problem that's causing all the pain and damage in your relationship. If you know the right thing to focus on in your particular case, and the right thing to do about it, your relationship will get better faster.

This is something life teaches us every day: only when you know what the real problem is can you solve it. For example, I turn my TV on and nothing happens. Oh my God! What do I do!

I could panic, but a much better solution would be to find out what the problem is. Is my TV suffering from Not Being Plugged in Disease? Has a falling tree limb snapped the cable? Did I forget to pay the cable bill? Or is there something wrong with the guts of my set? And if the problem's in my TV's guts, the repairperson has to figure out what the problem is there.

So the journey that led to this project fourteen years ago began with the faith that once I knew what the real problems were, finding the solutions that worked and that everyday people could use on their own would be the easy part. And that's how things actually turned out. *This is a book of solutions.* I don't have to teach you how to love. All any of us need is to be shown how to eliminate the problem that's threatening us. We can take care of the rest.

## What Is a Love Killer?

But what exactly takes you from the place where you're in love and everything's great to the place you're in now, where you still love your partner but the relationship is a terrible disappointment and is threatened with real trouble? *What problems have the potential to kill relationships?* That's what a love killer is. It's not just a problem people have in relationships. It's a problem that can destroy your love.

Here are two people talking about their relationship problems. Which one, Susan or Jim, is threatened by a real love killer?

SUSAN: *"It all began when I found out he was using my money, which I'd saved up before we even met, for his business. He hadn't asked. It was like a lie, a betrayal, and a robbery all in one package. That was a while ago and the money's all paid back now—it's not like he actually robbed me—but when I think about it, the hurt's still there like a cracked tooth that hurts when you bite down on it."*

JIM: *"We never spend a minute with each other. For years we believed it was because we're so busy. Too busy to ever make love. Too busy to say I love you. The truth is we avoid each other like the plague. We love each other, but why do we avoid each other?"*

By the end of this book you'll know which one, Susan or Jim, is under attack from a love killer.

## But What Are the Real Love Killers?

Finding the real love killers was a big job. For one thing, *I had to distinguish between things that are a pain in the neck in a relationship and things that could kill it.* You could spend your whole life complaining about headaches and lower back pain and then, God forbid, drop dead at sixty-two from something you'd never complained about once in your life. In the same way, getting into a fight with your partner about the same issue every time it comes up might be annoying, but is it a potentially fatal relationship disease?

For another thing, *I had to disentangle the symptoms from the disease.* People often break up because one of them has an affair. That's a symptom all right, and maybe the affair did cause the breakup. *But what caused the affair?* We ask this kind of question in medicine all the time: someone's death was caused by a heart attack, but what caused the heart disease that led to the heart attack? A high-cholesterol diet? Then *that* was the real killer, not the heart attack that was the final result of the poor diet.

It doesn't make sense to devote our precious energy to anything but the problems that can actually kill love. But what are they? For a long time I didn't know the answer myself.

## Common Sense

As you'll see, common sense triumphs once again. Our relationships do not boil down to one neat little theory, any more than we can understand what's going on in our bodies by focusing on one "theory" that explains everything, unless we want to get caught up in a fad. Our bodies, our relationships, most of the world are just too multidimensional for that.

I know this is true because you've told me it's true. Ellen captures this instinctive reluctance we have to pin all our problems on one explanation:

ELLEN: *"I never really believed that all of our problems came from our speaking two 'different languages' and if we could just 'translate' everything would be perfect. We spoke different languages when we fell in love, and things were perfect then. But I didn't know where else to get hope than to grab on to that one explanation."*

Now you can see why I got involved in hands-on research where I could plunge into the realities of regular people's lives. Why should I have a theory about what causes problems when I could make things real by discovering what was actually responsible for the problems we experience in our relationships?

### New Research, New Answers

As people who know my books have come to expect, everything you'll find here is based on research. For fourteen years, at The Chestnut Hill Institute under the research direction of Dr. Charles Foster, we followed the course of love in the lives of normal men and women, people like you, unhappy because something wasn't working well in their relationships.

By the end of the study period, it turned out that everyone we'd been talking to fell into one of two groups.

**When love died.** For one group of people, their relationship died. But we'd learned enough along the way to be able to conduct relationship "post-mortems" to determine exactly what killed them. Out of all the problems these people complained about and all the troublesome things we saw going on in their relationships, we wanted to know what were the real love killers.

To make a long story short, it turns out that there are ten

relationship diseases that threaten the health and happiness of our relationships.

If things aren't going well in *your* relationship right now, it's most likely that one of these ten love killers is responsible for all your unhappiness and frustration.

**When love stayed alive.** The second group consisted of relationships that stayed healthy. But guess what? In most of the relationships in the second group, the very same love killers also made an appearance. But instead of turning deadly, these potential love killers were eliminated by something the people did. So we conducted what's called "active ingredient" research to determine exactly what these people did that enabled them to overcome the very same problems that had killed love in the first group.

By seeing what regular people did on their own to eliminate the potential love killers threatening their relationships, we were able to develop the help you'll find here: a specific prescription for dealing with the specific problem that's been making your whole relationship feel lousy.

As a result, the help you'll get is a lot easier and a lot more effective than anything you've used before.

Instead of wasting your time and energy trying to solve many problems, you'll be able to focus your time and energy on solving the one problem that's been preventing your relationship from being healthy.

## Why You Should Feel Hopeful

Someone once said to me, "Ooohhh . . . *Love Killers!* That sounds like a horror movie. I'm being attacked by a *Love Killer!*"

Please don't get all shook up by the words *love killer*. I'm not talking about Godzilla here. Think of a love killer as the equivalent of a curable disease, perhaps a condition like pneumonia. Pneumonia can kill you if left untreated. But if properly treated, it can easily and reliably be cured. Timely diagnosis is 90 percent of the battle. That's the kind of love killer we'll deal with here. The kind that will kill your love if you don't do anything about it—that's the scary part. The kind you can eliminate easily if you diagnose it *before* it kills your love—that's the hopeful part.

There's a good chance that you're taking action in plenty of time. You've still got a long way to go before the love disease that's threatening your relationship passes the point of no return. But proper diagnosis is your only hope. What good are all your skills—and you're probably already a lot more skilled than you think—if you don't have the proper diagnosis?

## Why You Should Feel Good About Yourself

The analogy between love killers and physical diseases takes us even further. When someone gets sick, you blame the disease, not the patient. This is great for your relationship, because by diagnosing a potential love killer you can stop blaming each other. Any disease can have a kind of mindless agenda of its own. Cancer cells or infectious organisms proceed under their own steam. In the same way, there's something about the love killers that gives them their own momentum. But *a love killer is not part of who you are and doesn't represent anything that's part of your agenda or your partner's.*

On the contrary, in spite of your problems you deserve to feel good about yourself and your relationship. Too many people in trouble don't care enough to seek out this kind of help. Here's a fact:

If you're reading this book, that alone puts you in the top half of all couples.

I'm not telling you this to make you feel good. Regardless of the number of problems you have in your relationship—if you're right here, right now, that means that the foundation of your love is still strong and healthy. Yes, your relationship got sick. But it can recover and feel wonderful again.

## Where Do the Love Killers Come From?

What causes relationship diseases? How does it happen that two more-or-less sane, intelligent adults with life experience who have fallen in love with each other and who start out with a healthy relationship end up being threatened by a love killer?

The answer is surprisingly understandable. When you and your partner fell in love you recognized all kinds of ways the two of you were similar: you liked the same music, for example; you had similar opinions about people; you shared goals and values for your lives. You seemed compatible. You felt like soulmates. But there were also some ways in which you were different. Little differences. Ignorable differences. Seemingly unimportant differences.

But if some stress is added to your lives, it can cause these differences to start taking over and overwhelm your basic compatibility. Like the classic pinch in the shoe that you can't feel until you go for a long walk, or like the cold virus that sleeps in your body until stress and fatigue destroy your body's ability to keep that virus in check, ultimately your sense of how different you are can reach the point where you feel you have nothing in common.

> Relationship diseases come from the way the stresses and circumstances of your life can cause your sense of difference to escalate and ultimately make you feel you don't belong together.

Every love killer blows whatever differences there are between you all out of proportion, even though your basic underlying compatibility still exists.

Now you can see why it's been so hard for people to identify the true relationship killers. When a relationship gets sick, we all experience the *symptoms* of the disease, not the *cause*. These symptoms all too often have to do with the horrible sense of incompatibility, of poor fit. That's why we have the feeling that "it's all over" when our relationship gets in trouble, because these huge differences are shoved in our faces. But it's the ten love killers in this book that are the real underlying causes, and they can all be cured. When they are, your painful sense of incompatibility will go away.

### Real Life, Real Love

Let me underline what was perhaps the most shocking part of discovering where the love killers come from: there's a huge environmental component to most relationship diseases, just the way there is for cancer and heart disease. The difficulties and pressures we live with each day can aggravate our sense of difference. Either we feel so stressed that we can't resolve our differences, or we don't have the time we need to work out the problems that come up between us. It's this pressure from everyday life that opens the door to each and every one of the love killers.

> CHRIS: *"Okay, so we come home late from work and it's like, let's see how long it takes before things blow up, and maybe it's just five minutes or maybe we're lucky and it's a whole hour, but then bang! Something starts us off and we're fighting and we'll usually just keep on fighting and go to bed mad. Where did all this anger come from?"*

We don't live on the Love Boat. Maybe we wish we did, but we don't. As real flesh-and-blood people today we have too much on our plates. We work too hard. We have too much stress. Once things like work and children, time constraints, and money problems enter the picture, we all become simultaneously needier and more self-absorbed. We want more and can give less. And our partners are the same way. We live in a love economy of scarcity. And the sense of difference, of incompatibility, grows and grows.

Work on your relationship? If as a kid you ever tried to dig a hole to China—I know I tried several times—well, that's how most of us feel about the time and energy we put into working on our relationships. We can't afford it. It doesn't do what it's supposed to do. And it doesn't feel like love.

Fortunately, you now have a much better alternative.

## *Having Confidence in the Prescriptions*

For every love killer, I'll lay out for you a simple, easy-to-use prescription that will eliminate it. To find these prescriptions, I ransacked the research and clinical literature and talked to colleagues and ordinary men and women to uncover the best of what was already available, the things people did on their own that worked in the context of their everyday lives. That means all these prescriptions came pre-tested. Then I tested them again in a clinical setting to make certain that they really did cure the love killers, and that people could use them on their own.

Then I made sure these prescriptions could solve your problems in the context of your daily life. The prescriptions don't take much time. Most of them take no more than five or ten minutes a day. In many cases they take no time at all: you do things differently, but you don't do more things. None of us can afford to spend more time working on our relationship. So I've worked to make sure you have as little to do as possible and still get the full benefit from each prescription.

I wish I'd had these prescriptions years ago in my own relationship. I know what it's like from the inside to spend so much time working blindly on a relationship that you almost destroy it.

## My Life, My Love

The events of my childhood made me promise myself that if nothing else I'd have love in my own life. Have I succeeded? Good question, and you deserve an answer. I know that if any therapist said she could help me, I'd probably be wondering, "Yeah, but how many times has *she* gotten divorced?"

Well, here goes. As you know, I fell in love and got married while a crazy teen. Then, what's even crazier and more wonderful, I've stayed married to the same guy. Talk about your long journeys! In one marriage I've traveled from the romantic idealism of adolescence to the hopeful realism of middle age. I can still look at my husband's face and see the boy he used to be when we first met. When that happens I remember the impossible dreams youth has for love. Then, depending on how things are going that day, I experience how far I've drifted from my dreams or how close I still am to them. As you'll see, I wasn't always sure we'd make it.

### Sticking with It

If I'd gone through the process of getting divorced and remarrying, I'd have learned a lot. But that didn't happen. Whatever lessons I've learned in my own life have come from hanging in there when the going got tough.

When we were still kids ourselves we had two small children, no money, and days filled with work, anxiety, and stress. We'd often work in shifts so that one of us was always able to be with the kids. That's not good for love, but I hung in there.

Then when feminism got hot in the early seventies and I was struck by the chauvinist pig–like aspects of my husband, I hung in there to depork him. He'd now have to deal with an assertive woman . . . well, I was always pretty assertive, to tell the truth, but now I was more aware of being entitled to want the things I wanted and more insistent on getting them.

And a bit later when our busy lives caused us to drift apart, I hung in there. I sensed what we now know is a fact: everyday life can be a threat to love, but it doesn't mean anything's fundamentally wrong with your love.

And when sex started to get boring, I hung in there. I knew we'd have to find new ways to make each other happy.

But has a lifetime of learning about love helped me accomplish more in my own life than just being able to say I've been married for a long time?

### I Wish I'd Had What You're Holding in Your Hands

I'm not an easy person to live with: often I'm too intense, too emotional, too absorbed in what I'm doing. And my husband's a nice guy, but he gets impatient, he likes things his way, and at times he acts remote.

So it's only by using everything we've learned that my husband and I have made a satisfying life together. The things we share are deeper and richer than when we were kids. We're still each other's best friend. And here we are, both on the wrong side of fifty, and we're still hot for each other. My twentysomething daughters say we have a great marriage, but I'm sure they're each looking forward to having an even better one.

Let's be honest with each other. How can you beat that time when everything's new, and everything wonderful is happening for the first time, and you're busy naming each other's body parts? Today, when the pressure gets to us, we still step on each other's toes and get into fights.

So I know what the pain feels like when you're confused and overwhelmed by the problems between you and your partner. And I know what it feels like to be afraid of losing the good things in your relationship. After thirty-two years of "working on" my marriage, I wish I'd had years ago what you have now, this book you're holding in your hands. It would have saved me a lot of pain and confusion.

# How to Use This Book

My model "people helper" is this guy on the radio on Sunday mornings who talks to people about their gardening problems. "My rhododendron is drooping," a caller will say. This gardening guy is great. He doesn't tell people what to do right away, because he doesn't know. How can anyone prescribe without first arriving at a diagnosis? So he asks questions: "Have you been overwatering?" "Are there tiny white bugs on the underside of the leaves?" "How much sun does your plant get?"

Questions like these, plus the caller's answers, allow this gardening guy to diagnose what's wrong with that drooping rhododendron. After all, rhododendrons droop for all kinds of reasons. You don't treat the drooping; you treat the specific reason for the drooping. When you know why that rhododendron's drooping, you know exactly what to do to make it healthy again.

That's exactly how this book will help your relationship.

A question I'm often asked is whether you can use the material here on your own. You can. Of course the ideal situation is when you *and* your partner recognize your love is too good to feel so bad and you're both willing to discover what's necessary to bring your relationship back to full health. So I hope you and your partner will use this book together. But I know from long experience that it's often only one person in a relationship who's willing to get help or even admit there's a problem. So I designed everything you'll find in this book so, yes, it will deliver results that last if you're working on your own.

## Your Diagnosis

There are only ten love killers. I'll devote a chapter to each. In each chapter I'll talk about what that particular love killer is, where it comes from, and how it hurts relationships. And you'll meet people who've been struggling with the same issues you've been struggling with.

Then, like that gardening guy, I'll ask you a set of easy-to-answer yes-or-no questions—you don't need to know more about your relationship than what you can see with your own eyes and feel with your own heart. Your answers will show you immediately whether that particular love killer is threatening your relationship.

## Your Prescription

If that particular love killer *is* diagnosed, then . . . well, then you have to keep reading in that chapter to discover precisely what to do to eliminate it. The prescriptions that immediately follow each diagnosis are the heart of this book. They will tell you exactly what to do step by step to eliminate the diseases that have the potential to destroy your relationship.

Think of the prescriptions here just as you would a prescription you'd get from your doctor. All you have to do is follow the step-by-step instructions and the prescription will work its magic. You don't have to do anything beyond following the prescription.

You should be aware it may take days or weeks before you start to feel the full benefits of the prescriptions—something we're used to from medical prescriptions. Just be a little patient. Anyway, most people are surprised at how quickly their relationship starts feeling good again. Most important, once things start getting better between you, you'll find you've hopped on to the upward slope of the learning curve and your sense that things are getting better should pick up pace.

By the way, even though some of the prescriptions may take a little while to take effect, I worked hard to design them so that they don't take much of your precious time to actually put them into effect. Every prescription here had to live up to my "love shouldn't feel like work" guideline.

Then there's the issue of side effects, which we all know can be important when it comes to medical prescriptions. There should be none here. The prescriptions for eliminating the love killers have been tested to make sure they're trouble free.

## Your Relationship's Immune System

There's something that's part of who you are as individuals and as a couple that's always working to help you heal your relationship, just like your body's immune system. For each love killer there's a corresponding *love builder*, and you'll discover what it is and how it works.

The prescriptions here will help you eliminate the love killers, but in fact, just as with the body, you don't have to kill the love killer directly, any more than when you get whooping cough you have to search out and kill every *Bordetella pertussis* bacteria in your body. The prescriptions here will stimulate the love builders, and when your relationship's immune system gets its act going, it does the inside work for you.

And that's the book in a nutshell.

## A New Beginning

This moment marks a turning point in your life. No more working so hard on your relationship and having little to show for it. No more feeling baffled about what's causing your difficulties. You want love. You deserve love. You have the foundations for love. All you need is to answer some questions and then follow the prescription that's right for you. It should feel easier and more productive than anything you've done so far to heal your relationship.

In a sense, you're reclaiming your dreams. When a relationship functions properly there's no power struggle, there's no sense of deep inequality, there are no important needs that are aching to be met. There's a sense of being at home with each other. A troubled relationship drains your energy. A healthy relationship gives you energy. It's a place where you feel comfortable and alive with each other and at peace with yourself.

## A Note on the Order of the Love Killers

If you went to the doctor complaining of a stomachache, she'd have in the back of her mind a rough, experience-tested order to determine which diseases she'd check you out for first. For example, it's probable that she'd first check out whether the diagnosis was that you ate something that didn't agree with you before she checked out whether the correct diagnosis was that you had ulcers.

It's a basic rule of diagnostics: when you hear hoofbeats, think horses, not zebras. Out of all the things that *might* be going wrong, first see if you can diagnose the most common problems or the ones that are easiest to treat. That's why when your car breaks down and you call the auto club, for example, the first thing they check is whether you've run out of gas.

It works the same way with diagnosing which specific love killer may be threatening your relationship. The order in which the love killers are presented here is determined by what research and clinical experience show will work best and fastest on your behalf. You and I both want the same thing: to get to the heart of what's hurting your love as fast as possible and to cure it as expeditiously as possible.

Now you will appreciate why I put the following love killer first. When you combine how common it is with how easy it is to treat and how completely your relationship will improve if you treat it, there's every reason in the world to consider it before any other.

# · 2 ·

# Giving You the Best That I've Got

. . . . . . . . . . . . . . . . . . . . . . . . . . . . . . . . . . . . . . . . . . . . . . . . . . . . . . .

LOVE KILLER #1:
## Letting Essential Maintenance Slide

ISSUE:
Have you forgotten to do the essential things
you have to do to keep your love healthy?

There are places in the world where people die because they can't do the basic things we take for granted to maintain good health. Drinking enough clean water. Washing. Getting enough vitamins and protein.

Essential maintenance. It's what most of us remember to do most of the time when it comes to our bodies. It's what far too many of us *don't* do when it comes to our relationships. How tragic it is for love to die simply because you've lost sight of the basics. Or because you don't realize what the basics really are.

This first potential love killer seems so benign, so mundane, so easy to fall into, so easy to get out of that it almost doesn't feel right to call it a love killer, except for one fact. *Letting essential maintenance slide kills more relationships than any other love killer.* As you'll see, in my own relationship *this* is the love killer we were suffering from.

What's great is that it's incredibly easy to cure. You don't have to do anything new. You just have to do things you've done before.

The news here is that up until now no one has identified the dos and don'ts essential to maintaining love. Doing them, or not doing them, has been largely haphazard and unconscious. When the honeymoon is over and your energies get more taken up with daily life, you and I let essential relationship maintenance slide without thinking twice about it.

It's time we all understood and accepted that none of us is immune to this love killer. None of us is too smart to fall victim to it. None of us was ever so much in love that we can let essential maintenance slide. The next couple make this clear.

## ○ *Cathy and Will*

If any couple had a right to take each other for granted it was Cathy and Will. The beginning of their relationship was like a fairy tale. They met on the first day of their Peace Corp assignments in Kenya. In case you're not familiar with Kenya, its hills have one of the world's great climates and some of the most beautiful landscapes. It was close to paradise.

Cathy had training as an architect and Will had a bachelors in structural engineering. Theoretically they were supposed to go to Kenya to help the locals design and build housing out of native materials. Unfortunately—or *very* fortunately, depending on your perspective—they quickly ran into a buzz saw of local political problems that had one huge impact on Cathy's and Will's lives. It meant that they had little to do but wait, fall more and more deeply in love with each other, and roam around idyllic surroundings with some of the nicest people on the planet.

During this time they did absolutely all the things a couple should do to nail down their relationship. They spent hours and hours together getting to know each other extremely well. They opened their hearts and minds to each other without secrets and without hiding their true selves. They sang songs and made up stories. They had little adventures. In one Will saved Cathy's life by chasing away a hyena that started to attack her. In another adventure Cathy took care of Will when he came down with some strange stomach ailment far from their base camp.

**"Let's Put the Love Stuff on Hold."** They knew each other so well and had tested each other so thoroughly and had proven their love for each other so profoundly, that when they came back to the States, they felt ready for anything. They were eager to take on life, get married, have a child, launch careers, the whole nine yards.

Now get this. They felt they had such a solid footing that they actually planned a five-year period in which they would take each other for granted. They actually said (and I'm using Cathy's words), "Look, we've got so much going for us, we've spent so much time together, and we've gotten so close, we can put the love stuff on hold while we launch ourselves. It's not like anything bad could happen to a love like ours."

In this respect Cathy and Will were unusual. They actually made a decision to let love slide. For the rest of us, it just happens.

Three years later they had a child, jobs, a house, expenses. Nothing unusually stressful, just normal life. Here's what they were saying:

WILL: *"I know I'm not all that nice to Cathy now but she understands because we love each other so much and we know each other so well. She knows that this is just how I'm responding while I'm focusing on getting my career launched."*

CATHY: *"I get so frustrated sometimes with all the balls I'm trying to juggle—sometimes I have to let off steam and I let loose with all this pent-up anger and frustration, and I guess*

*a lot of it's directed at Will. But he understands because he
really knows me and cares about me. I think he knows I
love him even when I'm acting mean."*

What was a love like theirs for, they said, if you couldn't
take it for granted when you had to, even if you "had to" for a
long time?

But here's what happens. When you keep putting out poison
because you think your relationship can take it, at some point
you enter a new nightmarish state in which you see that the
only thing you can really take for granted now is all that poison.

Here's a bit of what Cathy said to me after she'd awakened
to the nightmare their relationship had become.

CATHY: *"We're just not affectionate anymore. It's not the
bad stuff—I'm sort of used to that now—but the lack of
good stuff that bothers me. Our relationship is like one of
those people who walk around feeling healthy but there's
some deadly cancer growing inside and it just hasn't reached
the point where you'd actually notice anything. When people
look at us all they see is our incredible politeness. But it's
just coldness; we're on our best behavior. It's like we're polite
to honor a memory of the love we used to have. But where's
our love now? I love him, and he says he loves me, but it
just doesn't feel like love anymore."*

That's where letting essential maintenance slide can take you.

Scientists call this *entropy*. You and I call this taking each
other for granted. Which anniversary are people more likely to
forget, their first or their eighth? You guessed right. People are
*twenty-three times* more likely to forget their eighth anniversary
than their first. And just think of all the other things we forget.
This means that as time goes by you get lazy. But whatever
we call it, when essential maintenance slides too far, it can kill
our love.

## *You're Okay, Baby*

If this is the only love killer threatening your relationship, I'm relieved. I can say to you the same words that make me happy when my doctor says them to me: *"There's nothing really wrong with you."*

And I mean it. Anyone can forget to do the basic things that will keep your relationship healthy, particularly since few of us were conscious of what they were in the first place. It doesn't say anything about you that you've forgotten to do them. You just have to remember to do them now.

Even when people have been struggling and fighting and getting stuck in misery and despair, you'd be surprised how often this simple diagnosis turns out to be the most correct one. You know from experience: sometimes when you feel lousy it doesn't mean there's anything really wrong with you. A bad headache, the flu, a pulled muscle—just go to bed and take care of yourself. All you need is a little basic care.

Here are two people in two different relationships who were convinced there was something deeply wrong. But when they understood what was required for essential maintenance, *their problems disappeared.*

GAIL: *"This goes on constantly, but let's just take one scene at random. We're having dinner. Theoretically we could be using our intelligence to talk about something interesting. But what made me think we were in trouble was my sister noticed that all that ever went on between us was constant little put-downs. There's no wit. There's no passion. All we do is zing each other and nit-pick. You can just feel our unhappiness."*

BOB: *"This money thing is like a dagger sticking into the heart of our relationship. We've both been married before, we're not kids, and we've each come into this with our own money, bills, expenses, income. And all we do is fight about dividing things down the middle so we both seem incredibly selfish and suspicious to each other. It's poisoning our relationship.''*

Most of us, men and women alike, started learning about relationships back in junior high school. By the time the average adult gets married, she or he knows more about relationships than about almost anything else. The sad part—but maybe, in a way, it's really the hopeful part—is that Bob and Gail, you, and I *already did* the things we needed to do to maintain a healthy relationship, which means that on some level, deep down, we *already know* what to do to eliminate this love killer.

## The Dos and Don'ts of Love

The dos and don'ts essential for maintaining a healthy relationship are an important research finding. It's not that any particular do or don't is all that earth shattering. In fact they should seem familiar to you.

What is new and important is that these dos and don'ts are the total of what everyday people have found works best to keep a relationship on track and prevent it from getting into trouble. So let's zip through the dos and don'ts that are the absolute foundation for a healthy relationship. Put on your seat belt. You're in for a fast ride.

### THE TOP TEN DOS FOR
### MAINTAINING A GREAT RELATIONSHIP

**1. Show how much you appreciate each other.** Show your respect and desire your partner. This includes being appreciative in your words and in your actions, doing and saying little things that say, "I think you're great and I love you." *Do this at least once every time you interact.*

**2. Touch more.** That means more affection, more hugs, more kisses, more sex, more foot massages, more hand-holding, more physical contact of every kind. *Do this at least once a day.*

**3. Say what you need.** Tell your partner what's bothering you, what you'd like more of or less of, to prevent problems from building up. Do it before it bursts out in a mean, angry way. *Do this whenever necessary.*

**4. Listen to each other.** We all need to feel we're heard and understood. When your partner talks, show you've listened and understood before you respond. Ask what your partner needs you to do to feel you've listened to her. *Do this whenever you talk to each other.*

**5. Be supportive.** Be each other's best fans. Praise each other's good qualities and encourage each other's projects and desires. Then do real things to help each other. Don't just support with words: make food, rub shoulders, put kids to bed, help with paperwork. *Do this whenever possible.*

**6. Spend time together.** There's a time for being busy and a time for being by yourself, but you have to put in a solid amount of time with each other to keep your relationship healthy. *Do this once a day for at least ten minutes.*

**7. Have fun with each other.** Do the things you did when you were first together that you both enjoyed. Keep nurturing shared activities and interests. *Do this once a week.*

**8. Make sure things are balanced and fair between you in your life together.** Keep on the lookout for one of you having less than her share of the good stuff or more than her share of the bad stuff. *Think about this at least once a month. Correct any imbalance or unfairness as quickly as possible.*

**9. Try to put yourself in your partner's shoes.** See things from her perspective. Always try to understand how she feels about you and why. *Do this every time a problem comes up between you.*

**10. Be open with each other.** Make your partner feel the two of you are intimate by opening a window to your heart and mind. Don't ever make him guess what you're thinking or feeling. *Do this at least twice a week.*

I've added it up, and doing all the dos should add no more than fifteen minutes a day to your busy schedule. Then think of all the time you'll save by not doing the don'ts. Here are the top ten things you *should not* do.

### THE TOP TEN DON'TS FOR MAINTAINING A GREAT RELATIONSHIP

**1. Don't lie or keep secrets from each other.** Lies and secrets create an atmosphere of distance and mistrust. (By the way, saying, "If you loved me, you'd know how I feel," is just another way of keeping secrets. If you love your partner, *just say* how you feel.)

**2. Don't put each other down.** An atmosphere of criticism and complaint destroys love, no matter how good your intentions.

**3. Don't shirk your responsibilities or shift them onto your partner.** Assume that 60 percent of your relationship and 60 percent of your lives together is your responsibility.

**4. Don't act miserable or gloomy.** Nothing says "get away from me" louder than negativity. And you can't excuse yourself by calling this "being real" or "being myself." Whatever you call it, it's putting sand in the motor of your relationship.

**5. Don't spend too little time together.** Every minute you spend really concentrating on each other is like putting money in your love bank.

**6. Don't have fights that go nowhere in which you say nasty things to each other.** Fighting is normal. But the real hidden purpose in fights is to bring out new information and create a basis for solving problems. Fights are not about assigning blame. And they're not about going over and over the same material you've beaten to death before.

**7. Don't try to control each other.** Being bossy, giving orders, and micromanaging each other kills warmth.

**8. Don't act like you don't trust your partner.** If you've got problems, solve them. But acting paranoid or treating your partner like a child is never justified.

**9. Don't do things to hurt each other, like cheating, abuse, undermining the other's attempts to reach her goals.** I'm talking about real damage here. It takes relationships years to recover from this stuff.

**10. Don't hold on to any of the ways you've been hurt.** Hurts need time to heal. But holding on to a hurt turns a wound into an infection.

See? You know a lot already, and the things you know are really important. Basic things such as appreciating each other, opening up to each other, not lying, not being selfish are the DNA out of which healthy, vital relationships are made.

Remember we talked about love's mysteries? Now you've just solved one. Now you know the first reason why relationships die even though nothing seems to have killed them. It was just this stealthy love killer. It's not that you aren't good people. It's that you didn't know exactly what to do to prevent your love from getting sick.

## A Little Gets You a Lot

It's a funny thing about smart, knowledgeable people. We're the first to think that the Essential Dos and Don'ts for maintaining a great relationship are beneath us.

Let me speak for myself. As you'll see when I tell you about some of the difficulties I got into in my marriage, the easiest thing for me was to think that I was too smart for these dos and don'ts to apply to me, if they would've occurred to me in the first place at that point in my development. Be appreciative? That's too simpleminded, I'd have thought. We can't solve our problems by just appreciating each other. *If somebody like me—a couples therapist—is having trouble in her relationship, there must be something deep, complicated, and important causing that trouble.* That's what I used to think.

Smart people do this all the time. A friend of mine who's a brilliant internist kept looking up rare diseases to determine why she was tired all the time. The real issue never occurred to her: *She needed more sleep.*

We're not too stupid for love. We're too smart to give essential maintenance the respect it deserves. But here are the facts. For at least 27 percent of couples who say they have struggled and failed to solve the problems in their relationship, understanding what's required for essential maintenance is all they need to make things better.

And I'll let you in on a nice surprise. If it turns out that you have this love killer, the prescription will be as easy as writing down a few things on a piece of paper and then putting it where you can see it every day.

# Diagnostic #1: Is Entropy Damaging Your Relationship?

We all let things slide from time to time and we could all do better when it comes to essential maintenance, but that doesn't mean you're afflicted by this love killer. Here's how to diagnose whether neglecting essential maintenance has started to damage your relationship.

## DIAGNOSING LOVE KILLER #1

Read the following seven statements and ask yourself if, *yes*, "This applies to me" or, *no*, "This does not apply to me":

1. "I'm tired of working on this relationship." YES___ NO___

2. "I spend more time feeling deprived in this relationship than I spend feeling how much I care about my partner."
   YES___ NO___

3. "Most of the time when we talk there's an undercurrent of anger." YES___ NO ___

4. "It's been a long time since I really asked myself if there's anything my partner might be needing from me."
   YES___ NO___

5. "We're more like roommates than lovers in the sense that too much of the time when we could connect we try to stay out of each other's way." YES___ NO___

6. "It's been a long time since I did something nice for my partner." YES___ NO___

7. "I feel I keep waiting for my partner to make things better between us." YES___ NO___

## How to Score Your Answers

If you checked off Yes *two or more times*, this love killer is at work. Entropy, taking each other for granted, habit, inertia, and frankly sheer ignorance have been forcing you to forget essential maintenance and are damaging your relationship.

If you checked off Yes "only" once, Love Killer #1 probably isn't damaging your relationship right now, but you really owe it to yourself to follow Prescription #1 anyway, because this disease can eventually kill your relationship.

If you didn't check off Yes even once, there are two possibilities: either you're doing a great job of keeping your relationship well maintained, or you're kidding yourself. Some people do kid themselves, you know. And you don't want your relationship to fall apart because you thought you were doing a good job when you really weren't. So if you didn't check off Yes even once, ask your partner to answer these diagnostic questions too. If she doesn't check off a single Yes either, you can feel confident that you're doing a good job when it comes to essential maintenance.

Remember: even if you're *not* diagnosed with Love Killer #1, you can still feel free to follow the prescription. It won't hurt you. It doesn't take much time. It can only make things better.

# Prescription #1:
# Follow Your Custom-Tailored Program
# for Essential Maintenance

The way to eliminate this love killer, and all the love killers, is to follow a specific, targeted prescription my research has proven will work to destroy it. You focus *only* on the love killer that's putting you at risk and *only* on the prescription for eliminating that love killer. It may feel as though everything is wrong with your relationship, but you'll probably only have to heal that one part of it. If you follow the prescription for eliminating whatever love killer you're diagnosed with, most of the things you thought were wrong with your relationship will get better by themselves.

## *How to Follow the Program*

The key is that you need to find out exactly which dos and don'ts you've fallen down on *most*. Take the first item on the list of dos. Probably you know you should be appreciative of each other. But maybe you've forgotten something like actually *being* appreciative of each other. Well, there you go. If that's your problem, you've saved yourself a visit to the therapist.

The lists of dos and don'ts themselves are most effective for custom tailoring a prescription for you. For each list, check off the *three* dos you feel you've been neglecting most and the *three* dos you feel your partner has been neglecting most.

## ESSENTIAL DOS

1. Show how much you appreciate each other.

> I've been neglecting this \_\_\_\_
> My partner's been neglecting this \_\_\_\_

2. Touch more.

> I've been neglecting this \_\_\_\_
> My partner's been neglecting this \_\_\_\_

3. Say what you need.

> I've been neglecting this \_\_\_\_
> My partner's been neglecting this \_\_\_\_

4. Listen to each other.

> I've been neglecting this \_\_\_\_
> My partner's been neglecting this \_\_\_\_

5. Be supportive.

> I've been neglecting this \_\_\_\_
> My partner's been neglecting this \_\_\_\_

6. Spend time together.

I've been neglecting this ___
My partner's been neglecting this ___

7. Have fun with each other.

I've been neglecting this ___
My partner's been neglecting this ___

8. Make sure things are balanced and fair between you in your lives.

I've been neglecting this ___
My partner's been neglecting this ___

9. Try to put yourself in your partner's shoes.

I've been neglecting this ___
My partner's been neglecting this ___

10. Be open with each other.

I've been neglecting this ___
My partner's been neglecting this ___

Now please check off the *three* don'ts you feel you've been violating most and the *three* don'ts you feel your partner has been violating most:

## ESSENTIAL DON'TS

1. Don't lie or keep secrets from each other.

I've been violating this ___
My partner's been violating this ___

2. Don't put each other down.

I've been violating this ___
My partner's been violating this ___

3. Don't shirk your responsibilities or shift them onto your
   partner.

   I've been violating this ___
   My partner's been violating this ___

4. Don't complain or act miserable or be gloomy.

   I've been violating this ___
   My partner's been violating this ___

5. Don't spend too little time together.

   I've been violating this ___
   My partner's been violating this ___

6. Don't have fights in which you say bad things to each other.

   I've been violating this ___
   My partner's been violating this ___

7. Don't try to control each other.

   I've been violating this ___
   My partner's been violating this ___

8. Don't act like you don't trust your partner.

   I've been violating this ___
   My partner's been violating this ___

9. Don't do things to hurt each other, like cheating, abuse,
   undermining the other's attempts to reach her goals.

   I've been violating this ___
   My partner's been violating this ___

10. Don't hold on to any of the ways you've been hurt.

    I've been violating this ___
    My partner's been violating this ___

## Follow Your Prescription

The prescription couldn't be simpler. You now know the three dos you've been neglecting most and the three don'ts you've been violating most. Your partner knows the same thing. Well, guess what?

Out of an overwhelming universe of possible things you should be doing to maintain your relationship in the pink of health, you've narrowed it all down to three basic things you need to do more of and three basic things you need to remember to stop doing.

This should be a relief. You are the proud owner of the most precious thing in the world: a relationship based on love. No one who owns anything precious—from a violinist with a Stradivarius to an astronomer with a telescope—ever fails to benefit from remembering to attend to essential maintenance. You've gone even further: now you know precisely *which* essentials you need to return to.

Whatever dos or don'ts you've been neglecting or violating, get going with them right now. Be organized about this. Here's what to do:

- Write down on a piece of paper *your* list of neglected or violated items of essential maintenance.
- Write down on another piece of paper *your partner's* list of neglected or violated items.
- Put both lists on the refrigerator or on your bathroom mirror or wherever you'll both see them every day.
- Make an agreement that if one of you sees the other falling down on one of his or her essentials, you'll simply point it out.
- When you point out a lapse to your partner, simply say,

"Honey, that was an example of number three [or what-ever] on your list." No nagging, no complaining, no blaming, because that itself is an Essential Don't.

Be *proud* of your lists. They're not a sign of failure. They're a sign of commitment, a sign that you're holding tight to the *most* essential piece of maintenance: a commitment to making your relationship healthy.

Let me sum up what this prescription is all about. It's about *highlighting* instead of *hiding* some basic weakness in your relationship, and doing so in a spirit of mutual support and cooperation. Never forget: because this is *essential* maintenance you don't have to learn to do anything. You already know how. You just have to remember to do these things more often and to remind each other gently if you forget.

## How I Forgot to Maintain My Own Relationship

If the story I'm about to tell you shows anything, it shows how important it is to remember essential maintenance and to keep doing loving things.

Turn the calendar back to a rare, cool summer evening in Manhattan, 1965. That's when I met my husband. We were both in college. I didn't like him at first because I thought he was a know-it-all. Somewhere in the next couple of days, though, we'd fallen in love. He *was* a know-it-all, but he was sweet and kind and funny and he was *my* know-it-all. I felt he respected me. Amazingly, because it was the last thing either of us would've predicted, a few months later we got married. Two crazy teenagers. Today, thirty-two years later, we're still crazy kids, still in love. We're just not teenagers anymore.

But we almost blew it. It was about nineteen years ago when my husband sat me down one Sunday afternoon and told me he was involved with another woman. He said they hadn't slept together. It was more like they were friends but he was very attracted to her, he said. He was telling me this because he'd suddenly gotten very afraid that we could lose each other.

His involvement with this woman hurt me deeply, and it still hurts a little when I think about it today, but I have to take responsibility for what I did to get us into that situation.


## Over the Top

I was a hot young therapist nineteen years ago. My head was filled with all the theories and techniques I was reading about and teaching other therapists. My marriage was my guinea pig. Talk about working on the relationship! I was actually proud of my attempts to bring "working on the relationship" to a whole new level. Forget "essential maintenance." If it wasn't advanced and deep, I wasn't interested in it.

Everything that went wrong between us, everything my poor husband did that was less than perfectly "functional" meant it was time to call out the troops. I remember getting upset once because he wasn't sitting still when I had something very important to say. He wasn't *not* listening, he was just fidgeting, and to me that meant he wasn't listening completely.

And of course the more he fidgeted, the more I wanted to talk about why he was fidgeting and the meaning it had for our relationship, and the more I "worked on" the issue of his fidgeting, the more he fidgeted and the bigger the issue grew.

Today I'm ashamed to say this, but we'd spend hours and hours at a stretch fighting and analyzing what we were doing and what to do about it. Really listening to each other *is* an item of essential maintenance. But we got completely tangled up in all kinds of side issues that had nothing to do with what was necessary to keep our love healthy.

## Stuck in Summer School

What I didn't see then was that working hard and working smart are two entirely different things when it comes to love. Working on your relationship is not like chopping wood. Chop, chop, chop, sweat and blisters, and eventually you've got a pile of firewood. No! Working on your relationship should be like cutting a diamond. Intelligence, experience, a careful diagnosis, one strategic tap with your hammer, and *ping!* you've turned a stone into a gem.

With my husband and me, every hour we spent turning our relationship into an out-of-control do-it-yourself project made love feel more like a chore and made my husband think I was only interested in criticizing him. It must've been like being married to a mental-health Nazi.

We fell into the same trap so many of us fall into. The more we worked on our relationship, the more we felt we *needed* to work on it.

## Love Hypochondria

That's when the relationship stopped feeling like love. That's when we were hungry to fall in love again, to start fresh, to enter that blissful state where you keep discovering new things about the other and keep being appreciated for the things the other discovers about you.

The sweet joy of acceptance is the major theme that runs through the symphony we call falling in love. You may have seen *Leaving Las Vegas*. How could a depressing movie like that be so well liked? Because beyond the self-destruction, it was a love story in which the theme of acceptance was powerfully highlighted. A nightmare in every other way, it opened a window onto a paradise of mutual acceptance.

Test this for yourself. Think about your favorite love story. Isn't one of its main ingredients something about acceptance?

Think about the last time you fell in love. Didn't the other person make you feel especially accepted for who you are?

At some point, struggling over your relationship does little more than loudly proclaim, "I don't accept you anymore, not the way you are." That's why my husband got involved with another woman. Of course he let himself get into this dangerous situation, but I'd made finding someone who'd accept him the most attractive thing in the world to him. It was his fault, and it was my fault, too.

We'd been trapped in a kind of *love hypochondria*. What is that? It's making a huge deal out of every sniffle in your relationship, turning every tiny dissatisfaction into a gigantic health scare. Love hypochondria is the opposite of what you and I are talking about here: focusing on the real threats and learning how to cure them.

### Love Makes You Do Foolish Things

Eventually I realized that love had made me stupid. I decided to get smart. I realized that our relationship didn't need me to run around like a crazy person. It needed me to do in my own marriage what I was doing more and more in my work with couples: *find out exactly what was making people sick, then cure that*.

So I made it clear to my husband that I'd kill him if he got involved with anyone, I went through my period of being upset, and I took a new turn in my journey to understand love's mysteries. I started down what was then only a barely marked trail that I've now turned into a superhighway: identifying and eliminating the love killers.

I'm ashamed to confess that for all my attempts to probe the depths of our relationship, the only disease we were actually suffering from was an advanced case of neglecting essential maintenance. How do I know? *When we remembered to do the Essential Dos again and stopped doing the Essential Don'ts, we got better.*

Specifically, I focused on being less critical, more affectionate, more appreciative. Besides, what could I lose?

### Relaxing

Soon we were *having* a relationship again instead of working on our relationship. When I relaxed, my husband relaxed. When my husband relaxed, he was a nicer, more pleasant, more fun person to be with. When he treated me better, I treated him better. We felt more compatible, less split apart by differences.

I remember the evening I realized that we'd finally climbed out of that deep hole we'd dug for ourselves.

We'd gone out for dinner and my husband spent the entire meal telling me the dishy details he'd picked up on a trip to the West Coast about Marilyn Monroe living with her psychiatrist and his family, and Judy Garland having all these uppers and downers prescribed for her by her psychiatrist. Our dinner conversation was the perfect mixture of gossip and shop talk. Fascinating on every level. I think that's where we all want to end up, having fun evenings like that.

That kind of activity made all the difference. You'll see why right now.

# Love Builder #1:
## Loving Feelings Follow Loving Actions

You have a whole series of inner resources right now that I call the *love builders*. There's nothing mystical about these love builders. They're just strengths and capacities that have evolved over time to help you function as a human being, and you're filled with them. If you cut your finger, there are a whole variety of forces within your bloodstream that automatically rush to the breach and begin repairing the walls, whether you want them to or not. You can help them (say by applying a bandage) or hinder them (say by picking at your wound) but they will keep trying to work for your benefit.

The love builders do the same kind of thing. They're strengths you already have that automatically work to repair breaches in the walls of love. You can see their effects in the simple things you had going for you when you were first together, like the desire you both had *and still have* to thrive as a couple, like the way you felt connected to each other *and still feel connected*, like the way it hurt you if your partner was in pain *and still hurts you*.

Now let's look at the specific love builder that comes into play to help you overcome Love Killer #1.

### *Making Love Happen*

Barbara, a woman who finally succeeded in making her second marriage work, said something that I think is very wise:

BARBARA: *"Inside us there's a box containing feelings of love. You know the box is there, so you figure the feelings are there. It's because you know the box is there that you say you love your partner. But to actually feel the feelings, some button has to be pressed to release them. Either you or your partner has to do something to bring out the love feelings that are in there. If you don't, your feelings don't just sit there, they eventually die. You can't just point to the box and say you love each other. You have to open the box and take stuff out of it."*

*If you do loving things, they'll release your partner's loving feelings, and they'll release your own loving feelings as well.* It's been proven a million times, in my research and in that of others, and it's incredibly important.

> The couples whose loving relationships we most admire don't sit around congratulating themselves on having huge reserves of loving feelings that no one sees or understands. They *do* loving things for each other, and then their *feelings* of love flow by themselves.

................................................

You know what I'm talking about. Of course you do. That's what essential maintenance is all about. It's not a list of things you should feel. It's a list of things you should do. Suppose you want to be in a party mood. Which will work best: sitting alone in your room trying to will yourself to be in a party mood or calling up people to come over and have a party? It works the same way with this love builder.

But suppose you want some extra help. Well, you're in luck. It just so happens that I've been talking to a lot of people about what you can do to get back some of those loving feelings fast. Here are some fascinating, useful suggestions people tell me they like best:

## THE TOP TEN FAVORITE THINGS TO DO TO REKINDLE FEELINGS OF LOVE FAST

**1.** Look in your partner's eyes and tell her how much you love her. If she says, "Well if you love me so much why do you . . ." say, "Because I take you for granted. You deserve better and I'll try to change."

**2.** Remind your partner about something romantic or special that happened the day you met.

**3.** Instead of kissing your partner on the lips, plant kisses all over his face.

**4.** Think about something you and your partner have been fighting over and tell her how she's been right and you've been wrong. Tell her what you're going to do differently.

5. Write your partner a one-page letter in which you list three or seven or ten reasons why she's special.

6. Remind your partner about something she said a while back that you thought was really smart.

7. The next time you start making love, before you get too heavily into the sex part spend time telling your partner how much you love her.

8. Tell your partner you look forward to the two of you spending all your years growing old together.

9. Slow dance in your living room or bedroom to music that's meaningful to you.

10. Do something the two of you did together at the beginning of your relationship that made you both happy.

But, hey, it's not for me to tell you how to generate loving feelings. You're the expert. Just ask yourself what you and your partner did when your relationship was at its best that gave you that special sense of being in love with each other. Do that again, as often as possible.

## A Special Love Tool

Here's the first of a series of Special Love Tools that will appear throughout this book. We noticed that successful couples used these tools to keep their love healthy, and you can use them too. I'll introduce one of these tools to you whenever I think you'll find it helpful.

One thing you probably did when your relationship was at its best is so important it deserves to be singled out. I call this particular Special Love Tool *Getting to yes*. To use it, you just talk about things the two of you agree about. It's as simple as that.

I know you may feel as if you and your partner are fighting about everything right now, but any relationship worthy of your commitment has huge areas of agreement you just haven't been tapping into recently (because you've been so busy emphasizing your differences). If you talk about something you know the two of you agree about, then you'll get to hear each other say, "Me too. I feel the same way," and then things between you will feel just a little bit more like being in love again. You can do this right now, even if the two of you are in a bad place at the moment.

## Love Is a Living Thing

Okay, you fell in love with your partner. But once you fall in love with someone, love is not a fact you can just forget about. You will not keep feeling love no matter what your partner does and no matter what you do. We get misled about this situation all the time because when we fall in love we say things like, "I'll always love you no matter what."

But anyone out of high school knows that commitment, no matter how deep, is a living thing. Living things can be nurtured and nourished. Living things can be killed. The mystery of love is the mystery of all living things: how resilient it can be and how fragile it is, all at the same time.

Because love is a living thing, it's dangerous to think of it as a kind of ol' man river that just keeps rollin' along. When you take love for granted, you're acting as though the feelings of love that are so important to you will always be there for you to tap into whenever you want them. But now you understand that if you want more love, you must do more loving things. That's what essential maintenance is all about.

## A Look Ahead

You might be surprised at the next love killer. It's simple, but it's potentially deadly—the love equivalent of a poisonous snakebite. The peculiar toxin in this love killer makes relationships so painful to be in that it robs you of your desire even to try to solve your problems. It's so important to eliminate this love killer, and this love killer is so easy to cure, that it would be a shame not to get it out of the way as soon as possible.

## · 3 ·

# Don't Say Nothin' Bad About My Baby

. . . . . . . . . . . . . . . . . . . . . . . . . . . . . . . . . . . . . . . . . . . . . . . . . . .

### LOVE KILLER #2:
### Making Your Partner Feel Small

#### ISSUE:
Has your relationship been poisoned by
destructive criticisms, put-downs, and
negative labels?

Sometimes nothing hurts more than a couple of words. And how easily it can happen that a couple of words will cut you down and make you feel like a nothing.

We all do it. The process of making your partner feel small takes place in the thousand and one ways we cut each other down once the honeymoon is over. I'm talking about a lot more than name-calling and digs. Saying "You bitch" or "You bastard" is the least important part of this love killer.

The most important part is the way words and names become labels, and the way labels serve to cut your partner into little pieces. Just the way the road to hell is paved with good intentions, here are some of the ways we make the people we love feel small:

- We say mean things in the guise of "having our feelings." ("I must've been crazy to think I was in love with someone so stupid.")

- We make our partners feel small because we're "just saying what's real." ("I'll never have nice things with the money you make as a teacher.")
- We "analyze" why our partners do the things they do. ("I don't think your mother paid enough attention to you when you were a kid.")
- We offer amateur psychiatric diagnoses in our attempt to "wake up" our partners. ("You know, only a psychopath would be so out of touch with his feelings.")
- We give "helpful" feedback. ("When you get to the party don't tell any jokes because you're not funny.")
- We say things we "don't really mean." ("You always fail at everything you do.")

As you can see, this is a game for smart people. The smarter you are, the more convincing a job you can do at making the person you love feel small. The labels you apply are more believable. They slip more easily under the other's skin. And the things that get under your skin can kill you.

We all know that it's bad to create an atmosphere of criticism and negativity, to call people names and put them down. There's nothing new about that.

What's new is that this is *such* a deadly love killer, that we have to determine whether it's afflicting your relationship before we can go on to do anything else. And it's also new to realize all the endless, subtle and indirect ways we cut the people we love down to size, even when we think we're helping them, even when we think we're being brilliant.

## Hidden Dangers

Of all the love killers my research uncovered, this is the one I least expected. Of course I knew it was bad to say rotten things to the person you love, but I didn't realize how *easy* it is to say rotten things when you think you're saying smart or helpful things. And I never realized how enormously destructive this was to every thread in the fabric of your relationship.

Do you remember how the movie *Jaws* changed how you felt about swimming in the ocean? Did you ever go into the ocean after seeing *Jaws* and suddenly feel afraid that there were sharks in the water? That's how it feels in too many relationships.

> TINA: *"Let me tell you how I destroyed a perfectly good relationship. I fell for stuff people were putting out about how a good relationship was a place where you let it all hang out. You know, you just say anything, whatever's on your mind. So we'd say horrible things and then add, 'Hey, I'm just being honest,' and blame the other if he couldn't take it. It wouldn't have been so bad if we'd just said things like, 'You're just a big fat pooh-pooh head,' just name-calling. But we thought we were sophisticated psychologically, so in the guise of being natural and open, we'd dish out these professional-sounding diagnoses. He convinced me that I was paranoid, and I convinced him he was suffering from all these personality disorders. But what did 'say anything' get me? I never felt any better, it didn't help me get my needs met, and I turned my best friend into my enemy. I'm never going to do that again. My next relationship—I'll ask for what I want, and I'll tell him what I don't like, but I'll never call him names, and I won't let him do it to me either, and I don't care if the mental health police come along and lock me up for 'not being honest.' "*

Here's the most dangerous part of this love killer. The smarter you are, the easier it is to fall victim to it. Like Tina, we call it being free and open and honest. We think we're using sophisticated psychological labels and explanations. We say we're trying to help our partners, to teach them lessons, to hold up a mirror so that they'll see who they really are.

But let's call it what it really is, *making your partner feel small.*

Words have a way of taking on a power or reality of their own, which is ultimately just a way of using them to make the people we love look sad, defective, emotionally shrunken.

We're doing what you'd have to say is the opposite of love. If you did the same kind of thing with a stick to a puppy, someone would call the ASPCA on you.

Of course you don't have a stick. But just think about how often in our lives a boss puts us down or someone we're dealing with in a bureaucracy makes us feel small. Too often we feel limited by our jobs. Everyone's ego is covered with black and blue marks, so when your partner throws a label at you that makes you feel small, it hits a psychological spot that's already tender and vulnerable.

## How This Love Killer Starts

When you get an infection, there has to be an entry point. A cut maybe. Inhaling infected air someone has exhaled. Well, what are the entry points for making your partner feel small?

## ○ Beverly and Zack

Beverly supervised all the cosmetics counters at the downtown branch of an upscale department store. She was a decent, hard-working woman married to Zack, a decent hard-working guy who was head of a technical support department for a major computer manufacturer.

Do you remember what it was like to fall in love? Well, with Beverly and Zack, the more they got to know each other, at first anyway, the more they liked what they saw. That's what falling in love feels like.

But after they reached a certain point, Beverly and Zack started noticing things they didn't like about each other. This happens to most couples, and maybe it's happening to you.

Maybe you see more of the things you don't like because as the relationship develops your partner has started feeling safer, more relaxed, less interested in monitoring himself, more willing to let his flaws show. Maybe you saw the flaws all along but maybe *you're* feeling safer, more comfortable attacking those flaws.

## When Anger Drives You to Make Your Partner Feel Small

Beverly and Zack started by calling each other names when they got angry. That's one entry point: anger. It would begin when Beverly wouldn't do something they'd talked about. After all, she was busy, so she'd forget to pick up the dry cleaning. She'd forget to tell Zack that her mother was coming to visit. Zack would say that he was tired of how she never initiated sex and she'd promise that she'd initiate the next time, but then she'd forget to do it.

There's a big difference between expressing anger and being infected by this love killer. There are two things that turn everyday anger into a love killer:

1. **Negative labeling.** When Beverly forgot things, Zack did more than get angry. If he'd just expressed his anger he might've said, "I'm pissed off at you," or "I can't stand this." But what turned it into a love killer was that he went on to say things like, "You're completely irresponsible," and "You always expect your father to take care of you." He'd found a label that turned Beverly into the "thing" he believed made her do what she did.

2. **Making the label stick.** We've all seen movies like *An Officer and a Gentleman* where the tough drill sergeant calls recruits all kinds of horrible names. The reason this is much less destructive than some of the labeling that goes on in relationships is that training is a relatively brief transition period. Several weeks later in their new status as full-fledged marines or fighter pilots, the

names they were called as recruits will fade into nothingness. But in a marriage, we never graduate and our status never changes. The longer we use labels, the more the labels stick.

But anger is not the only entry point for this relationship killer.

## When Helplessness Drives You to Make Your Partner Feel Small

Too much of the time in our relationships we feel helpless. Almost every person I've ever talked to who's made his partner feel small, when he's gotten a chance to open up, has used a version of the words Zack used: "But I just don't know how to get her to . . ." How to get her to *what?* Just supply any of the things you're trying to get your partner to do.

In frustration, we often turn to negative labeling to try to get our partners to do what we want. The incorrect theory we all subscribe to is that if you throw a label at someone—"You're such a loser" or "Why are you always so depressed?" or "You're just a computerized robot"—it will somehow wake him up.

This was what your parents were hoping would happen when you were a kid and they called you lazy. The idea was that hearing that label *lazy* would wake you up and make you sit up straight and force a kind of instant conversion. The seven-year-old you would smack herself on the forehead and say, "My God, I hadn't realized that what I was doing was being lazy! That's horrible! I don't want anyone to think I'm lazy! I'll change my behavior immediately." Instant diligence would set in. But it just doesn't work that way.

So out of our anger and helplessness, we make our partners feel small. There it is. The way lovers turn the people they love into people they hate.

## *How This Love Killer Happens Every Day*

The worst label Zack hung on Beverly, the most devastating way he cut her down to size, was his use of the word *silly*. Great poets couldn't have wrung more varied and powerful uses of this word than Zack did. Beverly would make a little suggestion about something. "That's silly," Zack would say. That was from earlier in their relationship. Later he would say things like, "Don't be silly," when Beverly would suggest that he might need help organizing their finances.

Almost any time Beverly tried to figure out why something was happening and offered her thoughts to Zack, he would call it silly. Still later in their relationship he'd confront her directly and say, "Why are you so silly?" After years of paving the way for this, he started telling her how she was an incredibly silly person. That's the essence of making your partner feel small: it doesn't just come from a label applied to something a person does—it comes from a label applied to the essence of that person.

## *Why This Love Killer Hurts Your Love*

Okay, so you apply all kinds of negative labels to each other out of your anger and helplessness. So what? Let me use an analogy to show you why this love killer causes so much damage. I have a cat, Tippy. She's safe in my house. I'm sure she feels it's *her* home. But suppose a dog got into our house. Out of fear, Tippy would hide from the dog. As he sniffed her out, he'd chase her from one hiding place to another. Eventually, if she were cornered, she'd fight.

Hiding and fighting. That's what animals do when they don't feel safe. *That's what people do when they don't feel safe. And that's what happens when we start cutting each other down to size.*

## Hiding

The labels, the criticisms, the put-downs that hurt—you can avoid them by hiding from your partner. Every minute the two of you stay away from each other is a minute in which your legs won't be cut out from under you.

You can also avoid being cut down by hiding who you are and what you do from your partner. How do you think Beverly dealt with Zack calling her silly? She'd never tell him what she was doing. At first she stopped sharing her plans with him. For example, instead of talking to him about buying new shrubbery for their house, she just went out and bought it.

But this cutting down never stops by itself, so the need to hide never stops. Beverly went further. She not only kept her plans from him, but whenever possible she wouldn't let him know how she was carrying out her plans. When she got sick with some kind of stomach problem, for example, she dealt with it completely on her own. Zack never even knew about her illness and he never knew about the treatment.

And that's one way this love killer turns lovers into strangers.

## Fighting

We not only hide, we fight. I don't have to catalog for you all the ways people in relationships fight with each other. A particular feature of the desperate fighting that goes along with making your partner feel small is the way labels escalate. Zack called Beverly silly? Fine. Beverly would call Zack sick. Then Zack would say, "I must be sick to be with you."

We're just protecting ourselves. We understand that sticks and stones *and names* can really hurt you. But it's a question of finding the right name.

## ○ *Martin and Elaine*

Martin hurtfully put Elaine down for twelve years and she kept fighting back, searching for a thermonuclear word to block Martin's words, and then she found it. Martin had just made some comment about her breasts looking like pancakes. Elaine said, "You put me down because you're an even bigger failure than your father was."

Ka-BOOM! Now she'd really hurt him back, hurt him badly. But all this caused was more fear and anger in their relationship. Yes, he was a little more careful about tossing off a casual put-down. But he was looking harder for his own thermonuclear put-down. Arms races always escalate.

## *Looking for Comfort*

After all the being hurt and hiding and fighting, we desperately need comfort, and we'll look for it anywhere we can get it. An incredibly high portion of the self destructive behaviors that ultimately destroy love—booze, affairs, compulsive shopping, overeating—grow out of our need to find shelter when we live in an unhappy atmosphere. You see why making your partner feel small is so monstrously destructive: it's psychological stress of the worst kind.

It's time to diagnose whether this love killer is present in your relationship. But we have to be careful. Some kind of negative labeling and name-calling goes on in almost every relationship. You can't call something a disease if everyone's got it. Exactly where do you draw the line?

# Diagnostic #2:
# Is One of You Making the Other Feel Small?

The challenge here is identifying the minority of cases where a true love killer has taken hold. I've always found that the best way to get what you want is to ask for it. So I asked couples and clinicians when they first became aware that negative labeling had become a serious problem for a relationship. Thanks to some wonderful input from people who've lived with this problem, I'm confident that the following questions do a good job of diagnosing when you've crossed the line from mild, occasional criticism to really cutting your partner down.

To diagnose definitively whether this love killer is afflicting your relationship ask yourself the following questions. The first group of diagnostic questions looks at whether *you* have been made to feel small.

## DIAGNOSING LOVE KILLER #2: PART ONE

Please answer each question *yes* or *no*:

1. Can you recite from memory phrases and expressions your partner has used to put you down?       YES____ NO____

2. Is your partner unwilling or unable to stop putting you down even though you've asked her to cut it out? YES____ NO____

3. Do you have an overwhelming sense that the ways your partner labels you aren't fair and don't really apply to you in any important way?       YES____ NO____

4. Do you avoid your partner in any way because of these put-downs?       YES____ NO____

5. Do you have fights where your partner tells you what's wrong with you and you try to convince him that what's wrong with him is even worse?                    YES____ NO____

### How to Score Your Answers

If you answered with a clear, heartfelt Yes to *two or more* of these questions, this love killer has afflicted your relationship. Even if you're not aware of your relationship being in serious trouble now, this problem can kill your love if you don't eliminate it. I'll show you exactly what to do in a moment.

But we're not done diagnosing yet. When it comes to this love killer, maybe you're not the person on the receiving end. Maybe you're the one who's dishing it out.

To determine that, the best thing to do right now is to ask your partner to answer the five questions you've just answered. But if you can't do that, answer the following five questions the way *you think* your partner would answer them. Please try to be objective.

### DIAGNOSING LOVE KILLER #2: PART TWO

Please answer each question *yes* or *no*:

1. Would you guess that your partner can recite from memory phrases and expressions you've used to put her down?
                    YES____ NO____

2. Are you unwilling or unable to stop putting your partner down even though she's asked you to stop?  YES____ NO____

3. Does your partner have an overwhelming sense that the ways you label her aren't fair and don't really apply to her in any important way?                    YES____ NO____

4. Does your partner avoid you in any way because of these put-downs?                              YES___ NO___

5. Do you have fights where you tell your partner what's wrong with her and she tries to convince you that what's wrong with you is even worse?                      YES___ NO___

. . . . . . . . . . . . . . . . . . . . . . . . . . . . . . . . . . . . . . . . . . . . . . . . . . . . . .

The scoring is the same here. If you answered Yes to *two or more* of these questions, then this love killer is threatening your relationship. It could kill your relationship if you do nothing about it, but it's easily treatable if you follow the prescription I've found works best.

## Needing Help

Let me describe in detail what will happen if you don't eliminate this love killer. Its effect on your relationship is very much like crack addiction. Let me explain by showing you what happened to Beverly and Zack.

Remember Zack had been calling Beverly silly, probably because he couldn't get his needs met and he was angry and he couldn't think of anything better to do. Then just the way it is with crack, Zack eventually stopped feeling that his using the word *silly* was as effective as it used to be, because Beverly became simultaneously angrier and more indifferent. Harder to control. So like any drug user chasing that high, Zack had to find more powerful and dramatic ways to let Beverly know how he saw her. By the end of their relationship, Zack was running around telling everyone who'd listen that Beverly was stupid, crazy, and "a nothing."

Just before they'd reached that point, in a desperate effort to make sense of what was happening, Beverly had gone into therapy half-convinced that she was somehow defective. She'd certainly swallowed a lot of the self-hatred Zack had fed her.

The therapist helped Beverly, because by the time their marriage ended, most of her anger was focused on Zack. This was good in one sense, because it was better than focusing it on herself. But they had two children, and those two children were victimized by their parents' mutual rage and contempt.

Every time you see a couple embroiled in postdivorce bitterness, suspect a marriage that was killed in part by this love killer.

# Prescription #2:
# What to Do Instead of Making Your Partner Feel Small

Suppose I told you that you could save your relationship by not saying the word *rhinoceros*—you'd think that was a pretty good deal. Well, eliminating this love killer is not much harder than that.

Here's the prescription. Let's use Chip and Jenny to illustrate.

## ○ *Chip and Jenny*

There wasn't just one bad guy here. Chip and Jenny both made each other feel small.

Maybe Jenny was just superorganized, but the labels Chip pinned on her all had to do with being a power-mad control freak, a castrating compulsive. Chip made her out to be a Hitler and called her that when he was angriest.

The labels Jenny pinned on Chip . . . well, I bet you can guess. If he was calling her a control freak, she was calling him a lazy, irresponsible good-for-nothing. And of course being a little smarter and more educated than average, Jenny went on to label Chip as being passive-aggressive and having a dependent personality, trying to turn her into his mother.

"I know you guys have a lot of issues, like everyone," I said, "but would you be willing to concentrate completely on this one love killer that we've diagnosed as being the biggest threat to your relationship? Perhaps if we kill this love killer your other issues will just dissolve." They agreed to follow my prescriptions.

So I asked them to begin with Step 1. I said, "Try this and if it doesn't work all by itself, there are more things you can do that will work."

Here's the first step of the prescription.

**Step 1: Acknowledging.** It's amazing how often you can eliminate this love killer just by understanding what it is and recognizing that it's threatening your relationship. So I had Chip and Jenny say the following to each other:

*In an attempt to deal with my frustrations, I've been calling you names, hanging labels on you, and painting a picture of you as a defective person. This is not good for either of us and I agree to stop. If something you do bothers me, I'll ask for what I need. If you can't give me what I need, I'll ask you why. If I slip and fall back into using labels, point it out to me and I'll do something else.*

What does acknowledging accomplish? It's a way to begin eliminating this love killer by admitting that it's going on and accepting the fact that it can destroy your relationship.

You've no idea how many couples made their relationship better—from who does what in bed to who does what in the kitchen—just by acknowledging that cutting each other down was a problem for them and then agreeing to stop. Rage and resentment fell away. The sense of helplessness was replaced by the sense that their partner was an ally, not an enemy. There was a lifting of the black cloud that once separated them.

It was this easy for many people—eliminating this love killer by acknowledging it was going on. But it wasn't quite this easy for Chip and Jenny.

Making your partner feel small is a bad habit. What happens is that people often start out steering clear of it, but then soon fall back into it. They need more help, more support. That's what steps two through seven provide.

**Step 2: Showing impact.** Almost everyone who throws a negative label at his partner feels justified. Like someone who tries to housebreak a dog by pushing its nose in its poop, people who use negative labels are just trying to get a point across. It's hard for them to imagine how bad it feels, how counterproductive it is, to be on the receiving end.

Showing impact stops this. To do it, you simply decide to let your partner know the impact it has on you everytime he cuts you down. Here are the words to use:

*"When you call me X, it makes me feel worthless and un- loved. Is that how you want me to feel?"*

The first time Jenny said this to Chip, he self-righteously explained what he was trying to accomplish: "I was only trying to get you to stop bossing me around." Well, whatever excuse your partner comes up with, just say, "Let's talk about what you want and not who I am, unless what you want is for me to feel lousy." Repeating these words every time they're needed will eventually drive this love killer out of your relationship.

**Step 3: Make a list of your "Don't say that to me" words and phrases.** This step is exactly what it says. You each write a list of the words and phrases you particularly want your partner never to use. "Call me this, call me that, but don't call me a dirty rat." This gives substance and focus to your attempts to eliminate this love killer.

Chip didn't know that Jenny particularly hated being called a Nazi. She'd had too many experiences of bosses and boyfriends whom *she'd* labeled Nazis, and they seemed like horrible, sinister people. Some people might shrug this label off, but for Jenny it stirred her worst nightmares about herself. She was all too ready to believe it, and at the same time all too ready to hate Chip for using it. So "calling me any kind of Nazi" was at the top of Jenny's list of words and phrases she never wanted Chip to use.

"Passive-aggressive" was a phrase Chip wanted Jenny to stop using. For him it conjured up the specter that he had a deep and hopeless personality disorder. Just as bad, it seemed like the kind of charge that's impossible to defend yourself against. It was at the top of his list.

Don't put more than ten items on your lists. Even ten is too much for most of us to remember. Five is better. But just having these lists and putting them where you'll both see them will keep them fresh in your minds.

**Step 4: Use do-overs.** Who says you never get a second chance? In love there should always be a second chance. When it comes to stopping this love killer, second chances are crucial. Most of us actually become dependent on the little labels we throw at our partners. How can they *not* slip out? Then what do you do? Go nuts? Throw around more labels? You can just feel the mess and the misery beginning. But just because you could travel down the road to disaster doesn't mean you have to.

Instead use do-overs. If your partner has said, "You're just like your mother," and that's something you've put on your list of never-use labels, say something like, "You've just used one of those labels we've agreed not to use. You obviously need something or are trying to get me to see something. Say it again, but please be more direct."

Obviously you don't have to use those exact words. Just don't use any words that will get you accused of making your partner feel small in return.

Here's what Chip and Jenny did. One day Jenny said, "I've asked you a million times to put your dirty dishes in the dishwasher." She was upset, because she felt as if she had asked Chip to do this a million times. But fighting over dirty dishes is not a love killer.

What Chip did next *was* a love killer. You know how it is in relationships: when one person gets upset, the other gets even more upset. "I'm upset with you for getting upset." What Chip *said* was, "Why do you have to be such a nut about where people put things!"

Uh-oh. *Nut* (along with its cousins *crazy woman* and *maniac*) was one of the words on Jenny's list. She asked for a do-over. She used words you should use: "I'm sure you're entitled to your feelings, and probably there's stuff I need to change, but we agreed that throwing names at each other could kill our love, so I'd like to ask you to do over what you just said."

Chip was smart enough to remember that dealing with this love killer was an absolute priority. He thought for a moment and said, "Here's my do-over. I'm sorry that my forgetting to put the dishes in the dishwasher upset you. I should've done it. I'll do it now." Of course that's not as punchy as calling Jenny a nut, but Chip either agreed with the general idea that he was responsible for putting his dishes in the dishwasher or he didn't. If he did agree, why not just accept what Jenny said?

Besides, let's not take our eye off the ball. Making your partner feel small is a fatal relationship disease. Following the prescription for eliminating it is an absolute top priority, a much higher priority than who's right about putting dishes in the dishwasher.

Now get this. If you do it over and get tangled up again, *you can do over the do-over*. Film directors will often call for dozens of takes before the actors get a scene right. You should care a lot more about your relationship than a director cares about some scene in a movie.

**Step 5: Fight prevention.** Let's face it. If you're having to "do it over again," right then at that moment, there's tension between you. Someone has *said something*. You're like two poker players in a cowboy movie where one has just accused the other of cheating. If the two of you had six-guns, shooting would break out. So you need to cool things down. Not by walking away.

Not by avoiding each other or the problem. But by talking *helpfully* about what you're on the verge of talking about *destructively*.

Is there ever a right time to walk on eggshells? This is it.

Let me start you off on the right foot. Here are the top ten vote getters in a little contest I held among people I interviewed for *the best phrases to lead off with when things are tense and you want to prevent a blowup.*

### THE TOP TEN FIGHT-PREVENTING PHRASES

1. "I'm sorry."

2. "You're right."

3. "I can see that that's very important to you."

4. "Is there anything I can do to help?"

5. "What do you need?"

6. "I'd like to hear more about it."

7. "What are you afraid of?"

8. "Would you like to hear how I feel about this?"

9. "When would be a good time for us to talk about this?"

10. "Let me tell you what I value about you."

Using this list is simple. Obviously you decide from the context whether it makes more sense to say, "I'm sorry," or to say, "What are you afraid of?" Just be honest. I don't only mean you should sound honest. But what you say should be whatever you most honestly want to say.

Another tip is not to swerve from your leadoff. For example, if you say, "Is there anything I can do to help?" keep going in the spirit of wanting to know exactly what help is needed and of wanting to give that help. Don't get deflected from your own goal.

Oh yeah, there is one last tip. If you use one of these remarks and the next thing you know the love train is headed off the tracks again, pick another remark from the list and lead off with that. And if you need to, keep leading off with these remarks until you hit pay dirt.

These are popular favorites for a reason. People who've walked down the same dark alleys of marital misery as you find these phrases lifesaving. Why cut each other down when you can avoid a fight?

There's a Special Love Tool that will help you avoid fights: ***Putting on the brakes.*** Do what smart lovers do. Have words you can use that will stop a fight from getting started. Say:

> *Let's stop this. I mean it. Let's stop. We're starting a big fight and I don't think either of us want to have a fight right now.*

Use this tool whenever you find yourself starting down the road to a fight, if you don't want to go down that road.

You wouldn't get into a car unless you knew the brakes worked. And yet most of us get into a lifetime relationship without any brakes at all. No wonder our emotional lives are filled with fender benders. No wonder so many of us get totaled.

We need this tool because every one of us is only three remarks away from a fight. One of you says, "You're going to wear those pants again?" The other says, "You always have to control everything I do." The first one says, "Well if you knew what you were doing . . ." And so the fight begins. We've all been down this road a million times.

Remember: just because you put on the brakes doesn't mean you can't step on the gas pedal again. And you may need to step on the gas pedal because even though you don't want to have an ugly fight, there are issues you need to deal with. So after you've said you want the two of you to stop, you have to say, "Why don't we get together [whatever time is best] and if there are any issues from this we want to discuss we can do it then."

**Step 6: Use put-down banks.** Get two jars. Agree that whoever uses one of the put-downs you've agreed not to use will put a quarter or a dollar or five dollars in the other person's jar. If one of you keeps making the other feel small, the other gets rich. Usually the sight of these two jars side by side on your bedroom dresser is a powerful incentive to watch what you say.

These banks also help you account, literally, for what's real in your relationship. For example, Chip insisted that Jenny had been putting him down just as much as he'd been putting her down. Jenny just couldn't believe this. But the dollar bills in Chip's jar matching the bills in Jenny's jar proved that Chip's memory was more accurate about this. And knowing that made Jenny feel less like a victim, and it made Chip feel validated. And the minute the money starts to pile up there's a huge incentive to stop making your partner feel small.

**Step 7: "A rose by any other name . . ."** Let's say your partner's made it clear that it really hurts when you call him lazy. But even if you stop, you still need to deal with your reasons for calling him that in the first place. It was probably because you didn't know how to get his attention, how to let him know that you need him to help around the house, and how to make him realize how important this is to you. Now you will. Here's where you eliminate your own need to put him down.

You can say almost word for word what Jenny learned to say to Chip. "Chip, you've left out the dirty dishes again. Look, I'm not calling you lazy, but this is exactly where I would've called you lazy in the past. And then you'd call me a kitchen Nazi and we'd be back to putting out all these bad images about each other. And that's all because I felt helpless. You tell me: how can I get you to stop leaving the dishes out?"

By saying this—just changing the words to fit the situation— you're getting almost everything you wanted from calling your partner names without actually calling your partner names. You're just saying,

> *This is where I would've put you down in the past. I'm not going to do that now. But I don't know how else to get through to you about how important this is to me. You tell me how to get through to you.*

Is this going to result in your magically getting your needs met all the time? Of course not (later we'll have a whole chapter that focuses on how to get your needs met). But that's the beauty of diagnosing these love killers, and I'm willing to repeat this point a million times because it's so important:

**Love doesn't die because everything isn't wonderful, or because sometimes you're angry and frustrated with each other. Love dies because of the love killers. Most of the things that make you angry will not kill your love. Making your partner feel small *will* kill your love.**

## Put-down–free Loving

What happened to Chip and Jenny? They still struggle with household chores, and like most couples, this will probably always cause conflict in their relationship. But here's why Chip and Jenny are happy now. When the name-calling stopped, the need to keep distant stopped. They no longer put off coming home from work, and even more important, while they are home together they aren't looking for ways not to talk to each other.

When they stopped being afraid that words like *lazy* and

*Nazi* would come flying at them, they started feeling more comfortable with each other. The more experiences they had where nothing bad happened, the closer they became. And the closer they became, the happier they were to find that nothing bad happened. They started feeling safe. They no longer were afraid that they'd look into the other's eyes and find an ugly monster reflected back.

One of the biggest payoffs was more and better sex, an area where they'd never really thought they had a problem. But in fact they made love more often because they felt safe and comfortable with each other. And when they made love it was more passionate and more intimate.

Chip and Jenny started feeling like a loving couple again. Because they were doing more of what loving couples do, it started being easier for them to be nicer and more affectionate with each other. Maybe Chip was a little more ready to put his dishes away. Maybe Jenny stopped caring so much when he didn't. But things were much better, so it didn't really matter.

# Love Builder #2:
## The Three Promises of Love

A wedding is a time when people make promises to each other. That's really what it means to get married to someone. It's a ceremony of promises. In a sense, the story of your relationship is the story of what happened to the promises you first made to each other. Here's one such story.

### ○ *Joyce and Ray*

Joyce and Ray were down-to-earth people. Joyce managed a small art-supply store near a local art college and experienced great satisfaction advising young artists on their careers, while making a decent living at the same time. Ray scrabbled to make a living managing local rock groups, and of course he was always looking for the next breakout band.

When they got married, as part of their ceremony, they read a list of promises to each other. One read a promise and the other read the same promise back. Nothing fancy. They just promised each other things like:

- "We'll always be there to talk out our problems with each other."
- "We'll always listen carefully to what the other has to say."
- "We'll never go to bed mad at each other without giving ourselves a solid chance to sort things out."
- "We'll never lie to each other or hold back the whole truth."
- "We'll always work hard to make sure that our needs, feelings, desires, and opinions are fully respected and given full weight."
- "We'll always try to be fair and see things from the other's point of view as well as our own."

They made the promises that mattered to them based on their past experiences. Joyce's mother had submerged her own need to have a career as a journalist for the sake of Joyce's father's career. In Ray's previous marriage, he and his wife had both ended up lying to each other.

It's funny though—we all have very different experiences in life, but we often end up learning the same lessons along the way. It hurts to be lied to, to feel misunderstood or unloved. That's why Joyce and Ray's promises seem so familiar to us.

And just as familiar is the need to promise. *Nothing is more satisfying than a promise that's kept.* Most good movies set up promises in the form of character and plot and keep those promises. If it's a good horror movie, it promises you that you'll be scared, and then it scares you. If it's a good comedy, it sets up the expectation that you'll laugh, and it makes you laugh. If it's a tearjerker, you walk in knowing you'll cry, and you walk out crying.

It works the same way in relationships. No relationship is more satisfying than one where the promises people make to each other are kept.

It's been a year and a half since they got married. As of today Joyce and Ray are working hard to keep the promises they made to each other.

For example, there was that time when:

- Ray took one of his bands out for a celebration dinner (they'd just been signed for a record) and didn't invite Joyce. She got mad and said something cruel to Ray about his hanging around with his loser bands. But they stayed up all night talking and fighting and crying until they worked it out with forgiveness, penance, and new promises.
- Joyce mentioned that there was a creamy Italian dessert, tiramisù, that she loved, and Ray spent an entire afternoon running around until he found some for her. After all, they'd made a promise that whatever was important to one of them would be important to the other.
- They stayed in bed for an entire Sunday, talking about their dreams, making plans for the future, reading, making love, tickling each other.
- Joyce told Ray's mother that one of his more successful bands had signed on with a new manager. Ray got furious and screamed at Joyce. She told him how upset she was when he yelled at her, and they got to talking and eventually made a long list of all the things they'd always do or never do, just to make each other happy.

During the period when you were settling into love, like Joyce and Ray, the two of you were also doing valuable and important work. Everything you're going through today is the result of what life has done to those promises you made to each other, to your ability to keep those promises.

It turns out that not only do we make promises as part of launching our relationships, but in spite of our incredible differences *we all basically make the same three promises.*

## The Records of Love

I've been going through all the records I have of all the couples who came to me because they were afraid they'd lose what brought them together. It's clear to me, when I listen to what people want from relationships, that love's three promises are

**1. *Honesty.*** "We'll always be honest and open with each other. We'll always tell the truth. We won't lie and we won't keep things hidden. Even if it's a truth we're afraid to speak or afraid for the other to hear, we'll speak the truth anyway. We'll get naked with each other not just physically but emotionally and in every way possible."

And how can you make each other feel small when you know that you're wanting to get naked with each other?

**2. *Respect.*** "We'll always pay attention to each other. It will matter to you if there's something I care about, and you'll try to give it to me or help me get it. And whatever you need that's important to you, because I respect you, I'll be aware of it and try to give it to you or help you get it. I think you're special and valuable and I want you to think the same of me. Whatever it means to treat each other lovingly, that's what we'll try to do. Showing respect is more than a matter of just saying words. It means acting respectfully. It means acting in such a way that we both feel respected."

The promise to respect each other is a promise not to cut each other down. Two people who respect each other can get through their lives without calling each other vicious, sophisticated versions of "pooh-pooh head."

**3. Passion.** "There will always be real passion and aliveness between us. Sure everyone grows up and grows old, but we'll always keep the flame alive and maintain real warmth between us. We'll never become like those married couples who lose interest in each other. We'll continue to give to each other, to be there for each other, to care about each other, and to have fun with each other."

Making your partner feel small destroys passion. But your desire to preserve passion helps you destroy this love killer.

The more I see of love's struggle to survive, the more I appreciate how these three promises provide a solid foundation for everything a relationship needs to be healthy. When you built your relationship on the foundation of these three promises, you were being very smart.

### A Look Ahead

Whew. We've gotten past the terrible problem of making someone you love feel small. Either that love killer wasn't threatening you or you're following the prescription for eliminating it. Either way, *everything* is easier when you aren't throwing daggers around. You're less ready to fight. You feel safer. You feel better about your partner.

Having made things safer by eliminating one poisonous snake in your love environment, let's take a fresh look at how the environment of love itself can get poisoned.

## · 4 ·

# I Can't Get Next to You

. . . . . . . . . . . . . . . . . . . . . . . . . . . . . . . . . . . . . . . . . . . . . . . . . . . . . . .

LOVE KILLER #3:

## When Everyday Living Pollutes Love

ISSUE:
Have the pressures and distractions of your
daily life eroded your relationship
to the point of causing serious, potentially
permanent damage?

## *The Ecology of Love*

I've seen it too many times. Good people with a good relationship find the spirit is being choked out of their love because their lives are stressful, distracting, and exhausting. But you don't need a perfect life to have perfect love. Ultimately, some of the healthiest, happiest relationships have survived the everyday pressures that get us all down. You don't have to change your life to heal your love.

But none of us can pretend that how we live doesn't affect how we love. It's tough earning a living these days. Most of our jobs have been "reengineered," forcing us to work longer and harder. Few of us have spouses whose main job is to make things easier for us. Your spouse is working longer and harder as well. Many of us are workaholics. Many of us have a hard time prioritizing. Many of us have crazy bosses and incompetent subordinates. Then add children to the mix. Even without children it's tough enough.

What does it add up to? The familiar complaint: "I don't have a life anymore."

Are stresses and pressures affecting *your* life? I'm sure you know already, but here's something that can help you know for certain.

## THE TOP TEN SIGNS YOU DON'T HAVE TIME TO HAVE A LIFE

1. You were so busy last weekend that you got through the entire weekend without having more than a two-minute conversation with your partner.

2. You can't remember the last time you did your favorite activity because it was so long ago.

3. At last count, you've lost at least one really good friend because you just didn't have any time to stay in touch.

4. The last time you had quickie sex, you were glad afterward because it didn't take up too much of your time.

5. Just the other day you realized you were communicating with your spouse by giving your kids messages to pass on.

6. The last time you heard about a couple breaking up you felt jealous because you figured each of them would have more time for him or herself.

7. You hate your clothes but you don't have time to shop for new ones.

**8. When you think about your children you feel guilty because you rarely spend time with them.**

**9. Every March you're in a panic because you don't have time to do your taxes yourself, but you don't have time to get your receipts together and find someone to do them for you.**

**10. Recently you've been lying awake at night with To Do lists scrolling through your head, and it's stolen sleep from you and made your days even more exhausting.**

These are the situations people describe as they tell me the story of their relationship, the story of how they journeyed from flirting with each other to flirting with divorce. Over and over the descent into painful difficulties started with circumstances ranging from a new baby to a new job. "And then real life struck" is how one man described what happened when his relationship got into serious trouble. A potential love killer indeed, as you'll see.

From time to time we all go through tough periods. But all too often the tough periods go on and on and on, making stories like Wendy's and Mike's all too understandable.

## ⟩ *Wendy and Mike*

For twenty-five years they were the All-American couple. Hard working, successful, family oriented. Mike had taken a corner gas station and built it up into a large, busy repair shop. Like most small-business owners, a forty-hour week would've felt like a vacation to him. Wendy taught English and coached the cheerleading squad at the local junior high school. They had three normal kids.

The logistics of romance and intimacy no longer fit into their lives. Sure they were nice to each other, and for a monkey-wrench kind of guy, Mike was surprisingly sweet.

But the pressure-filled years took their toll. Wendy learned early on that when Mike came home late—7:00 P.M. was the earliest he ever came home—there was no point in talking to him. He wouldn't listen. He wouldn't care. Wendy wasn't much better, she had to admit. A day of hassles with kids and administrators left her frazzled.

Without realizing it or intending it, they got to the point where they were acting like two diplomats in the service of family harmony. Politeness, silence, avoidance, and wariness were the four keynotes of almost every interaction between them. And they were proud of themselves. They were sure that they had a happy marriage, and that it would be there waiting for them when they finally had time to enjoy it.

**Face to face.** Then their youngest kid left for college a month early, at the beginning of August, and Wendy and Mike had a whole slow August to face each other alone for the first time in more than two decades.

By the end of a few days of chatting about the minutiae of family life, they found themselves with so little to talk about that they ended up planning the menu for Thanksgiving dinner, four months in the future. And when Wendy was brave enough to point it out, they had to face how little they had in common after all these years, during which real life had been working to undermine their love.

Was it threatening to kill their love? That's where the need for diagnosis comes in. What's news for some of us is the possibility that something about our daily lives could kill our relationships. But let's get real.

## *You Load Sixteen Tons and What Do You Get?*

I'm always impressed by how beautifully most of us cope with our high-pressure lives. We hang in there, we keep going, we take care of our responsibilities, we maintain our cheerfulness. But in spite of our heroic efforts, our relationships suffer.

What kinds of real-life situations bring us to this terrible state?

Let me see if I can briefly capture what far too many of us have been going through. If you're even remotely typical, then what follows is a description of your life:

- In the morning, you're so rushed that you rarely have time for more than a three-minute shower.
- If there's the slightest delay in getting your day started—a problem with the kids or a tie-up during the commute—your entire schedule is thrown off and panic sets in.
- During the day, you're so busy at work that it's hard to find time to call your partner. If the two of you do talk during the day, you find the call makes you tense and annoyed. Sometimes it seems as though all you have to talk about is logistics.
- Every day, your boss or your clients or your patients or your associates dump responsibilities on you that exhaust you emotionally and make you feel you have nothing left to give.
- When you get home at night, it's late, and it's a miracle if you have time to ask your partner how his day was or listen to his answer.
- You have work to catch up on or children to take care of every evening, and when you finally get to watch TV or read a book you soon discover that you're too tired to get up out of your chair and go to bed. Falling asleep becomes something that happens in front of the tube.
- You look forward to the weekend, but then you find you have a weekend full of chores to do every Saturday and Sunday.

I'm sure you do a great job of dealing with all this. Still, for most of us the busyness and pressure of daily life is getting really bad. We tell ourselves that we should be working on our relationships when in reality we don't even have time to have a life. But the question for us now is, When does this start hurting our love?

## What Makes Love Get Sick?

You might say you never expected life to be easy. Life is tough, but *you're* tough. You and your partner get away every now and then. You practice stress management techniques, or at least you know about them.

Fine, but real life has a powerful impact on genuine love. You and I know what actually happens. No matter how demanding and exhausting our jobs are, we hold it together all day because we're professionals, because our livelihood depends on it. Even if we're just running on adrenaline, we hold it together like a doctor on a MASH unit working eighteen-hour days. It's when work is over that we lose our ability to hold it together. We crash emotionally; we lose it psychologically.

That's how the stresses and pressures of everyday life bring out the love killers, just the way a polluted atmosphere brings out respiratory diseases. Polluted air doesn't make everyone sick. And some people get respiratory diseases even when the air is not polluted. But polluted air is bad news for lungs, and in the same way real life, as many of us live it today, is bad news for love.

## The Annoyance-Avoidance Syndrome

Let me show you how real life kills real love. Sadly, the process is all too familiar, all too natural.

## ◯ *Elizabeth and Bob*

Like a lot of women these days, Elizabeth had been so busy launching a career as a lawyer that by the time she was thirty-six she was eager to get married. When she met Bob, who is a hospital administrator, he was forty-two and in the same boat. She felt very lucky to fall in love with him because he was a terrific guy and they were on the same wavelength.

Elizabeth told me about the moment she first saw that their relationship was in trouble. Bob had picked her up after work and when she got in his car she started talking about something that had happened to her during the day. But Bob cut her off. "I can't listen to this. Be quiet, okay? I've had a really tough day and I can't talk to anyone anymore."

Elizabeth was shocked to find that she was relieved. Good, she thought, if he doesn't have to listen to me, I don't have to listen to him. It's better that way.

They both had too much on their plates. They were both exhausted and overwhelmed. Maybe things would've been all right if Bob's purpose in life was to make Elizabeth's life easier. But Bob was a real person with needs and opinions of his own, not a slave without a self. If you're under so much stress and pressure that every new straw breaks the camel's back, your partner's very existence threatens your peace of mind. "Shut up and leave me alone if you can't do what I want the way I want you to do it," is the way we're forced to feel.

But the same thing is happening for your partner. The stresses and pressures of life create what I call the *annoyance-avoidance syndrome*. The only way you can prevent your partner from annoying you is to avoid him. So you live as if you were enemies.

Like Elizabeth, sometimes we actually decide to do this. "If Bob can't listen to me, we don't have to talk to each other. I don't need to let myself in for this kind of aggravation."

How could this *not* kill love?

### Getting Through the Day

Inevitably, our partners become transformed in our eyes. The person we fall in love with becomes a mere tool, an accessory, an accompaniment to our everyday life. The beautiful young person you gave your heart to becomes like the car that you ignore when it gets you to work on time, which you hate if it acts up and has "needs" of its own. Of course we don't want it to be this way. We know we're loving, giving people. But when real life strikes, we expect our partner to help us get through the day.

So even if your relationship is one of the most important things in the world to you, you have no time to *have* a relationship. Certainly not as anything other than a handmaid to the pressures and responsibilities of everyday life. But just the way kitchens get dirty when no one has time to clean them and family finances go to hell when no one has the time to put them in order, if you have no time for your relationship, your relationship has all the time it needs to go from bad to worse and turn the love you were so confident about into a nightmare of coldness and anger.

If Bob wouldn't listen to Elizabeth—if he wouldn't open his ears to her—why should she have sex with him? It's not that this was a conscious thought. She just found that it was hard for her to open herself up to him.

Amazing, isn't it? Here's this thing that started out perfect. Here's this thing that I'm telling you can stay healthy and alive forever. And yet there's something about the hurly-burly of daily life that does something terrible to love. Bob and Elizabeth were one of my research couples. It turned out to be too late for them. Fortunately other couples have proven that it doesn't have to be too late if you diagnose this love killer. But you have to understand it.

## When Real Life Hits Real Love

You know that somewhere there should be a place where people have all the time they need to unravel the painful knots their love has tied itself into. Far off in the land of love, you'd have all the time you needed to do all the things that would strengthen your love, just the way in the land of fitness you'd have all the time you needed to get into perfect shape.

But that land is not your land. Like most people who live in the land of real life, even if by some miracle you found the time to work on your relationship, it wouldn't be a time that was good for your partner.

*You* can't relax until the two of you work things out, but *he* doesn't want to work things out until he gets relaxed. And so the two of you keep waiting for some open period when the frenzied cares of life subside and you can start working on your love life.

## Love Takes a Holiday

So maybe you go on vacation. And maybe by some kind of lucky break it's one of those really nice, relaxing vacations that are actually less stressful than the life you left behind. Suddenly the two of you are happy together again! You actually experience an hour, an afternoon that's just like those vacation ads on television with the handsome husband and the carefree wife.

But is that the time to start working on your relationship? Not for most of us. Sure, you "have some time now." But opening up the Pandora's box of problems between you is the last thing you want to do as you sit sipping piña coladas on the beach at sunset.

And so you're happy until real life strikes again and, thirty-six hours after you get back home, you're mad at each other all over again.

It's as if your relationship had come down with some weird

disease where you feel okay as long as you stay in bed, but you feel awful the minute you get up. You blame your partner. You blame yourself. You blame whatever the last book you read told you to blame. But what's the real problem? How did people like you—who loved each other so much and were so determined to make things work—end up in the one place you told yourselves you'd never get to?

## Thinking Like an Environmentalist

It's really not all that surprising if you think like an environmentalist; we've all become environmentalists these days. That means we've all become comfortable understanding things by looking at the contexts in which they exist. For example, when you hear that someone's gotten cancer, you wonder about the air he's breathed and the water he's drunk. When you hear that someone had a heart attack, you wonder about her diet or her stress levels.

We also understand that the world we live in has a tremendous impact on our individual mental health. Whatever role biology plays in problems ranging from depression to schizophrenia, there is no question that ecological factors—particularly a person's work and family environments—play an important role.

A psychologically toxic environment—a bad boss, an abusive family member, or money problems, for example—can blow up a slight predisposition to depression into a major illness. A psychologically nurturing environment—a loving family and rewarding work, for example—can protect someone with a predisposition to depression from ever falling into it.

## Love Conquers All, or Does It?

Yet the ecology of love has never been seriously addressed. If anything, when it comes to love, a lot of nonsense gets spouted about our ability to rise above our environment. For example, we sometimes say, "Absence makes the heart grow fonder." It's certainly true that when people we love go away, we miss them and feel our love more keenly. But let's get real. Does this mean that long-distance relationships are stronger and healthier than relationships between people who live together? Of course not. Long-term separation is an environmental *hazard* for relationships, and we need to look at the other ways relationships can be threatened, how they *are* threatened, by pollutants in the environment.

The ecology of love forces us to recognize the same kind of threat. If love is a living force, why not accept that even the strongest and most dominant of living things is a fragile castaway, always susceptible to being killed by toxic forces around it.

Take money problems. Just the way they can be toxic for individual psychology, they can be toxic for relationships.

## ○ *Sally and Al*

Sally and Al have been living together for almost two years. Sally moved in with Al after they'd been seeing each other for over a year. What started polluting their relationship was too little money. Sally doesn't make much as a teacher, and as a stereo salesman, Al's making a lot less than Sally thought he would when they got together. They both have student loans to repay, but most of all they can't seem to save for the down payment on a house.

Al and Sally feel trapped, unable to get out of where they are, unable to cope with staying there. They've gotten to the point where they're so tired of fighting with each other that they don't talk anymore.

But if you understand the real lesson in Al and Sally's story, plus the lessons contained in the stories of thousands of people like them, you'll see that there's really good news here. There's nothing wrong with Al and Sally. They're just living in a polluted love environment. When a pond is at risk of dying from acid rain, you don't blame the pond or criticize it for being weak. On the contrary, because you understand just how ponds can die from an environmental threat, you understand how to prevent one particular pond you might have fallen in love with from dying.

## Mean Streets

Like ponds and trees and frogs and flowers, our relationships exist in an environment of everyday life that in some cases can prove toxic. Of course just because love lives in a tough neighborhood doesn't mean that it necessarily falls victim to Love Killer #3.

Hey, I grew up on the mean streets of the Lower East Side. There was danger and poverty and limited opportunity there, and it was a tough neighborhood psychologically as well, because the air was filled with sexism and hopelessness and constricted horizons. There were probably toxic aspects of the physical and/ or psychological neighborhood in which you grew up too. And we survived and thrived. But to say that we can survive or even that if we do survive we're made stronger by the struggle doesn't negate the fact that the risk factors are real in a polluted environment and, like in any theater of combat, they take more than their share of victims. I'm just talking about two people who fall in love and then get so busy and stressed out that love falls by the wayside. That's what we'll try to diagnose with this love killer, to see if it applies to you. We all experience pressures and distractions. But have they reached the point for you where they've turned into a real love killer?

# Diagnostic #3: Is Your Life Polluting Your Relationship?

I know you've spent a lot of time thinking about how your relationship feels, but right now I'd like you to think about how *you* feel. In particular I'd like you to think about how your life makes you feel. Your life right now. Day to day. Do you feel calm and relaxed? Do things feel smooth and easy? Do you feel you have all the time in the world and no pressure whatsoever? If so, believe me, you're one of the lucky few.

After listening to thousands of people describe their lives and observing the conditions that put love at risk, I've learned that the following two-part question diagnoses Love Killer #3.

## DIAGNOSING LOVE KILLER #3

The pressures and distractions of your everyday life are eroding your relationship to the point of causing serious, potentially permanent damage if *both parts* of the following apply:

1. *You have an unusually stressful job or life situation.* We all like to complain about how tough things are. But this love killer obviously can't apply to everyone. Most of us are stress resistant enough to cope with average levels of stress. This diagnostic category is for people in *the top 20 percent* of stress levels. You can only say you have "an unusually stressful job or life situation" if what's going on in your life is as bad as or worse than the following examples:
   - you've just started a new job or you've just had a new baby
   - you have an unusually critical and demanding boss
   - you're working under continually hard-to-meet deadlines
   - you're working unusually long hours over a considerable period
   - you have difficult-to-achieve sales quotas or other performance goals always hanging over your head

- in addition to your normal duties, you're having to cope with some difficult, draining, chronic illness (such as cancer) or condition (such as menopause for some women), or with some family member's illness or condition
- you face constant serious worries about finances

This applies to me ＿＿

This doesn't apply to me ＿＿

2. *As a result of your unusually stressful job or life situation,* two or more *of the following examples apply to you:*
   - most days you feel that you have nothing left to give your partner
   - you carry around a sense of impatience or anger that rarely leaves
   - it seems as though everything your partner does irritates you
   - you'd have to say that you're doing everything possible to avoid your partner
   - you feel so depleted that you only want to be with your partner if he does things for you without expecting anything in return

This applies to me ＿＿

This doesn't apply to me ＿＿

If you checked off "This applies to me" to *both* parts, then stress from your life is clearly threatening to kill your love. Why is this question in two parts? The first part gets at what's going on *around* you. Life can't be the culprit if there's nothing so terribly stressful going on. The second part gets at what's going on *inside* you. Life can't be the culprit if it's not bothering you inside.

If you checked off "This doesn't apply to me" to *either* part, you and your partner might still be suffering from the impact of stress on your relationship and you might still benefit from following the prescription, but you're not immediately at risk from this love killer. Of course, it might be that the problem isn't your stressful life but your partner's stressful life. If Diagnostic #3 doesn't apply to you, ask yourself if it applies to your partner. Or better yet, ask your partner to answer these diagnostic questions.

**A note on denial.** There's a key reason why many of us are in denial about this love killer: sometimes we get down on ourselves when the pressures of everyday life make us feel and act less than our best. Most of us would like to feel we can rise above our circumstances, that if we were in a situation where other people were panicking we'd still keep our heads. So when the pressures and distractions of our lives get to us, we feel we've failed.

These feelings are normal, but they don't make sense, any more than it would make sense to get down on your lungs because they failed to "rise above" the impact of smoking two packs a day for twenty years. Having a new baby in your lives may make it harder for you to give to each other for a while, but it doesn't mean you've failed each other.

## What to Say to People

Here's what you can say to each other and to yourselves and even to your friends and relatives about what's going on if your relationship is suffering from this love killer:

*The long hours we've been putting in, the tension, the pressure, the endless distractions, the cost to our nervous systems—it just doesn't make sense that our love can survive in this environment. The lives we've been leading do nothing but make us see each other as obstacles and irritations. It's not us, and it's not our relationship—it's the way we've been living that's polluted our love and put it at risk. We can't count on our relationship to be strong enough to survive the stress of our lives, but we can be strong enough to change the things in our lives that create this love killer.*

# Prescription #3:
# Have a Life That Supports Your Love

If this love killer is afflicting your relationship, there are ten things you can do to eliminate it. Most of them are easy or fun or pleasurable or life enhancing in some way. They're not work.

I'd like you to do all ten of these things, but I know that when stress levels are at their worst, even a short to-do list can seem like too much to bear, so I've written down the exercises in order of priority. If you can do only one thing now, do the first one. If you can do only two things now, do the first two. And so on. But eventually do all ten of them.

## THE TOP TEN WAYS TO PREVENT LIFE FROM HURTING YOUR LOVE

**1. Rest.** Do you know what happens to people in one of those sleep-deprivation experiments? To make a long story short, they go mean and crazy. They lose all perspective and become willing to turn on the people who are closest to them. Torturers in police states know that if you deprive someone of sleep long enough, he'll betray his parents, his children, and his lovers.

Okay, fine, you're not *that* tired, you say. But every time I've diagnosed Love Killer #3, at least one of the people in the relationship was chronically fatigued and suffering from a sleep deficit. The most overlooked part of what happens to you when your life is filled with pressure and difficulty is that you get incredibly tired, because the more stress you're under the more sleep you need.

Even if your real-life problem seems to have nothing to do with time—like money worries, for example—worry can exhaust you.

What's that you say? You're too busy to get rested? I understand. But think about what you're saying. You're saying that you're too busy to have love in your life. Your job and all your other responsibilities supersede your relationship. You're saying, hey, throw the relationship overboard, and if it can keep up with the ship of my life by swimming alongside it, that's great.

Some people really do feel this way. It's better to be honest with yourself if you do. But don't kid yourself about what's at stake and how love actually works. The stars are beautiful, but they run on the simplest of all atoms, hydrogen. Love is beautiful, but it runs on simple things like getting enough sleep. If you care about love in your life, then you'll organize every evening around making sure you get to bed early enough to get close to eight hours of sleep. As sure as the sun rises, "mettle fatigue" kills love.

**2. Avoid special situations that will stress you out.** Love Killer #3 works like a trick knee: you've got to be aware of the situations that will make it go out on you, and you have to avoid them. Here are some ideas people who've faced this love killer came up with for avoiding situations that will exacerbate it:

- Never bring up problems the minute your partner walks in the door.
- If you know you're going to go through a period of particular stress—a deadline at work, a relative's illness—warn your partner.
- Protect yourselves from the telephone. Use caller ID or your answering machine to save you from taking calls you don't have to take. If you answer the phone and it's for your partner, *always* say he's busy and can he call back. If it's really important, he can call back.
- Keep a notebook on the kitchen table in which you both write down practical, daily-living-type questions or requests for each other to deal with as they come up. This is where you remind your partner to pick up the dry cleaning, where your partner reminds you to show up for your kid's school play. Read this notebook every day.
- Don't be too quick to react when your partner baits you. When one guy told his wife he couldn't listen to her telling

him about her day, she felt insulted and was ready to attack him. But to avoid making a bad situation worse, count to ten before you say something that drops a match on the gasoline your partner's poured.

Here's a Special Love Tool that will help you avoid stress-producing situations. After all, what's more stressful than those situations where one of you wants to do one thing and the other wants to do something else and you're threatened with horrible conflict? I call this Special Love Tool **"On a scale from One to Ten . . ."** You will not believe how often you'll use this tool or how much trouble it will save you.

Here's how to use it. Let's say, with all the time pressure you're under, you find you want to go to different restaurants. To prevent stress and conflict one of you says, "Before we get all tangled up, let's each say on a scale from one to ten, ten being highest, how important our preferences are. You say how important it is to you to go to a Chinese restaurant and I'll say how important it is to me to go to an Italian one. When we each have a number, let's say it."

*What you'll find over and over is that one of you cared more about his choice than the other.* It was a nine for you to go to a Chinese restaurant, but it was only a six for your partner to go to an Italian restaurant, even though you'd thought she was passionate about her preference. Nine beats six. You go Chinese.

Here's another example. A couple is having a bitter fight about how one of them spoils their child by getting snacks for him whenever he asks, even though at six he's old enough to grab an apple or a piece of bread himself. They even get to the point where they're talking about how the other had been damaged by his or her own parents.

Suddenly one of them remembered to use this love tool. It turned out that it was a ten for the person who wanted the kid to get the snacks himself, but it was only a seven for the one who wanted to get snacks for the kid. Ten beats seven. The kid got his own snacks. The couple dropped the fight immediately, and each apologized to the other.

**3. Brainstorm ways to give yourselves more time by giving yourselves less to do.** Pressures and distractions getting you down? *Eliminate some of them. Let things go. Do less.*

I heard something the other day that shocked me. In some circles, being incredibly busy has become a status symbol. Our new hero is the White Rabbit: I'm late, I'm late, for a very important date, no time to say hello, goodbye, I'm late, I'm late, I'm late. The way it works is that you lose status if you're ever seen as having an opening in your schedule. Of course you and I aren't slaves to fashion, so there's no way this could possibly apply to us. That means we're free to organize our lives so we have more, not less, free time. Let me help you with this.

I've asked around and I've come up with what I believe are the ten biggest-bang-for-the-buck ways to give yourselves more time in your lives to be with each other. Do any or all of the items on this list to give yourselves more time for each other and eliminate Love Killer #3.

## THE TOP TEN WAYS TO HAVE MORE TIME FOR LOVE

1. **Spend less time in pointless socializing.** Most people report that over 50 percent of the time they spend socializing is not very pleasurable nor is it with people they especially like.

2. **Buy time for yourself.** Hire people to perform time-consuming chores. There's almost nothing you do from shlepping the kids places to getting your computer to run right that someone else won't do for you.

3. **Let things go.** So your house is a little messy. So your dinners are not so fancy. If it's not something that, on your deathbed, you're going to wish you'd spent more time at, don't spend time at it now.

4. **Buy fewer things.** Shopping takes a lot of time.

5. **Send the kids somewhere.** You know—grandma, camp, a friend's house overnight. We've all learned the importance of spending quality time with our children, but you also need to make time to just be with each other.

6. **Find something to do together.** Exercise together, for example. Going for long walks together on the weekends can give you couples time and cardiovascular time simultaneously.

7. **Write down the seven things you do that take up most of your time, in order of importance.** Eliminate the two least important.

8. **Never ever watch a rerun on television.** Also, give up the last or first hour of TV watching every day.

9. **Never have the same fight twice.** If a fight starts that sounds familiar, say, "Haven't we had this fight before?" If so, ask each other how it ended. If neither of you can add anything new to this fight that will give it a different ending, just say, "Okay, we've had this fight," and move on.

10. **Spend more time saying I love you and less time talking about who did what, who's going to do what, who should do what, and who forgot to do what.**

Talking about getting a divorce takes an incredible amount of time. Being busy with divorce lawyers takes an incredible amount of time. Looking for a new postdivorce place to live takes an incredible amount of time. Explaining to your friends why you got divorced takes an incredible amount of time. Dating frogs while you're looking for that new prince or princess takes a *ton* of time. So saving your love now will save you a lot of time later.

**4. If your life's in combat mode, carry on an underground love affair with your partner.** Couples fall into a trap when stress makes their normal methods of keeping love alive impossible. For example, if they're too tired and stressed out to make love, they go from good sex to no sex. If they can't manage to have a long chat with each other, they stop talking altogether. If they can't go out to a restaurant together, they do nothing with each other.

This happens for a very simple reason. Couples learn how to connect during a period when they have relatively more time for each other. You made more time for each other, and other distractions (children, a mortgage) probably weren't factors. So even in the best of relationships, there might be no pattern in place for making quick but real connections. Here are some ideas to remedy this:

- Never let a day go by without doing something nice for each other, no matter how tiny. Let's say you have two small kids, incredible pressure at work, a cold you can't shake, and you're getting ready to move. And your mother-in-law has shown up to stay with you. Fine. You can still take your partner's hand when you get into bed and hold it for thirty seconds. You can still say, "Hey, good lookin'," when you pass your partner in the hallway.
- Remember to tell each other "I love you." You'd have to be pretty close to a nervous breakdown to be literally unable to say "I love you." By doing this you avoid the surprisingly common situation in which your stressed-out state makes your partner start thinking you've stopped loving her.
- You might laugh at this one, but it works. If you don't have a pet name for each other, get one. If you have old tired pet names for each other, get new ones. Use them as often as possible.
- Quickie sex is not the answer. But not touching is not the answer either. Touch each other a lot, whenever and wherever possible. Don't just hold your partner's hand, massage it.

**5. Avoid each other when you're stressed out.** It's much, much better to avoid each other before you start picking at each other. Sometimes solutions that seem radical work very well. For example, just because people who are in love are supposed to be happy to see each other doesn't mean you have to interact with each other when you first come home from work.

I've seen couples make good use of the "Let's pretend we're invisible" tactic. For the first hour or two they're home together every evening, they don't talk to each other, they don't even hang out in the same room. Unless having dinner together is a big deal to them, they don't even eat together. Maybe they just walk in the house, grab a sandwich, throw together a salad, toss something in the microwave, *and wait until they feel the stress leave their bodies* before they spend any time with each other.

But you've both got to agree to this. Otherwise it's just one of you being mad and giving the other the silent treatment.

Something else you can do to minimize contact when you're stressed out is agree to be in charge of separate domains, so you don't have to talk about so many decisions.

I knew a couple who were both busy lawyers, and I thought it was unfair that the woman always made the dinner. I asked her about this and she described some of the fights they'd get into when they were both exhausted and they'd start talking about what to have for dinner and then they'd go to the kitchen to make it together. One day she said to her partner, "I'll tell you what. If you say absolutely nothing about dinner, and I can make whatever I want, I'll prepare it alone." He agreed and life was much happier and less stressful for both of them as a result.

If your love is being polluted by real-life stresses, you still have to solve the problems that come up between you, but you can also avoid discussing problems when you're most stressed out.

Follow this rule: if something is important enough to talk about, it's important enough to save until the right time. So:

- Never bring up anything stressful just before bedtime.
- Never bring up anything your partner's going to ask you

questions about just before you're going to leave the house.

- Never bring up problems or decisions just before guests are due to arrive.
- Never bring up important issues just before your partner's favorite TV show is about to start.
- Never bring up *anything* if there won't be time to talk about it.

Here's the best tip of all: ask your partner when in general is the best time to bring up stressful issues, and tell him when the best time is for you. And then keep to those times.

**6. Make appointments to be together.** Quality time is such a cliché that I'm almost embarrassed to mention it. But we all need to be reminded of it so I'll mention it anyway. The emphasis is on the word *quality*. *Quality* time. And that means time when you have something to give each other, because how can you produce quality *anything* when you have nothing to give? To put the quality back in quality time, many couples have made an arrangement like this: they've designated Sunday morning (or whatever time suits you best) as inviolable, time that belongs only to them as a couple together, to no one else, to nothing else.

In effect they make a date, and we're all used to getting ready for a date, to feeling we have to have something to contribute to the occasion. So they treat their partners as if they were people they were having an affair with, where their time together is special and precious.

Let me be even more radical. If your relationship is really threatened by Love Killer #3, then *every* time the two of you are together should be chosen and designated as relationship time, *or* it should be time the two of you stay out of each other's hair. Good time or no time. But never stressful, annoying-the-hell-out-of-each-other time.

When crunch time is crunching you up emotionally, the less

time you spend getting on each other's nerves, the better. Years from now, when your relationship is still alive and healthy because you've eliminated this love killer, it won't matter that you spent only a few hours a week together. It will matter that you've spent as little time as possible feeling irritated and deprived.

**7. Add some missing piece.** Because of your busy stressful lives, almost everything enjoyable that you used to do together has fallen by the wayside. For now, most of it will probably have to stay fallen by the wayside. But I know that there's *something* the two of you used to do together that you enjoyed that doesn't take much time and that you can add back into your lives, particularly if you subtract some of the stressful parts.

In the last few years my husband and I got so busy that Monday through Friday we never connected except to talk about work or to collapse like idiots in front of the TV for an hour before we went to bed. It was horrible. Then about nine months ago—I don't really know how it happened—we realized two things: we had all these great recordings we hadn't listened to for years and we really missed connecting with each other during the week.

So we started a new ritual. We begin every day by sitting down together and listening to one piece of music for about fifteen minutes. If we're under a lot of time pressure and the piece of music is long, we'll listen to part of it. At the rate we're going, we figure it'll take about three years to get through all our music. But a relationship is like a community. The glue that holds a community or a relationship together can be strengthened or it can crumble. By listening to a little music every day, we do just that much more to strengthen the glue that holds our love together.

I hope you'll find something similar to do.

**8. Don't think that you or your partner really are what stress has turned you into.** If this love killer is operating, that means that if your partner is acting like a jerk, it's not because he *is* a jerk but because the pressures and problems in his life are making him *act* like a jerk. He's no more a jerk than a coal miner who comes home from work covered by coal dust is a dirty guy. He's a clean guy who got dirty from his job. That makes all the difference.

And it will make all the difference in your relationship if you understand that being irritable and pushing your partner away because your life has stressed you out doesn't mean that you've actually changed. You may still be the same patient, warm, loving person you were when you fell in love.

**9. Make a long-range plan to eliminate the level of stress and overwork that's keeping this love killer alive.** Having a long-range plan for eliminating this love killer is important because it gives you hope. If the major stressor in your life is a newborn baby, your long-range plan might be nothing more than figuring out how you'll survive the years between now and when he starts school. Much more serious for most people is work that's making them crazy, one of those divorce-making professions like medicine, sales, finance, entertainment, law, high-tech, or long-distance truck driving.

There are always two ways you can go. You can move into a low-stress area of your field, or you can do your current job in a more low-stress way. Someone in sales, for example, can go into management or go into selling something that involves less stress or can decide to accept making less money.

The point is that by pushing less, or being willing to change direction in your career, you can make your life easier so that you don't have to push your partner away. Acknowledging that this love killer is at work means making a long-term commitment to eliminate the pressures that create it.

**10. Don't take your eye off this love killer.** Being so stressed by your life that you lose your interest in or ability to interact with your partner plays a role in *at least* 40 percent of divorces. If people deal with nothing more than this love killer, I'll have done more than my share to cut down on the relationship death rate. Here's a story that illustrates why it's so important to keep your eye on this love killer.

## ○ *Tom and Arlene*

Tom and Arlene closed their eyes and ears to the impact their all-absorbing jobs were having on their love. They ignored this love killer until Arlene was shocked to find herself having an affair. An affair is the heart attack of relationships. Sometimes it kills love, sometimes it permanently diminishes love's vitality, sometimes love completely recovers. But it's always painful, messy, and scary. And it's always possible to look back and think that if you'd led your life a little differently, you could've prevented it.

Tom and Arlene had been married for three years. They had no children. They'd met on the first day of a two-week vacation at Club Med. It was love at first sight, and so in a way their relationship began with a honeymoon. Maybe that spoiled them. Back in the city, they spent weekends together, during which they'd pretend that work wasn't weighing on them. They wanted to spend their lives together, but their secret reason for wanting to get married fast was to get to the stage where they wouldn't have to devote so much time commuting to each other's apartments and nurturing their relationship.

## When You Forget About the Impact of Real Life

The day they settled in together after the wedding marked a dizzying reversal from love time to no time. A month later Arlene found herself crying and told Tom they couldn't go on seeing so little of each other. But they ignored that warning sign. Three years later a guy Arlene knew from work took her to dinner and asked her to go back to his place. She accepted so fast she couldn't believe it. Afterward she hated the idea that she'd been unfaithful. But she was even more pained to realize that she'd been starved for love. It was the way she and Tom had been living that had starved her.

So here's how to make sure you don't take your eye off this love killer. First you have to acknowledge the dangerous power real life has. We've all had the experience of going to the doctor and being told that if we don't cut something out—drinking, smoking, high-cholesterol foods—we'll get into big trouble. Sometimes we take the doctor's warnings seriously, sometimes we don't. And let's face it, it almost never happens that within mere days the doctor's warnings bear fruit. So it's very easy to ignore the risks we face when we're diagnosed as suffering from this love killer.

But I'll promise you something. If this love killer applies, sooner or later it *will* mess you up. What do you think years of bickering and annoyance and avoidance and angry silence will do? Will you just be able to forget it? Will you just be able to pick up your old loving ways as if nothing had happened? Of course not. The life or death of your love is at stake.

## The Buddy System

Once you've acknowledged this to yourself, you have to make sure that you and your partner admit it to each other. Just ask your partner to answer the questions in Diagnostic #3. If your partner gives you any resistance, ask him this question: "Which is more important—keeping our love alive or pretending that the way we live isn't hurting our love?"

The most important part of involving your partner in keeping your eye on this love killer is seeing that whichever one of you is incredibly stressed out is *not* the bad guy. He or she is not even the responsible party. The pressure is a fact of both of your lives, and you're both responsible for eliminating it.

## Live the Program

If you're suffering from a love killer, *no more business as usual*. You have to put this program into effect the same way you would if your doctor scared you into realizing you were risking serious damage to your body.

I'll let you in on a secret. *You don't have to eliminate this love killer completely to take your relationship out of the danger zone.* Just *trying* to eliminate it will give you a whole new sense of closeness and comradeship that will be wonderful for your relationship. And *reducing* the amount of this love killer in your system will make things go much more smoothly between you. Love was not designed by nature to be able to exist only in 100 percent pollution-free environments. It's a lot hardier than that.

# Love Builder #3:
# Not Wanting to Lose What's Special

Some people worry that the pressures in their lives are too big to overcome. But you're not alone in this fight. The love builder you have working for you is that deep down you know there's something special about your relationship. There's something precious there, something unique. Something as valuable as a species of bird that might be threatened by extinction. The world will be a slightly poorer place if your relationship disappears.

The sense of specialness has been a powerful ally in the fight against environmental pollution as it will be in your fight against this love killer. We clean up our lakes and beaches and the air over our cities because these things belong to us and we care about them. And we're proud of them. Once upon a time that beach was clean. Once upon a time the air above that city was breathable. Well, once upon a time you felt your love was special. You felt you had something special going for you. Maybe some people didn't applaud your getting together, but you were proud of things in your relationship that other people didn't see. Maybe everyone thought you were perfect for each other, and you were proud of having such a great relationship.

If you reconnect to that sense of specialness, to that sense of ownership and caring, you'll be particularly motivated to clean away the gunk in your lives that's been poisoning your love. You'll follow the prescription—you'll get more rest and spend more time together—because you want to save something special from becoming extinct.

## A Look Ahead

If you're doing the essential dos for maintaining love and not doing the essential don'ts, and if you've stopped making each other feel small, and if you've carved out some stress-free space for your relationship from the jungle of real life, you've already come a long distance toward getting what you want most in your relationship. It's easier to talk without fighting. You feel a little closer.

You've started solving some of the mysteries of love. Now it's time to take another step. You're ready to face each other. But many people in relationships wake up one day to find they're strangers in paradise.

# 5

# I Heard It Through the Grapevine

. . . . . . . . . . . . . . . . . . . . . . . . . . . . . . . . . . . . . . . . . . . . . . . . . . . .

LOVE KILLER #4:
## The Chain of Silence

ISSUE:
Are you able to talk to each other freely, openly,
and easily?

LISA: *"All I can think of is that our relationship is like this* Twilight Zone *episode. We've somehow turned into alien beings who look and act the same as before, and yet we no longer feel connected to each other. How does a lover turn into a stranger overnight?"*

Do you feel distant and disconnected from your partner? I know there was a period when I did, and it feels awful, as if your love is a lie and your relationship is dying. Too often we put up with it. Too often we think it's inevitable. But it can be a love killer.

To understand this love killer, we need to see it more clearly. There's distance between you and your partner? If so, what kind of distance is it? There are three kinds of estrangements couples fall into. Mad distance. Sad distance. Cold distance.

## Mad Distance

With mad distance, you go around angry with each other all the time. You make a point of being in separate rooms, but then you slam things around for your partner to hear. In fact the only thing that keeps you from being more distant is your need to let your partner know how mad you are.

But that's exhausting and few couples can maintain a high level of angry distance for very long.

## Sad Distance

With sad distance, you feel as if someone has died. This happens when couples get into that walking-on-eggshells existence where they stay away from each other as if any kind of contact will just prick a wound. Sometimes with sad distance, if you should happen to come in contact, you'll actually be nice to each other but only in passing and only until you can get away from each other again.

## Cold Distance

With cold distance, you've got a relationship that's gone through a lot of hurt and damage. Don't think of "cold distance" as people acting icy and making an elaborate point of ignoring each other. That's just a version of mad distance. Believe it or not, the keynote of cold distance is politeness. I'm not saying you'd go out of your way to be nice to each other. You've just gotten to the point where it's safest not to care. It's not that you're trying to avoid each other, but you've lost the desire to connect with each other, and politeness is a way to maximize avoidance.

### The Chain of Silence

Whatever kind of distance you've fallen into, you've gotten caught in what I call the *chain of silence*, a sequence of events that actually begins when you're still strangers to each other at the beginning of your relationship and ends with your feeling almost completely cut off from each other.

This chain of silence is Love Killer #4. If you were being dragged down to the bottom of the ocean by some chain wrapped around you, which link in the chain would be the killer? No link. It's the whole chain. Break any link in the chain, and you're free.

You don't need the chain of silence to be together because you've already lived without it when your relationship was at its best. And you'd be surprised how easily you can live without it again. But you can't ignore it.

I'm going to use Esther and David's story to illustrate all the links in the chain of silence. This is not a story with a lot of fireworks and bombshells. The power of this story comes from the way well-intentioned everyday people can dig themselves into a terrible trap. I think there's a good chance this will seem familiar to you. Once you see how this chain of silence gets forged link by link you'll be in a better position to answer some diagnostic questions to determine whether this love killer is actually dragging down your relationship.

### ○ Esther and David

Esther is forty-one now, David is thirty-nine, and they've been married for eleven years. They met at a Jewish singles dance. They were both lonely and tired of first dates that led nowhere. They were both all too eager to hook up with someone as fast as possible.

Esther was a third-grade teacher. Today she admits that she'd hoped David would get the idea that she was a playful, happy person who got pleasure from taking care of other people. David worked in purchasing for a large, prestigious hospital. Okay, he wasn't a doctor, but he was vaguely in the medical field and today he's willing to say that he wanted Esther to get the sense that he'd be a good provider, that he was interested in being in control (in a good way), being responsible, being organized, that he'd be a success.

It's not that anyone was faking. But Esther and David did what so many people do. They wanted to give the best possible impression. And they helped each other too, because each wanted to see what he or she was searching for.

**Link 1.** Without their realizing it, Link 1 in the chain of silence was being forged: *seeing what you want to see*. This link is all too natural. We close our eyes to warts and warning signals. Who wants to be like Jerry or Elaine from *Seinfeld*, rejecting everyone for the slightest imperfection?

Because they only saw what they wanted to see, it was only natural that David, for example, would fail to ask himself if it was realistic for someone to be as cheerful and giving every minute of their lives together as Esther was on their dates.

Esther was similarly blind to the real David. For all his talk about wanting to be successful, he was a lot less driven by the need for success than he could admit even to himself, much less to Esther. In fact, work was so grim that when he got home he needed to give vent to the lazy, goofy side of himself.

Just think of it. When she came home, Esther was hungry for grownups. When he came home, David was hungry for acting like a kid. But I'm getting ahead of myself. Anyway, I'm sure you can guess what the next link in the chain of silence is.

**Link 2.** Their not wanting to see the other clearly led to Link 2 in the chain of silence: *unrealistic expectations*. Because they didn't want to see who the other really was, they formed expectations of each other neither could fulfill. All this could have easily been prevented if, for example, the night they'd met

David had said, "I know I seem like this really together guy who'll be able to manage things and take care of you, but I actually need to be taken care of myself."

But who wants to show his less attractive side to someone he's hoping will fall in love with him? *Even during that stage of relationship formation where we're being vulnerable and self-revealing, we have an instinct for keeping quiet about that one part of us that we know will turn the other person off.*

**Link 3.** The next step is inevitable. Sooner rather than later, unrealistic expectations will run smack into Link 3 in the chain of silence: *startling revelations.* Imagine a peaceful Sunday morning. David and Esther have just made love and they're both feeling incredibly relaxed and secure. Esther is so comfortable that she starts telling David about how obnoxious her third graders are and how she can't wait for the day when she can have a kid of her own and stop having to go to work.

**Link 4.** Life's filled with startling revelations. But this was a devastating head butt to the solar plexus of David's unrealistic expectations. And this helps forge Link 4 in the chain of silence: *disappointment.* When David saw that Esther was so much *not* the person he'd thought she was, his heart sank and his gorge rose. He got depressed and angry at the same time.

This wasn't an isolated incident and disappointment didn't just happen to David. It also happened to Esther. The first year tax time rolled around for them as a couple, David complained about how annoying and confusing he found the whole business. Esther was incredibly disappointed. This was exactly the kind of thing she was *not* looking for in a husband.

I don't want to give the impression that links 3 and 4, *startling revelations* and *disappointment*, are isolated, one-time-only events. For most people, as it was for David and Esther, there are always many little moments during the first years of a relationship where you reveal things about yourself that your partner finds incredibly disappointing. Each one of these moments is an opportunity for the next link to be forged.

**Link 5.** We've all been there. We all know what happens next. Usually you know it best when you're on the receiving end, but if you've received it, you've probably dished it out. Link 5 in the chain of silence is *rejection*. When your partner says something to you that disappoints you, you respond as if you'd eaten a bad oyster. You're disgusted, and you can't help letting the other person know it. Maybe you get angry, maybe you act sad, maybe you mock the other person.

You know what it's like to be on the receiving end of this kind of thing. In Esther's case, David said things like, "What's wrong with you? Is this who you really are? I thought you were a person who cared about making a difference. I thought teaching was this creative expression of your soul or something. Now I wonder who I really married." Esther felt as if she had been slapped in the face, like when you make an innocent remark to a colleague at work and he blows up. Rejection is usually physically palpable.

**Link 6.** What had Esther done? She'd shown herself naked. Not physically naked, but naked in a much deeper, more intimate sense. She'd shown a dark side of her soul. And when you show yourself and get rejected, and if the rejection's strong enough or happens often enough, you learn a very simple lesson that's Link 6 in the chain of silence: *it's not safe to show yourself.* You know the cliché: once burned, twice shy.

A sad lightbulb goes off. "When I tell David how I really feel," Esther might've said to herself, "he makes me feel sorry I ever said anything. In fact I'm not really sure what I can reveal to David. I'm not going to feel safe saying things like that again."

Notice how I said that Esther "might have" said something like this to herself. We rarely *actually* say things like this to ourselves. We're tough, independent people, as was Esther. She was not one of these people who look like they're skulking through life, as if their sole mission is to avoid being hurt. She was a hearty woman with a loud laugh and a strong voice. She wasn't afraid of confronting people. If people criticized her at teachers' meetings, it didn't bother her. Not feeling safe to show yourself isn't a sign of weakness. It's the way anyone would respond when he or she is attacked for being emotionally naked.

**Link 7.** So what do you do when you don't feel safe? It's obvious. You forge Link 7 in the chain of silence: *you hide—you stop talking.* But you don't just stop talking about the little subject for which you got jumped on. You stop talking about a broad range of things that connect to it, that might cause the other person to jump all over you. It doesn't happen all at once, once and for all. That would make it too noticeable. In real-life conditions, you shut up for a while, then you leak something out, then you shut up for a while—you keep testing the waters.

David did that. One way or another he'd reveal some glimpse of his feeling careless and lazy. And Esther wasn't perfectly consistent in slapping him down. But over the course of a year or two David got the picture. *Shut up about who you really are.* That's ultimately what we go silent about. Because we feel unsafe being naked, the easiest solution is to reveal nothing; otherwise, there's a good chance we'll get slapped down. What can you hope to gain to make the risk worthwhile? You no longer need to offer intimacy to win your partner. You've already won her. Now you can go silent.

It's always both people who go silent. Maybe one more than the other. But the point is that silence itself starts infecting the relationship. The day-to-day sharing of little things—the scraps of feeling, thought, and experience out of which we build our sense of life together—stops.

**Link 8.** That brings us to Link 8 in the chain of silence: *estrangement.* You almost literally become strangers. In a way you teach each other to become strangers: that's precisely what the chain of silence is all about. Just the way some couples learn that they can't cook together in the kitchen, many couples learn that showing yourself to your partner too often leads to disaster, and the things your partner shows you too often make you wish she'd kept them to herself. Why have anything to do with someone like that?

## THE CHAIN OF SILENCE

Link 1: seeing what you want to see
Link 2: unrealistic expectations
Link 3: startling revelations
Link 4: disappointment
Link 5: rejection
Link 6: realizing that it's not safe to show yourself
Link 7: hiding—not talking
Link 8: estrangement

The chain of silence is a terrible love killer. It kills love the way all love killers do—by making the things that go on in the relationship not look like love. You go on a picnic to enjoy yourself eating outside and hanging out with friends. If you add rain and wasps and ants and people with boom boxes to the picture, it soon stops looking like a picnic. There's almost nothing left to the experience that looks like why you went on a picnic in the first place.

The chain of silence does this to love. It destroys that sense absolutely necessary to love that you're two people who can speak from the heart and appreciate each other for doing so. With the chain of silence, instead of being soulmates you become inmates—strangers locked together who have to maintain maximum distance to prevent hostilities from breaking out.

# Diagnostic #4:
# Are You Trapped in a Chain of Silence?

You have to diagnose the true cases where the chain of silence is strangling the relationship. But I don't want to scare you too much. Every relationship, even the healthiest ones, has areas filled with landmines. You can talk about almost anything with each other, but you can't talk about *that*.

I've been guilty of being judgmental in my own marriage, and I've worked hard over the past thirty-two years to make it easier for my husband to throw open all the windows to his soul. But I'm sure if you asked him, he'd tell you there are things about which he just won't open his mouth to me.

I wonder what those things are?

Let me go ask him. I'll be back in a minute. . . .

Interesting. *First* he said that at this point with all the stuff we've worked through he could really tell me anything now.

But I found that word *anything* just a little hard to believe. So I pushed on him a little; I said it wasn't completely normal to feel you can say absolutely *anything*.

He thought a bit, but he wasn't saying anything so I asked him, "Well, what about things you spend money on, like stuff for the garden, for instance. How much did that new tree that you had put in cost? Aren't you sometimes afraid to tell me about that stuff until after you've spent the money, like you're afraid I'll argue with you about it?"

## Silent Little Traps

Here's how intimate communication can sometimes feel like a hall of mirrors. He was open and honest enough with me to say, yes, he sometimes does try to avoid telling me he's spending money until after the fact. Amazing. He was saying he *wasn't* completely open, but what he said *felt* like openness because he was admitting it, and I remembered one of the prescriptions I offer here, that you never punish openness.

It's interesting what happened next. We got to talking about other things, and he remembered having heard about a high school classmate who'd just died, a guy who was handsome and popular back in high school but later had gotten involved with alcohol and drugs. My husband said, "I have a feeling he might have killed himself."

Now check out what I said next. "You always think the worst." I just wanted to understand how my husband works. But my remark came across like a judgment, and no one likes to be judged. You could see in my husband's face a decision to be more careful next time about sharing his hunches with me. And did I really want him not to tell me his hunches?

That little offhand remark of mine—"You always think the worst"—was just the tiniest of examples of how we keep forging the chain of silence in spite of our best intentions, how we have to keep being vigilant in trying to break the chain and prevent it from forming.

## Falling out of Closeness

The chain of silence is all about your ability to be emotionally naked with each other. The idea is that nakedness promotes closeness, and closeness is what we want from a relationship, what makes us feel good about a relationship.

So if you think closeness is a good thing, and if you envy people in those relationships who can say, "I can tell my partner anything," here's how to diagnose whether the chain of silence has taken hold in your relationship.

## DIAGNOSING LOVE KILLER #4

Ask yourself the following diagnostic questions and check off the answers that are truest for you:

1. Would you say that your partner is a judgmental person?

VERY MUCH SO____ MORE THAN I'D LIKE____ NOT VERY MUCH____

2. Are there a lot of things that are important to you that you discuss with your best friend that you can't discuss with your partner?

VERY MUCH SO____ MORE THAN I'D LIKE____ NOT VERY MUCH____

3. Has it been quite a while since you and your partner talked about how you felt about things?

VERY MUCH SO____ MORE THAN I'D LIKE____ NOT VERY MUCH____

4. Do you find yourself censoring and editing a lot of what you're thinking of saying to your partner because you don't want to deal with his or her response?

VERY MUCH SO____ MORE THAN I'D LIKE____ NOT VERY MUCH____

. . . . . . . . . . . . . . . . . . . . . . . . . . . . . . . . . . . . . . . . . . . . . . . . . . . . . . . . . . . .

If you checked off even one *very much so* or if you checked off even two *more than I'd like* options, then Love Killer #4 applies to you, based on comparing your answers to the answers of people who are definitely caught in a relationship-killing chain of silence.

Think about it. If you can say, for example, that it's "very much" the case that "my partner is a judgmental person," then what do you think you've just said? You've said that you're in a relationship with someone who can and will come down like a ton of bricks if you let loose with the wrong remark, even if that remark shows a little bit of who you really are. I don't need to know whether the two of you fight a lot. If you don't fight, it's probably because you've gotten good at avoiding the areas your partner is judgmental about.

By the way, if you and your partner are both judgmental about the same things, then you're made for each other and you wouldn't have checked off "very much so." We never think of people who agree with us as being judgmental. You can open up with each other because you're not going to get slammed down for the things you open up about.

# Prescription #4:
# Forging Bonds of Openness

The crucial link in the chain of silence is Link 5: rejection. One of you shows yourself and the other shows how she feels about it. "Okay, you were open with me. I'll be open about how I felt about what you said: it sucks."

It seems fair on one level. If you can be free to show yourself, your partner should be free to show how she feels about what you showed her. But it doesn't work that way. You won't have people feeling free to say what's on their minds and in their hearts if other people are free to make them feel awful for speaking out.

The battle between openness and rejection is unequal. Rejection always wins. It's like a fight between a Doberman and a bunny rabbit. The Doberman of rejection always rips the bunny rabbit of openness to shreds. *Being open* and *being rejecting* don't have equal status in the land of love. To end the chain of silence you need less rejection so that openness can flourish.

That's how it works in general. Here are the steps to follow.

**Step 1. Accept the need for more openness.** Talk to each other and see if you can both agree with the following statement:

*We've not been as open and honest with each other about what we think and feel as we could, and we'd like to change this.*

All you're doing here is declaring that you want to make *more openness* a top priority in your relationship. It's one thing for me to tell you that the Chain of Silence is a love killer. It's quite another for you to make a commitment to do what's necessary to end it.

Okay. So you're committed to eliminating silence, distance, and rejection from your relationship. You're sure? Okay.

**Step 2. Identify what's been making you shut down.** Tell your partner what he or she does that makes you wish you hadn't opened your big mouth.

Most of the time our partners don't realize what they're doing. I like to think I'm very accepting of what my husband says. And yet I say things that make him wish he hadn't said a word. The impact on him of what I say is the important thing, not how horrible it is in itself.

For example, he'll agree with one of our daughters, and I'll say, "Oh you always defend her." He'll say he doesn't care about getting older, and I'll say, "Oh you always deny realities that make you feel uncomfortable."

Making people feel rejected by explaining them to themselves is just one of dozens of ways we make our partners wish they hadn't opened their mouths. If I speak without thinking, my husband's liable to jump all over me and demand to know why I'm saying what I'm saying or what he's supposed to do about it or what my words all add up to. That's another way of making someone wish she hadn't opened her mouth. When he does that, he makes me feel stupid, and the chain of silence starts being forged.

So in Step 2 you just lay out what you specifically need from your partner to feel safer speaking from the heart. If you need a bit of help identifying the openness-destroying responses that lead to silence, here are some of the major categories:

- **Anything that makes you or your partner feel stupid:** for example, "That doesn't make any sense," or "You obviously don't understand what you're talking about." The

chain of silence is often forged by people treating a relationship like a business meeting or a conference.

- **Anything that conveys the sense that only an emotionally
  disturbed or psychologically damaged person would say
  it:** for example, "What did your mother do to you?" or
  "Don't be so paranoid." You can't promote openness and
  play amateur shrink at the same time.
- **Anything that says your partner is immoral for thinking
  or feeling what she does:** for example, "Don't you have a
  conscience?" or "What's wrong with you to say something
  like that?" No one wants to open up to someone who's
  going to make moral judgments.

Here's what some people have said, talking about how their
partners got them to go into hiding:

- "She'd always make me feel so geeky, like I had the soul
  of a nerd."
- "He'd start instructing me, even in ways that seemed to
  have little to do with what I was saying, like there was
  always a right way to do things, and by opening my mouth
  I showed that I didn't know what it was."
- "She'd tell me, 'Oh I know that's not you, you don't really
  feel that way, you're just saying it.' Why should I be open
  with her if she's going to make it seem like I'm not telling
  the truth?"
- "Every time I said something he didn't like, he knew just
  how to get me. 'You're just like your mother.' I once spent
  a year where I didn't tell him a single thing that was really
  going on for me, although he didn't know it, just to avoid
  being told I was like my mother."

You get the picture. If your ideas make your partner sorry
he's shared his ideas, very soon the free exchange is over.

**Step 3. Work at being more open.** Practice makes perfect. The
beauty of zeroing in on the love killer that's the biggest threat

is that you can focus on one issue in your relationship and let everything else go. The issue you're focusing on here is getting naked, except we're talking about a nakedness of the mind and heart. So you set up a game with very specific rules:

1. More sharing is good and wins you points.
2. Saying things that make the other person feel slapped down is bad and loses you points.

Keep score. Add up your points. Every day, whoever has the most points is the winner. But you both win because you've broken the chain of silence.

A really good exercise you can use to accomplish Step 3 is to try to listen to each other for five minutes at a time without responding. The more you talk without getting slapped down, the safer you'll feel to talk in the future.

**Step 4. Stay out of trouble.** Now you have to troubleshoot why Step 3 would be hard for you. It's easy enough to say, "Don't respond in rejecting ways," but something I've found amazing is that it's hard for many people to respond without coming across as being judgmental. All their habitual responses make their partner sorry she'd spoken. So Step 4 requires that you learn openness-promoting things to say when your partner talks to you.

Here are the top ten comments that work to prevent your partner from feeling sorry she opened her mouth:

### THE TOP TEN OPENNESS PROMOTERS

**1. "So let me hear more about what you're saying."**

**2. "Why do you feel that way?"**

3. "Then what happened?"

4. "What makes you think so?"

5. "What else do you think is going on?"

6. "How did it start?"

7. "Exactly how badly do you feel about it?"

8. "How important is this to you?"

9. "Tell me what you'd like me to do."

10. "I'm glad you told me."

I know the things on this list don't sound as pungent as saying, "What kind of a person are you to say something like that?" Well, as any prison inmate will tell you, there's nothing as pungent as starting a riot. These top ten items *prevent* riots. They also prevent emotional flare-ups, and they promote true warmth. Why do you think a child babbles on and on with complete honesty? Because he knows he'll be accepted for whatever he says. And that climate is one of the reasons the parent and child love each other. Adult relationships need more of this kind of openness.

**Step 5. Ask questions.** This step helps you move closer to forging bonds of openness. All you have to do is ask questions. Draw each other out. Your "interviews" might last for only one question. But the point of them is to help your partner tell his story (so you feel closer to him) and to make your partner feel more comfortable telling his story (so he feels closer to you).

Esther and David did this. They'd both been liberal Democrats. One day David came home and said he was sick of Clinton. This was during their chain-of-silence period. Esther responded by saying, "I hope you're not going to turn into one of those guys who become conservative when they hit middle age." David had some comeback but Esther's response made him lose interest in talking about how he felt.

A few years later they were trying to feel closer to each other and Esther asked David what he thought about politics. As he talked, the biggest surprise for her was realizing that David had been thinking about the way things were going in America. If anything his sympathy for the little guy was stronger than ever.

In a couple of areas he had changed. He was now for capital punishment, for example. Esther was tempted to jump all over him for this and say something like, "How can you be one of those electric chair people?" But then she remembered the cardinal principle of forging bonds of openness:

## Never punish honesty.

Esther got her reward later. The next day David said, "How do you feel about all that political stuff I was saying? When I said I was in favor of capital punishment, I was sure you were going to let me have it."

Esther said, "Do you really want to hear how I feel about capital punishment?" David nodded. Esther was smart enough to remember to be open about her own feelings, without making David feel rejected for his feelings. "I think that . . ." and she laid out her position on capital punishment.

I realize that 99 percent of the things we need and want to be open about have nothing to do with politics. They're personal. They have to do with our private lives, with the details of our bodies and the people we know and our daily routine. But openness has an amazing way of promoting more openness, and that has a miraculous way of bringing relationships back to health.

### *Getting Naked in a Nutshell*

This prescription is really about breaking bad habits. It's so easy to fall into the pattern of rejecting what our partners say that we don't even realize that we're doing it. And there's a part of us that wants to maintain the rejection: we want to feel free to respond the way we want to. This freedom is so important to us that we fail to see how it ends up creating chains of silence.

Here's what this prescription amounts to. You're in the park with a bag of peanuts. There are semi-tamed squirrels there. You want them to eat out of your hand. They're suspicious, but if you're patient you can persuade them to trust you. So here's a stupid question: if you're holding out a peanut and one of these squirrels starts slowly and carefully approaching you, do you *jump!* at him? Or do you hold still, acting as nonthreatening as possible? If you know the answer to this question, you know how to follow Prescription #4.

# Love Builder #4:
# I'll Show You Mine If You Show Me Yours

You meet a stranger on a train. You talk about nothing important. Then the stranger reveals a personal detail. How do you respond? Oh no! You can't help it! You find yourself revealing a personal detail as well. Before long, the stranger confesses a personal detail that's unflattering to her. Oh no! You can't help it! You find yourself confessing a personal detail that's unflattering to you as well.

This is the inevitable, natural process of mutually escalating personal disclosure: the more one of you reveals, the more the other reveals. The more both of you reveal—well, it's called openness, closeness, intimacy. If you show me yours, I'll show you mine. It's a way of acting as if you liked each other. Since you really do like each other, why not act that way?

When people like each other, nakedness begets nakedness, just as when people don't like each other, walls beget walls. Right now you're trying to break down the walls, and Prescription #4 is the way to do it. What you should find encouraging is that in spite of having felt unsafe, the more open one of you is, the more open the other will be. Just follow this prescription and the love builder here will carry you forward on its own momentum.

## A Look Ahead

More good stuff, less bad stuff. More openness, less feeling shut off from each other. More feeling comfortable, less hostility and criticism. All these are part of the foundation of a relationship, part of what you get when you eliminate the four love killers we've looked at so far.

Now it's time to take the next step. Only when you know that your foundation is solid does it make sense to tackle whether you feel you can get your needs met in this relationship with this particular person. And what's more important than that?

# 6

# What Have You Done for Me Lately?

. . . . . . . . . . . . . . . . . . . . . . . . . . . . . . . . . . . . . . . . . . . . . . . . . . . . . . . . .

LOVE KILLER #5:

## Needs Disease

ISSUE:

Why is it so hard for me to get my needs met?

Think about why you fell in love with your partner. Make a little list. Now out of all the things you fell in love with, what are the things you fell in love with that feel smart to you today? It might be that you intuited that your partner had a kind soul. It might be that you had the strong sense that your partner cared about his family.

Why was it smart of you to fall in love with that? *Because you knew what you needed.* It's somehow thrilling to the core to feel we're hooking up with someone who can meet our deepest needs.

Too often, though, time goes by and we find ourselves saying, "I don't know how to get him to start . . ." or "I don't know how to make her stop . . ."

Saying things like this signals that you have unmet needs. When you and your partner met, it might be that you respected her for being smart in her field. And you thought you had a free pass to be the fun-loving guy you are when you're being yourself. But a few years later, you find you can't get your partner to talk about anything you're even remotely interested in. And she can't get you to take things seriously.

What do we refer to when we talk about "needs"? Basic wants and desires such as:

- Make love to me.
- Be nice to me.
- Be involved with the children.
- Stop undermining my authority with the children.
- Don't raise such a ruckus when I want my mother to come to visit.
- If you say you're going to do something around the house, do it.
- Talk to me about our finances as you said you would.
- Have our friends over.
- Be willing to go out.
- Stop leaving messes for me to clean up.
- Don't say no whenever I suggest something.

Unmet needs are what every couple is talking about whenever they have a fight. For example, here's a condensed version of the kind of fight that goes on in most relationships:

SHE: "Are you going to wear *that* shirt with *those* pants?" ["I need to feel my partner looks good when we go out together."]

HE: "You're always criticizing me." ["I need to feel appreciated."]

SHE: "I'm just giving you feedback." ["I need to feel I can say what's important to me."]

HE: "I didn't ask you for feedback." ["I need to know that I'm not going to be ambushed with criticism at any moment."]

SHE: "Well, I just want you to look nice." ["I need to be proud of you."]

HE: "Well, I don't want to hear it." ["I need to know that I can ask you to stop talking about something and you'll respect me."]

SHE: "I've got to tell you how I feel." ["I need to feel there's room in this relationship for me to be the person I really am."]

HE: "But it's none of your business how I look." ["I need to feel I have some part of my life I can call my own."]

SHE: "Okay, so you want us never to talk . . ." ["I need to feel I'm in a relationship where we can talk to each other about anything."]

Who needed what? It's hard to tell from this little dialogue. Clearly it seems as though someone wants to feel less criticized and someone else wants to feel free to speak her mind. But the real needs here are lost in a tangled mess. Instead of helping each other, they're like two octopuses playing Twister. Criticism. Feedback. Saying how you feel. Minding your own business. Asking for things. By the time they're all tangled up with this, it's too easy for them to be completely disgusted with each other.

And all they wanted was to get their needs met.

## What Happy Couples Say

Why do you think it was so important to you to meet the "right" person? Why do we all dream of finding a soulmate? Because a soulmate is someone with whom it will be easy for us to get our needs met.

Good sex; free, open, intimate conversation; acceptance; fun—things like these are important to us. So let's repeat out loud the Happy Couple's Mantra:

> We're both entitled to get our needs met.
> We both want to help each other get our needs met.
> There is a way for both of us to get our needs met.
> If we hang in there, we can both come out of this
> feeling satisfied.

There's something almost miraculous about this mantra. All you and your partner have to do is believe it and act on it, and it becomes a reality.

All this is easy when needs disease hasn't afflicted your relationship. If it has, then you've got a real love killer on your hands. You can cure it, and when you do your relationship will feel 100 percent better, but you can't ignore it.

## Toward a Solution

What's the real problem when people are struggling over unmet needs in a relationship? It might help to have a conversation about needs—you, me, all of our smartest friends. Let's pick up some of the remarks that would come out during this conversation:

". . . It's just not worth the struggle to get my needs met. . . ." "When we got together I thought it would be automatic that we'd meet each other's needs, and every time we don't, I get depressed. . . ." "I don't know if I have a right to all these needs of mine. . . ." "You just meet each other's needs or you get divorced. . . ." "When you tell someone what you need, he feels put down, as if you're saying he's not good enough. . . ." "I think most of us are just too needy. . . ." "A relationship isn't about getting your needs met. . . ."

If you read between the lines, you'll see that these quotes contain clues about the problem. Unmet needs aren't the result of one disease but a group of closely related diseases. Here are snapshots of people in relationships haunted by unmet needs. In each snapshot something is blocking the ability of the people in that relationship to meet each other's needs. *But that "something" is different in each case.*

SNAPSHOT: A man wants to have sex with his wife. She almost always says no. From his point of view not only is this whole issue a problem, but he's convinced his wife has a problem that's causing her to keep saying no. But she refuses to discuss anything about the topic of their not having sex.

SNAPSHOT: Two men have been in a relationship for twelve years now. One makes a good living as a graphics designer. The other calls himself a writer, but he's written little and drifts from one low-paying job to another. The first guy needs his partner to pay more of his fair share. The second guy's open to talking about it but every time they do, his feelings get hurt.

SNAPSHOT: A man says his wife is depressed. Most people who know them agree that she certainly seems that way. He knows he can't expect her to be a Happy Hannah all the time, but they're at loggerheads because she refuses to go into therapy or to consider the possibility of taking Prozac. They fight about this constantly. "Do something." "Leave me alone." Over and over.

Just the way many different infections can attack the body, and we can fall victim to multiple infections at once, when it comes to unmet needs there are a number of different little diseases that can cause problems, each with a different diagnosis and a different prescription.

By the end of this chapter you'll know two things:

1. Whether or not unmet needs are killing your relationship, and

2. If unmet needs *are* killing your relationship, you'll know which of the needs diseases is causing the problem and how to cure it.

We all have needs in our relationship that aren't met. I remember one patient of mine who was a fitness expert whose husband weighed 270 pounds. It embarrassed her, it made her feel he was mocking her, and it made her scared he'd die on her. So she had a lot of unmet needs. The question was—and this is the question we're going to answer here for you—do *your* unmet needs point to a real love killer: Needs Disease?

This chapter is going to be a little different from the others. First we're going to diagnose whether you have some form of Needs Disease. Then, and only then, will we get down to diagnosing and treating the specific form Needs Disease has taken in your case.

# Diagnostic #5:
# Are You Suffering from Needs Disease?

## DIAGNOSING LOVE KILLER #5

To diagnose whether your symptoms point to a needs disease, all you have to do is answer three preliminary questions:

1. Would you say that, for whatever reason, more often than not you don't bother asking your partner for important things you want?  YES ＿＿ NO ＿＿

2. Do your unmet needs make your relationship more undesirable than desirable, and if these needs were met would you then say that your relationship was desirable?  YES ＿＿ NO ＿＿

3. Think about the times you and your partner are together—for example, lying in bed at night, sitting down for a meal together, making love, driving somewhere together, or having a conversation on a Sunday morning. Because of your unmet

needs and the way you feel about them, are most of your times together unsatisfying?                    YES ____ NO ____

. . . . . . . . . . . . . . . . . . . . . . . . . . . . . . . . . . . . . . . . . . . . . . . . . . . . . . . . . . . .

If you answered *yes* to any one of these three preliminary diagnostic questions, you have some form of Needs Disease. It doesn't matter how many or how important your unmet needs are, how big a fight you've had about them, or how bad you feel. You've got a needs disease if you can't even ask anymore, or if your unmet needs and your anger and disappointment over them spoil the relationship for you or spoil the times you have together.

## *If You're* Not *Suffering from a Needs Disease*

Just because you don't have a needs disease doesn't mean you wouldn't like to get more of what you want in your relationship. Well, you're in luck.

I've performed many tests and here's what I've found works best. Assuming you *don't* have a needs disease, here's what you can do to increase your chances of getting your needs met:

### THE TEN FUNDAMENTAL STEPS FOR GETTING A NEED MET

**1. Get the other person's attention.**

**2. Tell him you need something that's important to you.**

**3. Ask if it's all right for you to tell him what you need at that time.**

**4. Tell him how terrific he is in any way you can, in any area connected with your need.**

5. Say what you need as simply and specifically as possible, so your partner knows exactly what to do to meet your need.

6. Ask your partner if he understands what you need.

7. Ask what would help him meet your need.

8. Discuss all the practical details about exactly how it's going to work for him to meet your need: who does what, when, to whom, and how.

9. Troubleshoot any problems that might occur in carrying out the plan, including what will happen if your partner fails to meet your need.

10. Since he's going to be meeting this need of yours, ask him what you can do for him.

Here are the ten steps in action. As you'll see, you can accomplish these steps in a few sentences. They're easier to carry out than you think.

## ⊃ *Margaret and Peter*

Peter had said that he wanted to be a good father. That was before they had kids and before work started piling up at his accounting firm. All Margaret needed was for him to be there sometimes for the kids—to meet with a teacher, to show up at a soccer game, to read a story.

Here's how Margaret could've asked for what she needed: "Can we talk now, because there's something I need that's very important to me? [Steps 1, 2, and 3.] Look, you're a really good guy, and I know you care about the kids, but I need for you to put in substantially more time with the kids than you're doing now. [Steps 4 and 5.] Do you understand what I need? [Step

6.] Can I help you with this? For example, do you want me to write out a schedule of the kids' activities so you can meld it with your own, and then you can put it in your appointment book? [Steps 7, 8, and 9.] I know it's costing you something to do this—is there anything I can do for you? [Step 10.]"

In this case, Peter agreed to do what Margaret wanted, and he did do it. These ten steps don't always magically give you everything you want. It's just that *they're more likely to give you what you want than anything else.*

There are also five things it's important *not* to do because they hurt you even more than they hurt your partner:

## THE TOP FIVE THINGS *NOT* TO DO IF YOU WANT TO GET A NEED MET

1. **Never make your partner guess what you need.**

2. **Never be anything other than highly specific about what your partner needs to do to meet your need.**

3. **Never bring up more than one need at a time.**

4. **Never fail to say something nice to your partner while you're talking about your need.**

5. **Never fail to appreciate him for trying to meet your need, even if what he does isn't perfect.**

The things you shouldn't do if you want to get your needs met can be summed up very simply: *Watch out for how deprived you feel.* The angrier you are, the more you feel your partner doesn't care; the more desperately hungry you are for whatever it is you want, the more likely it will be that your asking will feel like an attack on your partner. It's only natural. You've felt very hurt, and maybe you're desperate. But as natural as it is, if your request feels like an attack, your partner will respond to the attack and not to your need.

# Prescription #5:
# Discovering Your Particular Needs Disease and What to Do to Cure It

Okay, here's what we're going to do. If your answer to the three preliminary diagnostic questions showed that you have some form of needs disease, you're in the right place. We'll zip through the twelve different needs diseases and as quickly as possible help you understand what they are, diagnose whether you have a particular disease, and understand exactly what you have to do to eliminate it.

*Follow the prescription for each individual needs disease you're diagnosed with.*

### Needs Disease #1: Need Overload

Consider the possibility that one or both of you simply needs too much from the other. Let's face it, our partners are not Superman or Superwoman. With all the love and energy in the world there's only so much I can do to meet my husband's needs if he starts bringing them to me by the shovelful. And if he runs around "suffering" from need overload because one day I wear a jacket he doesn't like and the next day I eat my food too quickly and the next day . . . maybe there aren't too many unmet needs, there are too many needs period.

**Diagnosing need overload.** You have to keep count. Does the person with the "needs" bring up the subject of one unmet need almost every time you talk to each other, and are these unmet needs rarely the same from one conversation to the next? If *yes*, you've got need overload.

**Prescription.** The person complaining about unmet needs—and maybe it's both of you—should make a list of his or her unmet needs. Then ask yourself, "Are all these needs necessary for me?" Throw away every one you can't persuade yourself is important.

Here's the rule. Don't pay attention to more than five very important unmet needs in your whole relationship. Otherwise you're overloading the system, especially when most of us lead busy lives these days. Your partner can probably cope with your five unmet needs without feeling overwhelmed. More than that, though, and your partner will start feeling confused and inadequate.

> If you're wondering whether to let go of a need, just ask yourself: "If this need never gets satisfied, *will I respect myself for suffering over it?*"

One man had trouble because when he and his wife were going somewhere together she always had a lot to do at the last minute, which usually held them up. Then he'd make a big deal about how unhappy he was about his unmet need for the two of them not to be late, and they'd have a big fight. But the minute he asked himself if he could respect himself for suffering over this need not being met, he was able to let go of it.

It's not that I can tell you what you should need, but you've got a lot of buddies out here who've walked down the same path you're walking down, and they're the ones from whom I've learned this. The simplest way to deal with unmet needs is to just let go of the needs that aren't really all that important to you.

## Needs Disease #2: Hidden Hostility

Okay, you've got some need that's very important to you, and you're suffering because it's not being met. But what have you been putting out to your partner? In many cases, the only way you've felt you can convey the intensity of what you feel is to let loose with all kinds of negativity and criticism and anger and misery. What started out as "I need you to call me if you're going to be late," becomes "You're a selfish bastard for not calling when you're late," which becomes "You're a selfish bastard."

What's the problem with this?

## You're making TOO MUCH NOISE.

The intensity of your negativity drowns out your need. It just doesn't get heard. The thing you do to get heard prevents you from being heard.

**Diagnosing hidden hostility.** Does the person with the need seem to her partner to be too critical, angry, and miserable? Does she seem to be on the attack? Do you keep having fights about the ways your partner expresses herself about her unmet needs? If you answered *yes* to all three questions, then you've got a case of hidden hostility.

**Prescription.** Say what you need one more time, as calmly as you can. Be very careful to leave all complaints and criticism out of what you say. Then ask your partner if he understands what you need. Ask him if he knows how important it is to you. Ask him if he has any problem meeting your need. If he does have a problem, then *talk about solving his problem.*

### Needs Disease #3: Freedom Freaks

Of course we all love our freedom. But freedom freaks are especially troublesome people who don't get the idea of doing something because they have to, or because another person needs it or wants it, or because they've agreed to it. As one classic freedom freak said, "No one should have to do anything he doesn't want to do. So I'm not going to agree to start dinner when I get home first, because, I mean, whoever feels like doing something should be the one to do it."

Don't get the wrong impression. Freedom freaks probably *don't* come across as mean. If anything, they can be very charming, friendly, interesting people. They'll just make you so angry that *you'll* come across as mean.

**Diagnosing freedom freaks.** Does your partner say things like, "Why should I . . . ," "No one should have to . . . ," "You should just do it yourself . . . ," "We should just let it happen however it happens . . ."? Does your partner try to argue you out of your needs, and then if you should ever get some kind of agreement it's soon broken? A *yes* answer to either question means you've got a case of freedom freaks in your relationship.

**Prescription.** This strain of Needs Disease is more tenacious than any other. That means that you can help your relationship if you jettison as many of your less important needs as possible. As for your most important needs, here's what works best. Appeal to his sense of fairness: "Is it fair that I should have to . . . ?" Watch out for being too vehement—it will just make him feel more trapped. Relentless but quiet persistence is your best tool: make him feel far less free not meeting your need than if he meets it. Show him the benefits that he'll get if he meets it. Don't expect too much. But never stop persisting.

## Needs Disease #4: Reality Wars

When you were a kid, you probably took part in a fight where your mother said clean up your room and you said, "It's not even messy!" Fights like these come up all the time when it comes to needs and relationships. You say, "We need to talk more," and your partner *doesn't* say, "I don't want to talk more." Instead, he says, "Why? We talk plenty."

You get the point: you are told your need either doesn't exist (like with the nonmessy room) or is already being satisfied (like with the way you're already talking plenty).

In one couple I worked with the husband had been suffering from stress. His wife wanted him to get treatment because she needed to live with someone who wasn't so stressed out. He said that he wasn't stressed at all *and* that he was doing things anyway like taking yoga to deal with it. This was a double attack on his wife's sense of reality.

**Diagnosing reality wars.** Fortunately, this is incredibly easy to diagnose. Has your partner told you that the thing you need doesn't exist, or that your need is already in the process of being satisfied? If *yes*, you guys are stuck in a reality war.

**Prescription.** You have to tackle this on two different levels.

First, don't get caught in terminology. That husband could deny he was stressed but it was a lot harder for him to deny that he'd sit around the house all weekend saying there was nothing worthwhile in life. His wife made more progress when she told him that her need was for him to have more upbeat energy on the weekends. Remember: your real need isn't for your partner to agree with you about what's real. It's for your partner to try to meet your need. What you can do is say something like this: "Fine, we can call it whatever you like, but I still need you to . . ." and then say what you need without using the old label.

Ask for actions, not agreement about labels.

Second, if your need to know what's real is about something serious, choose some expert whose opinion you both trust and ask her to arbitrate. For example, one sixty-six-year-old man said he needed to make love with his wife more than once every three months. His sixty-three-year-old wife said he couldn't need that because people their age didn't make love anymore. The husband said to his wife, "Let's make an appointment with your gynecologist, and if she says that people our age don't have sex anymore then I won't ask you to have sex anymore." His wife agreed and in the end found that treatment was available to both raise her libido as well as relieve a number of other symptoms she'd been experiencing.

Following this prescription doesn't automatically mean your need will get satisfied. There may be other needs diseases that will get you stuck in the process of trying to satisfy them. But at least you won't get stuck fighting about whether your need has a basis in reality.

## Needs Disease #5: Sliding

This may be the most common Needs Disease. A need should be definite. So should the solutions. Sliding is going on when things that should be definite aren't. You are victims of sliding when

- one day you say you need something, the next day you don't need it
- one day you need one thing, the next day you need something else
- you keep talking about solutions, but nothing definite is ever proposed
- you propose solutions, but you never agree on solutions
- you come to an agreement, but then it turns out you had widely different views of what you agreed to
- you come to an agreement, but then don't follow through

Anyone who's been through this will recognize what I'm talking about. Bottom line: needs don't get met because there's nothing solid under your feet.

**Diagnosing sliding.** With respect to your important needs, would you say there's just no follow-through, no sense of moving from discussion to solution to implementation in a solid trust-building manner? Do you feel nothing gets resolved? If *yes*, you've been sliding into a case of Needs Disease.

**Prescription.** Some people don't like this prescription but ultimately sliding can be a real love killer, and this prescription is a small price to pay for keeping love alive. If you've diagnosed sliding, then to cure it you're going to need paper and pencil. Here's how you'll do it.

**1.** If you have a need, you talk to your partner about it on May 1, for example. You write that date on a piece of paper, write down the need you brought up, and write down where you were at the end of this first discussion. "I told John we needed to have the kitchen remodeled and he said he'd think about it."

**2.** Then get a definite date for when you'll talk about it next.

**3.** The next time you talk about it, you write down that new date on the same piece of paper and begin exactly where you left off. "John, last time we talked, you said you'd think about getting the kitchen remodeled. What do you think now?" Maybe new issues have come up. For example, maybe he says okay except that he doesn't see how the two of you could afford to spend more than ten thousand dollars. Maybe you agree with him and say you'll see what you can get done for ten thousand dollars. So on that piece of paper you write down this next step and the date on which you'll reopen the discussion.

**4.** Then make sure that by that agreed-upon date you've gotten the new information you need.

You see the point. Sliding means nothing gets pinned down, as when the guy proposes but then refuses to set a date for the wedding. The solution is to pin things down. You don't have to solve everything in one step. You just have to be definite at each step.

## Needs Disease #6: Off-the-Table-Itis

"I just don't want to talk about it." That's what off-the-table-itis really is. It's when you or your partner, one way or another, throw roadblocks in the way of talking about a need. It's taking any discussion about that need off the table. It is *not* the same as saying you don't want to meet a need—for example, "Honey, the thought of spending a vacation walking through the hot streets of Europe from one boring museum to another is just awful." It's when you'd say, instead, "We always go to the Cape and we're not going to talk about doing anything else."

No. No. No. You *can't* refuse to talk about doing anything else. That kills relationships. Relationships can survive people disagreeing about what they want, but they can't survive the consequences of people not being able to talk about their disagreements. Suppose you were in a restaurant and complained to the manager about extremely slow service. It would be one thing if he explained that they were extremely busy that day and short of help. But suppose he said, "I refuse to discuss the problem."

In a healthy relationship, both people are comfortable saying "Let's talk about what we need and try to find a way to meet those needs."

Off-the-table-itis violates this basic principle.

**Diagnosing off-the-table-itis.** You've got to go with your feelings on this. Do you feel your partner makes it hard for you to bring up your needs? If *yes*, your relationship has come down with a case of off-the-table-itis.

**Prescription.** There are three steps to eliminating off-the-table-itis.

**1. *Confront your partner.*** Say something like this: "You've been making it very hard for me to bring this up, but if we don't talk about it it's just going to fester and hurt both of us."

**2. *Appeal to her sense of fairness.*** For example, "Don't you think it's only fair for us both to be able to say what we need and then talk about it?"

**3. *Persist.*** If your partner is saying she doesn't want to talk about something, you've got to make it clear that you *do* want to talk about it. That means you keep bringing up your need to talk about it. If you drop it because she's asked you to drop it, you're saying that you also agree to take it off the table. But if you don't agree, don't drop it.

## Needs Disease #7: Undercutting Your Own Need

I used to think it was mostly women who did this—you know, because we're so shy and sweet and hate to make trouble. But a lot of research has erased this idea. Men do it just as much.

What I'm talking about is the problem that comes from not letting the other person know how important your need is to you. In a way, this needs disease is the opposite of hidden hostility, where you hurt yourself by putting forth your need with so much anger and intensity that you drown out the other person's desire to meet your need. Here, instead, you *downplay* how important your need is to you so much that your partner doesn't understand why he should try to meet it.

I can't tell you how many times the following scenario has played itself out:

A couple comes in for therapy. One partner sobs about unmet needs. The other partner indignantly protests about not knowing that these needs had even existed. I start thinking the second person is the bad guy for not listening. Then we do some exercises in which the first person is supposed to present his needs. Guess what? He'll say something instead like, "I think it might be nice if sometimes you . . ."

Ten minutes earlier he was ready to end the relationship because he wasn't getting a need met. Now he's saying it "might" be "nice" if "sometimes"—no wonder he's not getting his needs met. His partner wasn't the bad guy. She was in the dark because he'd been keeping her there. When there's a fire in the building, you set off a fire alarm. You don't send a memo saying there might be a "heat surplus" somewhere.

**Diagnosing undercutting.** Does the person with the need typically use phrases like, "Why don't we . . . ?" "What do you think about . . . ?" "Wouldn't it be nice if . . . ?" "You know, some people . . . ," "Sometimes I wonder if . . ."? Or, does the other person frequently and sincerely end up saying things like, "Gee, I never knew that really mattered to you so much." A *yes* answer means you are undercutting yourself.

**Prescription.** It couldn't be simpler. You just use the old *One-to-Ten-Scale Love Tool.* If you need your partner to do more chores around the house and it really is a nine for you that he does so, then you say it's a nine for you, and act like it's a nine.

## Needs Disease #8: Obstructionism

One man's great negotiator is another man's obstructionist. Obstructionism, however, is not about whether a particular need

of yours is a big problem for your partner. In some of the healthiest relationships, some needs just can't be met. Obstructionism
is different. It's about *your* feeling that your partner is throwing
up obstacles to avoid meeting your needs.

These obstacles can come up at any time—

- *When* you bring up your need: "I can't listen to you now"
  or "What, you need something else?"
- *While* you're talking about your need: "How can you want
  that?" or "Do you realize how impossible it would be for
  me to do that?"
- *After* you think there's been an agreement: There are endless "misunderstandings" about what you actually agreed
  to, or the other person keeps forgetting to do what he
  agreed to.

You have to look for a pattern. One man I interviewed complained, "All she thinks I'm good for is bringing home a pay-
check. If I do that and shut up, then things are fine. But if I
should want anything, like for us to go for a three-day weekend
or to have some friends over or to buy a pool table . . . anything—well, it's just a huge fight from beginning to end and I
almost never win. Here's the deal, from her point of view: she
says, 'I'm happy, so *you* should be happy.' "

There's a real clue to obstructionism in this man's statement.
It has to do with the way one partner gets far fewer needs met
than the other. It's the imbalance that makes obstructionism
particularly destructive.

**Diagnosing obstructionism.** Do you have this experience
fairly frequently: You talk to someone close to you about something that makes you unhappy in your relationship, and she says
to talk to your partner about it, and you say it's just not worth
all the trouble (because you're thinking of all the ways your
partner will make asking for something an ordeal)? If *yes*, then
obstructionism has brought a needs disease to your relationship.

**Prescription.** The key to curing obstructionism is to make sure that this disease itself is out in the open as an issue. Your partner will deny that he's an obstructionist. He'll blame your being too needy or having unrealistic needs. He'll say that there's no problem, that it's just the way things have worked out because he's just taking things need by need.

So you have to make a commitment to show him the pattern. Every time you bring up a need, write down what that need was, when you brought it up, and what happened. Do the same with the next need that comes up. And the next need. Do the same with all of your needs. Document a pattern of needs that you bring up and that are obstructed. This is not a time to wail, "You never do anything I want." This is a time instead to make the kind of well-documented case that would persuade anyone with an ounce of fairness that there's a pattern.

You're not doing this to play gotcha. You're doing this to save the relationship.

## Needs Disease #9: ''Huh?''

It often happens, even when there are two bright, articulate people in a relationship, that one is complaining about an unmet need, but the other doesn't have a clue about what her partner needs or what to do to meet his needs. People who get in trouble with this needs disease are like people who die of thirst in the desert when they're a few feet away from an oasis. They're incredibly close to solving the problem, but clear communication is the obstacle.

I think of one woman who was at the point of consulting her lawyer about divorcing her husband because he just wasn't warm, affectionate, and romantic. "I've complained and complained and complained," she said.

Now get this. When I was called in I discovered that *he* thought the problem was with who he was, not with what he did. He thought she was describing him, not asking for something. Then I asked a simple question that struck them both like a lightening bolt. "What would Mark do if he were the warm, romantic person you'd like him to be?"

She started reeling off a list of generalities, but I stopped her.

"Wait," I said, "let's start with the first thing on your list: Be more affectionate. What would he do if he were being more affectionate?"

"I don't know," she said.

"Well, name something, anything," I said.

"Well, he'd touch me when we talk, and he'd hold my hand."

"Can you do that?" I asked him.

"Of course," he said.

They were suffering from the needs disease "Huh?" because she didn't break down what she needed into something he could easily understand and do something about.

**Diagnosing "Huh?"** The only way to diagnose "Huh?" is to treat it. If you respond to treatment, you're on your way to being cured of it. So go directly to the prescription.

**Prescription.** The prescription is a joint exercise. You take a need you've been suffering from because it's not being met. You sit down with your partner and say exactly what your need is. Then say, "And here's one thing you could do to help meet my need." Make sure your partner knows exactly what to do. No confusion. No ambiguity.

One man who complained of "not feeling loved" got the response, "Well, if you don't know that I love you . . ." Classic "Huh?"

This time he said, "One thing you could do that would make me feel loved would be to ask how I'm feeling every couple of days and then listen to my answer."

Their progress was enormous, as yours will be. You're not communicating your needs if your partner doesn't know exactly what to do to meet them.

## *Needs Disease #10: Not Working It Through*

We now know that Communism can end in Russia and that the Israelis and Palestinians can engage in peace talks. What many people in relationships don't seem to know is that much lesser miracles can be accomplished between two people when it comes to getting needs met. White-dominated rule in South Africa ended, but John and Mary can't figure out how to have a vacation that will give her interesting things to do and yet allow him to do nothing.

The culprit here is not working it through. When you *don't* have this disease, you work your way through the inevitable conflicts and roadblocks that come up between different people with different needs. John and Mary find a beach somewhere in the world that's not far from museums and ruins and stores.

Another couple finds a way to satisfy *her* need for another child even though *he* doesn't want any more children. They work out a way for her to identify his main concerns (he's fed up with the thought of being awakened in the middle of the night again, particularly since he's older now, needs more sleep, and has a more demanding job), and then they work out a way to satisfy them (he'll wear ear plugs and she'll get up during the night).

But to be able to do this, you have to be able to get beyond that stage where the two of you simply say Yes! No! Yes! No! Yes! No! Okay, forget it! And *that* means you have to be able to talk until you identify what your partner's real concerns are and brainstorm ways of meeting those concerns.

But sometimes in our relationships we get angry and discouraged, and we give up on the possibility of working things through. Because we give up, our needs don't get met. Because our needs don't get met, we feel like giving up. All because we're not letting ourselves do what comes naturally to smart people like us: working it through.

**Diagnosing not working it through.** Do you find that the minute one of you brings up an objection or says No to a need, the other person immediately says, "Fine, forget it"? If *yes*, then your relationship is suffering from this strain of needs disease.

**Prescription.** What you have to do first is *open up your conversations*. Bring out more information. *Talk to each other.*

For example, when someone has a need, he may not know exactly why he has the need or exactly what he wants in order to feel that his need is being satisfied. Suppose you "need" for the two of you to have separate bank accounts and to keep your finances separate. Okay, but *why* do you need that?

What exactly would you want to happen for you to feel that need is being satisfied? Is it that you don't want to be judged by your partner for the way you spend money? Is it that your previous partner ripped you off? Is it that you make a lot more money than your partner? Talking about the real issues is what is involved in working things out, because then you can solve the real problems.

Let's look at the other side. Your partner may not know exactly why he wants to say No or what he might need in order to be able to say Yes. If you're saying you want to keep your finances separate, what needs or fears are making your partner refuse? Is he afraid that this is a sign that you're not committed? Is this what another woman did just before she dumped him? Would he be satisfied if the two of you went in together on a big purchase, like a house?

All this should be brought out. Instead of assuming that these things can't be talked about or are somehow automatically talked about, you have to make the assumption that you must talk about them. Couples who are geniuses at working things out *bring out* all the real issues.

When you have a knot in your shoelace, do you grab a pair of scissors if you can't undo the knot in one second? Or do you say, "Okay, there's a knot, so I'll have to take the time to untangle it."

The second thing you have to do is *actually work things through*. The key to working things through is to understand that inside the intensity and commotion of a person's need, or another person's objection to that need, is a *small kernel of concern* that's easier to deal with than what the person has been putting out. You have to *crawl inside of what they're saying* to get at the kernel that's really important. So ask, "What's your *real* concern here?"

For example, one couple had been having a lot of trouble because the wife didn't want to move to the Midwest where her husband had been offered a job and where his family still lived. "I like the East Coast," she said, "and I'm not moving out to the sticks."

When they looked for her kernel of concern, it turned out there were only two small obstacles. The woman was a writer and she had a lot of friends on the East Coast. It turned out that all the treasures of the East Coast for this woman boiled down to having access to a good university library. Well, as it happened they could very easily move near a university with such a library and still be close to her husband's job. As for her friends, she realized, she almost exclusively talked to them by phone. So they worked out an arrangement whereby she'd have an unlimited long-distance phone budget, as well as a generous budget for trips back east a few times a year.

Everything's possible when you get down to brass tacks.


## Needs Disease #11: Loggerheads

Sometimes, even when couples try to work things through, they run into this problem. One person needs something very badly. The other needs the opposite very badly. They can't seem to split the difference. They can't seem to find an alternative.

They're at loggerheads.


### ⊃ Joan and Frank

Joan and Frank lived in an old townhouse on Beacon Hill that Frank had inherited from an uncle. Old, expensive to maintain, dark, and cramped. But it was in a prestigious location at the heart of the city. Frank loved it.

Joan hated it. She wanted their kids to grow up in the suburbs far from the city. She wanted land, light, space. Joan hated the thought of their kids going to the Boston public schools. She wanted her kids in one of those highly rated suburban school systems. Frank thought, *If Boston Latin was good enough for me, it's good enough for my kids.*

Total loggerheads! They'd either stay in the house Frank inherited or not. You can't half-live in a house. If one of them was the big winner, the other was the big loser.

It matters where you live. The essence of loggerheads is that some need eating away at you is so important you wonder if the relationship itself is worthwhile. People who are at loggerheads typically threaten to end the relationship. Whoever makes the most convincing threat wins, and the other is left with a huge sense of an important unmet need.

**Diagnosing loggerheads.** If you and your partner are at loggerheads over some huge issue that is vital to both of you, which you can't resolve and keep fighting over, you already know you're in trouble. You just didn't know it was a needs disease.

**Prescription.** You've got to approach this problem indirectly, because you're already banging your heads together. When you approach it the right way, the *sense* of being at loggerheads fades. You *feel* less like two people at war. Then whatever solution was possible in the first place will become clear to both of you. You just can't see what's possible as long as you feel at loggerheads.

Here's what you do. To cure loggerheads, you stop trying to solve the problem and start listening to each other. It's the sense of *not being heard* that's the worst part of this needs disease. So you agree to talk to each other and listen to each other as best friends. You forget winning and focus on hearing. You "win" when you each listen to how the other feels.

That's what Joan and Frank did. They agreed to postpone talking about what to do for an entire year. In the meantime, they *would* talk to each other about what staying in the house meant to Frank, about what his connection to Boston meant to him, about why Joan was unhappy in the house, about what living in the suburbs meant to her. There was only one rule: as long as one talked and the other listened, they were both winners.

In the end it worked out the way it always works out when people are at loggerheads. There are real forces that will ultimately determine your decision. Someone will win something and someone will lose something. But because you both felt heard, it will seem fair, and the person who comes out on the losing end will feel better.

What ultimately will determine who prevails? Here are the forces at play. Let's trace them in Frank and Joan's case, then you guess who came out ahead.

**1. Who already has what he wants?** Not always, but most of the time, one person is already getting his way. They were already living in Frank's house, just as if the two of you were at loggerheads over whether to keep your cat (because one of you is allergic to it), the person who's not allergic to the cat is already having things the way he wants. Whoever is already winning stands the greater chance of coming out ahead in the end.

**2. Who cares most about the relationship?** The ultimate threat, of course, is my way or the highway. Joan might say, for example, "I'm going to move to the suburbs with you or without you, but I'm going there." The person who cares most about the relationship is most likely to give up what he needs for the sake of the relationship. What emerged gradually with Frank and Joan was that she cared most about the relationship. They both loved each other, but Joan was terrified of being alone and Frank wasn't.

**3. Who cares most about whatever it is you're struggling about?** You probably think you both care equally, since you're at loggerheads. But deep down someone always cares a little bit more. Frank loved the city. It was part of who he was. Joan hated the house, but they'd be moving to a suburb where she didn't know anyone. Frank cared more.

**4. Who can wage war most effectively?** I know "war" sounds negative but all I'm talking about is who's most able to nag, act depressed, get friends to agree with him, cry, persist—you get the point. Joan definitely seemed to have the edge here because she literally *was* most able to nag, act depressed, get friends to agree with her, cry, persist, etc. Sometimes Frank was tempted to give in just to make Joan happy. But remember, he had possession. He could wage war by delaying. And his ability to delay rendered most of her tactics ineffective.

I'm sure you can see the outcome. Frank won, of course. He had all the forces on his side. But here's the thing. Frank could have won at the cost of destroying their relationship. But because they spent a whole year listening to each other, Joan didn't feel beaten. She just felt she was bowing to the inevitable. Most of all, she didn't feel Frank was her enemy. He wanted what he wanted. But because he really listened to her, he was on her side. Listening destroys loggerheads.

Of course, listening has to be more than just an empty gesture. If Frank had done nothing more than listen, Joan wouldn't have felt so good about the ultimate solution. But he made Joan a promise: Buying a summer house would be his top priority. And she believed him. Listening is great. But listening and delivering on what's heard is even better.

## *Needs Disease #12: Flying Blind*

When I first started writing I was going to have lunch with an editor whom my agent thought could be a big help to me. I was all set to do what I always do: get right down to business the moment we sat down. My agent must've known about my pattern because he warned me: "This guy is going to feel pounced on if you jump right into talking about your book. Don't bring up business at all. Let him talk about this and that the way he does. But he's got to feel he knows you as a person before he can begin to talk about anything you're interested in."

That's a lesson in avoiding flying blind. You have needs. But the people you bring your needs to work in a certain way. There's a way they like your needs to be presented to them. How many guys totally ruined their marriage proposals by not making a romantic moment of it?

Maybe you're pissed with your partner for needing to be talked to in a certain way. Or maybe you feel she's screwed up for wanting you to say your needs the way she does.

Well, you can do it the way you want. Or you can find out the way that works best. Now let's see, which makes more sense . . . ?

**Diagnosing flying blind.** Has your partner told you more than once that she didn't have a problem with what you were asking for—it was *how* you asked for it that caused all the problems? If *yes*, you've been Flying Blind.

**Prescription.** This prescription is perfect for flying blind but it's so healthy for almost everyone that you could think of it more as a needed vitamin than a medicine. It's just medicine if you've got this needs disease.

Here's what you do. You get together with your partner and say this: "I think we'd both like to have a relationship where we get more of our needs met. One way we could do a lot better than we've been doing is to let each other know what to say. Here's what you can say that will make it most likely that I'll want to meet your needs . . ." Then you tell your partner the script he should follow, both what to say and what not to say.

When you avoid flying blind like this you avoid terrible tragedies. Take my husband and me. I'm always afraid my needs won't get met. So my tendency has been to make a big deal of what I need, as if the magnitude of my suffering will motivate my husband to meet my needs. But that's just flying blind. The minute I start with a shrill, "I can't stand it anymore that we . . . ," he's immediately launched into a state of denial and defensiveness. Instead of focusing on meeting my need, he's focusing on the "I can't stand it part" and trying to make the "I can't stand it" go away.

When we exchanged scripts with each other, imagine my amazement when my husband said that what would work best would be for me to say what I need in a simple, flat way and then say, "It's important to me." At first it was hard for me to believe that something so elementary would ever help me get my needs met. *But it worked.*

# Love Builder #5:
# The Willingness to Do Things for Each Other

Let's face it, you and I don't like talking about unmet needs in our relationships. We got together with our partner in the first place because we thought we fit together, and that meant that we automatically would meet each other's needs. What? Unmet needs? That means we don't fit! Oh no!

That's why we don't like to think about needs at all. But we all have a real Love Builder working for us in this area of needs, something that should make us feel hopeful and energized. Love Builder #5 is *the willingness to do things for each other.*

In a sense this love builder goes back to the roots of romantic love. Gallant knights, damsels in distress, and all that jazz. Good lovers show their love by doing things for each other.

DAMSEL: "I need you to go kill a dragon for me."
KNIGHT: "Sure, but I need you to sit in a tower and pine for me."
DAMSEL: "You got it."

I don't think too many dragons were actually killed, but there probably weren't that many dragons to begin with. And I don't feel that all that many damsels were truly pining either. But the *idea* that being in love with someone means wanting to do things for that person was real, powerful, and is still very important to all of us.

Let me put it this way. Every case I've ever heard of in which two people fall in love, somewhere near the beginning at least one of the people did something incredibly generous, incredibly loving for the other. It might've been nothing more than driving across town in a blizzard to be together or buying a special gift. But we all understood in our bones that the ship of love floats on a sea of this willingness to do things for each other.

And that's what we need to remember when we confront unmet needs. Just because we have needs doesn't mean we don't fit. It just gives us an opportunity to do things for each other. And that's what you do when you're falling in love.

## A Look Ahead

We're halfway through the love killers. The first five love killers had to do with the foundations of your relationship. The last five deal with issues that build on those foundations. We'll start with sex.

# 7

# Sexual Healing

· · · · · · · · · · · · · · · · · · · · · · · · · · · · · · · · · · · · · · · · · · · · · · · · · · · ·

### LOVE KILLER #6:
## Sexual Depression

#### ISSUE:
#### Have sexual dissatisfactions hurt your relationship?

Let's have sex. Well, not literally you and me, but I think it's time we talked about sex. You were probably wondering how sex fits into a book of love killers and now you'll find out.

In case you didn't know, the evidence is overwhelming. You don't need great sex to have a great relationship. But sometimes when sex is starting to get boring, or if you're not having sex at all, you can feel as if something's eating away at the core of your relationship.

Come with me into Betsy and Jeff's bedroom. We're going to play sexual detective. Don't worry—no one's home.

### ○ *Betsy and Jeff*

Betsy, thirty-four, is senior executive assistant to the managing partner of a downtown law firm. Jeff, thirty-six, is senior statistician for a major life insurance company. They've been married for eight years. Let's rummage through their night tables to see what we can learn about Betsy and Jeff's sexual history.

**Looking in their drawers.** Okay, here in the bottom drawer of Jeff's night table is a copy of *The Joy of Sex* and a book on how to drive your wife crazy in bed (you know, the tease-her-till-she's-ready-to-explode book).

So we know that Jeff has tried to spice up his sex life and has tried to understand how his wife "works" to make things better for her. How many of us are like Jeff, with sex books lying in our drawers, looking for the tools and tips and tricks that will solve our sexual problems?

Let's hop over to Betsy's night table. Sort of shoved into the back of her top drawer is a plastic vibrator loosely wrapped in its original packaging. It has an inexperienced air about it. It's hard to tell—how would a vibrator show wear and tear?—but it doesn't seem much used. Was it a solution for which there was no real problem, or is there a real problem that it couldn't solve?

At the front of the drawer, right at the top, are a couple of books. One is a book on tantric sex, something about having a deeper yet more cosmic connection sexually. If books could talk, you can just imagine the kind of conversation this book would have with Jeff's how-to-satisfy-a-woman-every-time book. There's a yin and a yang here somewhere.

Then there's a book that consists exclusively of long quotes from everyday women talking about their sexual problems and practices, first-hand accounts from the sexual frontlines. You get the idea that Betsy is wanting something from sex beyond what the mechanics can give you, and that there's something missing she can't even formulate as a question, and that she desperately needs to talk to someone and share experiences. Why isn't she talking to Jeff? If she is, why isn't that helping?

**Table talk.** If Betsy and Jeff's night tables could talk to each other, Jeff's might be saying, "I wish sex were better for you and less boring for both of us," and Betsy's might be saying, "I'm not sure what better is but I wouldn't define it as narrowly as you do."

Jeff and Betsy are typical. They've already found most of the easy answers. It's the hard answers that still elude them. I did with Jeff and Betsy what I often do with couples who come to me for help with sex. I asked them to describe to me what they have in their bedroom that they use to help with sex and what else they've tried. That speaks volumes about the road they've already traveled.

Most of us are like this. If you examine our bookshelves or play back conversations we've had with friends over the years, there's a gold mine of information and advice about sex, most of it good, much of which we've put into practice. We, too, have moved beyond the need for easy answers.

**Beyond easy answers.** I asked Betsy and Jeff exactly what was bothering them about their sex life. They mentioned some specific complaints. But their complaints quickly degenerated into wrangles that were predictable to all of us:

BETSY: I wish we could have sex more often but you're always too tired.

JEFF: I'm not too tired. But if you want sex, why don't you initiate?

BETSY: You know it's hard for me to initiate. Anyway, you're never into it unless it's your idea.

JEFF: Well remember that last period we were making love a lot? And you started complaining that it's always the same and that it's not special . . . ?

BETSY: (interrupting) Well I'm not asking for much. Why can't we just get close and feel connected to each other? Why does it always have to be about moving the show along to orgasm? There are people who spend hours just kissing each other.

JEFF: (turning to me) You see, that's the kind of complaining she does that's supposed to get me to initiate sex. And then (turning to Betsy) you want us to have more sex but you want us to do stuff that no one has the time to do.

BETSY:   I just wish you were *interested* in sex being more than it is.

JEFF:   There are all kinds of things I want more of in sex. . . .

Now you know a little of what it's like to do sex therapy for couples. They—you—*we* have used up all the easy answers. This dialogue, plus Betsy and Jeff's night tables, prove it.

Whatever the specific problems are that have frustrated you—and I've dealt with them all clinically—you've tried your best to solve them. Here's what most smart, knowledgeable people have tried already.

### THE TOP TEN BEST WAYS TO IMPROVE YOUR SEX LIFE

1. Ask for what you want.

2. The things you did that turned you on when you were first together: do them again.

3. Make love in a different room, at a different time of day.

4. Sit down and talk about your lovemaking, what you like and what you don't like, what you want more of and what you want less of.

5. Tell your partner, and show him, how your body works sexually.

6. Add a little fantasy or role playing.

7. Read a sex book that's filled with new ideas for positions or techniques and try some.

8. Have a sensual, naked encounter—including massage, stroking, kissing, etc.—without anyone having an orgasm. You could try this in the bathtub.

9. Watch a dirty movie together and either during or after do some of what the people in the movie were doing.

10. Listen to a different kind of music while you make love, or start listening to music, or stop listening to music. Do *something* different with music.

Since you know to do this already, since you've *done* most of this already, you need new answers. That's where I come in. There is a love killer that's specific to the sexual relationship, but before we get to it we have to investigate the impact of all the other love killers on sex.

## When Love Killers Become Sex Killers

Suppose you get out of breath walking up a long flight of stairs. Do you have a lung problem? Maybe. But in many cases, you're experiencing *in* your lungs what's really a problem *with* your overall physical fitness. If you were to work out twenty minutes a day, three days a week, the "lung" problem would disappear.

It's like that for many people when it comes to sexual problems in their relationship, particularly when they've already tried things to make sex better. Let me be very specific. Based on my research, if I know that you or your partner has read one sex book and has talked to one friend to get advice for your sex problems, then there's a 60 percent chance that identifying and eliminating one of the *other* love killers here will solve your sexual problems. If you fall into this group, the love killer that's hurting your relationship is afflicting your sex life as a side effect.

Eliminate that love killer and your sexual problem will go away by itself.

For example, was the chain of silence diagnosed as threatening your relationship? That means one or both of you wasn't being open. Eliminate that love killer and you're talking more and revealing more to each other. Most sex problems get better when the couple talk more and reveal more to each other. In the same way, every other love killer has a bad effect on sex. Eliminating any love killer will make sex better.

How do you know if this applies to you? The love killer that's specific to sex is sexual depression. Answer the diagnostic questions designed to reveal whether your relationship has a case of sexual depression or not. If it does, following the prescription here for eliminating sexual depression should solve your problem. If you're *not* diagnosed with sexual depression but you're still unhappy with your sexual relationship, then eliminating whatever other love killer is threatening you will probably solve your sexual problems as well.

## The Real Problem When It Comes to Sex

Here's an analogy that will make clear what sexual depression is and where it comes from.

You're about to leave the house and you quickly check to make sure you have your car keys. Wait a minute! You don't have them!

They must be on your dresser. So you look there. Okay, they're not there, but . . . oh yeah, that coat you were wearing yesterday. But the car keys aren't in those coat pockets either. You're starting to get annoyed, maybe even a little panicky, but you're not really discouraged. You check in a couple more obvious places, and then you get smart. You say to yourself, "Okay, I had the keys when I came home yesterday. Let me retrace everything I did."

You start retracing your steps still filled with hope, but by the time you've reconstructed everything you did you still haven't found your car keys. That's when you start getting really bummed out. You've tried everything. You don't know what else to try. You can just picture yourself slumped in a chair immobilized by discouragement.

And this is exactly where you've gotten when it comes to sex. You've tried everything. You've looked everywhere for the answer. Now feeling bummed out about it is taking over.

Sexual depression is exactly like psychological depression. You feel very sad about your sex life. You feel immobilized or helpless about your sex life. You feel bad about yourself because your sex life isn't what you'd like it to be. You've got low sexual self-esteem. Accompanying all this, deep down, is a sense of anger with someone, about something.

### It Doesn't Have to Be Perfect

It's not that things aren't perfect sexually that brings on sexual depression. I once heard a woman in her seventies say, "We don't do it as much as we used to—we're not kids anymore—but we still get it on and we still like it." She was expressing a positive sexual attitude. A man in his thirties said to me, "We're way too busy to make love as often as we'd like, and I wish we could change that, but I really think we make love as often as we reasonably can, and thank God we continue to feel that spark." He was expressing a positive sexual attitude too.

Feeling upbeat sexually makes many things in your life better, sex among them. When has this ever not been the case? From cooking to playing golf, from gardening to bowling, when we feel positive, we try harder, we're more open to criticism, and we're more creative. It's the same with sex.

But sexual depression is a real love killer. It's one thing to say you have problems in the bedroom. But if you reach the point where you feel helpless to do anything about your sex life, for whatever reason, then for most people it's impossible to prevent this from contaminating their sense of who they are to each other.

# Diagnostic #6:
# Are You Suffering from Sexual Depression?

Here's the best way to diagnose whether you're suffering from sexual depression.

## DIAGNOSING LOVE KILLER #6

Read the following seven statements and think about which of them, if any, are statements about which you could say, "*Yes, this is true for me.*"

1. "We've had a big drop-off in our sexual activity in the past several months, and it has nothing to do with some fight we've been having or with our being too busy."

    YES____ NO____

2. "When I think about our making love I think why bother."

    YES____ NO____

3. "I feel badly when I think about our sex life."

    YES____ NO____

4. "There's got to be something wrong with at least one of us for sex to be so crappy."      YES____ NO____

5. "Sex was so good between us, and now it's not."

    YES____ NO____

6. "My partner refuses to do most things I ask him to do to please me in bed."  YES____ NO____

7. "I know that all hell would break loose if I told my partner how I really felt about many things when it comes to sex."

YES____ NO____

. . . . . . . . . . . . . . . . . . . . . . . . . . . . . . . . . . . . . . . . . . . . . . . . . . . . . . . . . . . . . . . . .

If you said Yes to *two or more* of these statements, then you're suffering from sexual depression.

Okay, suppose it turns out you are suffering from sexual depression. What does that mean for you? What is the best way for you to think about it? Well, remember the car keys analogy? There's this person who's mislaid her car keys, and she's looked and looked until she's done everything she can possibly do to find them. She feels completely helpless. She sits in her chair, feeling more and more discouraged, which means she's started to feel depressed.

That's what the latest research shows is the psychological roots of depression: you get depressed because you get discouraged, and you get discouraged because nothing works as you try to do something about an issue that's important to you, and that makes you feel ineffective. The more ineffective you feel and the more important to you the thing that you feel ineffective about, the more depressed you get.

This makes it clearer what the problem is when it comes to sex. It's not about sex per se at all. It's really about not feeling effective when it comes to this incredibly important part of our lives. And that's really good news for you. It's surprisingly easy to start feeling more effective when it comes to sex—I'll show you how—and *that* will make this love killer go away.

# Prescription #6:
# Feeling Sexually Effective

There are two ways out of sexual depression. Remember: you're feeling ineffective because you want to do better but nothing you've done works.

One way out is to *accept where you are*. People always forget that when you're feeling terribly frustrated from trying to change things that don't change, letting go of the desire to change things ends the frustration. Suppose something's making you unhappy about your sex life, and you've gotten depressed because nothing you've done to fix it has worked. If somehow you could find a way (and I'll show you ways in just a moment) to let things stay the way they are without being unhappy about them, then your frustration would go away, taking your depression along with it. This is the *finding acceptance* option.

The other way out is to *become more effective*. It may make sense for you to keep trying to change things, but if you've run out of ideas, you need new ideas. No matter how discouraged you get, you're only one really good idea away from success. And if you *become* more effective, you'll stop feeling ineffective and your depression will lift.

Both ways out are possible solutions for sexual depression. One of them will work for you. Let's see which one.

## ○ The First Way Out: Finding Acceptance

Let's see if *finding a way to accept things the way they are* makes sense as the best way for you to overcome sexual depression.

Remember how bummed out Betsy and Jeff were about their sex life? Suppose, in spite of all the issues they had to deal with, they'd been able to look each other in the eye and say, "You know, it could be better, but you have to admit that we have a healthy, normal sex life." If they could've done that, and meant it, they'd have been able to accept where they were sexually and that awful gnawing need to try and try and try would have lifted. And their sexual depression would have lifted with it.

Defining "a healthy sex life" is important because many people are depressed over their sex lives unnecessarily. I think we're all entitled to want what we want when it comes to sex, but I've struggled with this for many years and I've come to the conclusion that you can have a perfectly healthy sex life without it being everything you want. It's stupid to think there's something wrong with your sex life just because it's not *everything* you want.

To illustrate. If I, as a fifty-year-old woman, can run three miles in fifteen minutes without collapsing, then in that respect I'm healthy by any reasonable standard, no matter how much I might complain about not being able to run a marathon. I can complain if I want, but that doesn't entitle me to say I'm not healthy.

And if I have to admit that I'm healthy, I'd be nuts to be depressed about not being able to run a marathon. I could deal with feeling ineffective by letting go of that sense of emotional urgency I'd had about running a marathon. I can continue trying or not trying, but I can do so as a happy warrior, not as someone who needs to meet her goal to lift herself out of misery. If I'm already healthy, then I've already met the critical goal.

### How Healthy Is Your Sex Life?

So—do you have a healthy sex life? Let's make it easy for ourselves.

I define *healthy* here the way you define *healthy* when it comes to your body: something's healthy when it's within the norm, when it promotes day-to-day functioning, and when it's not involved in a disease process. What else could the word *healthy* mean?

There are three questions that get right to the heart of whether your sex life is healthy or not:

. . . . . . . . . . . . . . . . . . . . . . . . . . . . . . . . . . . . . . . . . . . . . . . . . . . . . . . . . . . . . .

1. Whenever I think about our sex life I get really angry.

YES____ NO____

2. One of the strongest feelings I have during sex is humiliation.

YES____ NO____

3. One of the strongest feelings I have when I think about having sex is fear. YES____ NO____

. . . . . . . . . . . . . . . . . . . . . . . . . . . . . . . . . . . . . . . . . . . . . . . . . . . . . . . . . . . . . .

A *yes* answer to any *one* of these three questions would be a sign that there's something *not* healthy about your sex life. If your answer is *no* to all these questions, then you really need to think about accepting the possibility that your sex life is healthy. And if it's healthy, why not accept it the way it is (even though you still might wish it were better)? And if you can accept it the way it is, why be depressed about it? And if you're not depressed about it, you've eliminated a love killer!

If you'd like more reassurance, here are some things that some people *think* are signs that there's something unhealthy going on with sex. But these are all false signs. They are all perfectly consistent with healthy, normal sex:

### THE TOP TEN *FALSE* SIGNS OF SEXUAL PROBLEMS

**1. You don't have sex very often.**

**2. You wish there were more passion or intensity in your lovemaking.**

3. The woman in your relationship can only have an orgasm if she rubs her own clitoris.

4. One of you likes to do something in bed that the other doesn't like much.

5. Sex feels predictable. You usually do the same things in the same way.

6. One of you doesn't always find the other very attractive physically.

7. One or both of you likes to masturbate.

8. Sexual intercourse doesn't last very long. (The average man reaches orgasm four minutes after he puts his penis in a woman's vagina.)

9. One of you takes a long time to have an orgasm or has trouble reaching orgasm.

10. One of you fantasizes about someone else when the two of you are making love.

None of these issues are necessarily signs of sexual problems. There's only a problem if the two of you are battling over one of these issues and can't find solutions or compromises. If you *want* to solve problems like these, I'll have plenty of solutions for you in just a little while when I talk about sexual sticking points. What I want to say here is that you don't *have* to solve these problems.

So let everyone who has a healthy sex life acknowledge it. I had a patient once who complained bitterly about her sex life. Jasmine reeled off all the ways sex was less than perfect. I tried to help her see that her sexual relationship was healthy enough, no matter how many ways it could be improved. I wanted her to get the distinction between what's healthy and what's ideal.

A bit later the subject changed and she started expressing anger about something that makes me angry too (because I see all the damage it does): the way supermodels' bodies are held up as a kind of norm so that real women with normal bodies end up hating the way they look. I said to Jasmine, "Look, it's fine with me if you want to be in better shape in any part of your life. But why let yourself be victimized by standards of perfection in sex when you would never let yourself be victimized by standards of perfection when it comes to your body?"

Okay. No more beating ourselves up unnecessarily for having less than perfect sex lives.

## ○ The Second Way Out: Becoming Effective

The other way out of sexual depression is to find new ways to feel effective about your sex life. Well, when I get through with you, boy, are you going to be feeling effective.

Our little journey here toward feeling more effective is going to proceed in two stages. First I'm going to present to you an all-purpose technique to use when you've tried everything you know to do already and you're still unhappy with the way things are. Second, we'll diagnose just where you've gotten stuck sexually, and I'll offer you specific, proven ways of getting out of each of these sticking points.

## Stage One: Taking Turns

Let me introduce to you a Special Love Tool that's the single most powerful tool that I know for uplifting a couple's sex life. This tool is called *Taking Turns*. It couldn't be simpler and there's nothing technical about it. What's more, it gives you all the opportunity in the world to be yourself.

The way it works is this. Flip a coin to see who goes first. Let's say you win the coin toss. That means the next sexual encounter between you and your partner is *your turn*. Here's what *your turn* means. It's your turn to initiate. It's your turn to decide who does what in bed, when, to whom, in what way. It's your turn to have things be the way you'd like. It's your turn to have this be the most satisfying sexual encounter you can make it. The stuff you wish your partner would do that he never does because you never ask or because he's reluctant— well, it's your turn, so just ask for what you want, because he's got to do it.

*Taking Turns* only requires two things. First, follow the rules. Think of *Taking Turns* as a simple game with simple rules (like tic-tac-toe), but you have to follow them. Second, be patient. It should feel good while you're doing it, but it's not going to solve everything at one stroke, so to speak. It usually takes two weeks to a month for all the benefits to start kicking in.

**When you're in charge, you're in charge.** Let me make something clear about the rules for *Taking Turns*. When it's your turn, you're the one who says what happens. It's violating the rules for the other person to give you an argument or make objections. It's also violating the rules for you not to make clear what you want. If making love were a movie, *your turn* means you're the director.

Your turn is over when you leave the room where you made love. Then it's the other person's turn. Your responsibility for initiating the next sexual encounter is over until it's your turn again. When the other person initiates, since it's his turn, he can request what he wants from the sexual experience.

So *Taking Turns* means you completely and thoroughly rotate who's in charge, from beginning to end, each time you make love.

**What an accomplishment!** Here's what this accomplishes. First of all, at least one of you should be satisfied every time you make love. For couples in the throes of sexual depression, or for couples just not happy about parts of their sex life, *one person always happy* is almost always an improvement over *two people almost always* not *so happy*.

Second, *Taking Turns* gets you over the no-sex hump. When people aren't making love, it's usually because no one is really responsible for making it happen. And if one person is always the designated initiator, he's usually sick of it. According to my research, *Taking Turns* makes more sex happen.

Now for the most important benefit. On top of happier sex, and more sex, *Taking Turns* amounts to a sex tutorial for both of you. The person in charge, while she's getting her needs met, is teaching her partner how she works and what she likes. Usually there is some spillover, so that when it's her partner's turn he'll do a little bit more of what she likes, because making our partners happy makes sex feel better for us.

**Making it work.** Three questions come up with the *Taking Turns* technique.

• **There's the selfishness question.** Couples ask, "How selfish can I be when it's my turn? Does it mean my partner's my sex slave?"

If your "selfishness"—getting your needs met your way—makes things awful for your partner, then that's being too selfish. If your "selfishness" doesn't make things happen in a way you'd like, then it's stupid.

But if your "selfishness" feels good to you and doesn't bother your partner—given that he always has the next turn—there's nothing wrong with it. What happens with some couples is that they try a bunch of "selfish" things, but then they learn what works and they usually report several months later that sex feels much less selfish.

• **Then there's the ringmaster question.** This is like one of those philosophical paradoxes: "If it's my turn and I get to have things happen the way I'd like, what do I do if what I want is for my partner to call the shots?''

But this is not really such a paradox. Here's the way out. A lot of people, when it's their turn, don't like spending the whole time saying, "Now we'll do this, now we'll do that, now we'll do this other thing," like a circus ringmaster. So what you say is this. "It's my turn, but I just don't feel like playing ringmaster. I'd love it if you were the one who made things happen this time, but since it's my turn I'm just asking you to do things you know I like. For example, you know I like it if you kiss my back, so you could do that if you want to—I just don't feel like asking you to do it."

• **And then there's the trying-to-please question**. Call it a failure of selfishness. This arises when people don't make good use of their turn—instead they orchestrate the experience so it would be okay for their partner.

The solution to this is simple. If you sense that your partner has been too much focused on trying to please you when it's her turn, gently say, "I just want you to know—when it's your turn you really can ask for what you want."

**A lifetime solution.** At least two-thirds of the couples who really give *Taking Turns* a fair chance continue to use it all the time. That's just how good it is. As for the people who don't use it all the time, two-thirds of *them* report that what they learned while taking turns helped them overcome at least one sexual problem that had been nagging them.

The only objection I've ever heard to *Taking Turns* is that it destroys spontaneity. But no one's made this objection after they've given it a chance. If perfect spontaneity had really been working for you, you wouldn't need any tool. But if things could be better, this tool will give you as much spontaneity as most people can handle. Plus it will make things a lot clearer, and your sexual satisfaction will rise.

## Stage Two: Getting Unstuck

*Taking Turns* was a general solution to feeling more effective at dealing with sexual issues. It's time to zero in on the specific problems you've tried to solve but that have so far resisted your efforts.

Well, I have good news for you. These sexual problems certainly are sticky, but many people *have* found solutions to these problems. They're not any smarter than anyone else or more gifted sexually (whatever that is). They've just hit on good solutions. Isn't it time that all of us benefit from that?

Here are the most common, most frustrating sexual sticking points. For each one, there's a prescription that real people use and that real people say gets them unstuck. As you read about each sticking point, ask yourself if it applies to you, and if it does, follow that particular prescription.

## Sexual Sticking Point #1

*Do you get stuck here?:* "We're open about other things but it's hard for us to talk about sex."

I'll never forget the locally prominent sex therapist who came to me with her husband and it turned out that *they* had trouble talking about sex with each other. Here's a woman who talked about sex for a living, but to tell her husband the truth about how she felt and what she wanted—that stumped her. The point is that it's really, really hard for most people to talk about sex. But if you can't talk about it, how are you going to get unstuck?

Here's some help. Both of you answer *The Sex-tionnaire.* Write out your answers to these questions and exchange your pieces of paper.

## THE SEX-TIONNAIRE

1. What I most wish you understood about me and sex is ___.

2. Three things I'd like you to do more of are _____.

3. Three things I'd like you to do less of are _____.

4. Three things I'd like you to let me do more of are _____.

5. Three things you can do to make me feel you want me are
_____

6. I'd like us to make love between ___ and ___ times a month.

7. Here's what I love most about you as a lover and about making love with you _____.

The Sex-tionnaire makes it easier to talk about your lovemaking. But there may be still more obstacles to overcome, and the solution, it turns out, is more diagnosis. Pinpointing the problem is always best. The reason you have trouble talking about sex may be that you're afraid of something. Identify what you're afraid of, and you can overcome your fear. Here are the major fears people have when it comes to talking about sex, and what to do to overcome them.

*Fear of being critical.* "If we talk about sex, then my anger/disappointment over [you fill in the issue or complaint] will come out and my partner will feel hurt and rejected, and he'll pick a fight, and he'll criticize me, and we'll both feel so lousy we won't make love again for six months."

**Prescription.** First say that you want to make your sex life better. Then tell your partner how much you love him. Then praise him as a lover. Be specific: praise something about his lovemaking that's important to you and that he'll believe you would praise him for. Then instead of talking about what's wrong with your partner talk about what you need.

For example, instead of saying, "I don't like the way you touch me," say, "I'd like to tell you *how* I want you to touch me." Then if he says, "Are you saying there's something wrong with the way I touch you?" say, "There's nothing wrong with you at all, I'm just saying what I need," and then praise him again and tell him how much you love him. If you want to give a Tylenol tablet to a child, you grind a little bit of it into a lot of applesauce. It's the same with remarks that might sound like criticisms.

***Fear of making things worse.*** "Let me tell you what happened the last time we talked about sex. I was going to do this and she was going to stop doing that, but what we thought would work turned into a disaster and we ended up feeling incredibly self-conscious."

**Prescription.** When guests were coming to dinner my mother would get it into her head to prepare a new recipe because she wanted to make something special. She kept forgetting that it takes a couple of tries to figure out how to make a new recipe work. So every time people came for dinner, my nervous-wreck mother would end up serving a disaster dish to the guests. And then she'd always say she should never try anything new. The answer of course you've already guessed. Talk about sex, make your plans, *but give yourself a chance to work out the kinks in your new recipe.*

## Sexual Sticking Point #2

*Do you get stuck here?:* "Sex is okay, but for a long time I've felt something was missing. I'm not sure what, and we've done all these sexy things to try to supply what's missing, but nothing has really worked."

In most cases, when people felt the above statement described their situation, their problem had to do with affection, not sex. More affection, not better sex, is the answer. When people were more affectionate with each other, the sense that something was "missing" from sex magically disappeared.

The biggest problem when it comes to affection in relationships today is that what *you* think shows affection isn't at all what makes *your partner* feel you're being affectionate. Because she doesn't respond the way you'd like to what you think is affection, you get mad and stop wanting to be affectionate. And you're both doing this. It's a stupid misunderstanding.

**Prescription.** Stop thinking you know what makes your partner feel loved. Stop thinking your partner knows what makes you feel loved. Most of all, stop thinking that if you really loved each other, you wouldn't have to sort this out.

Instead, do this. Sit down with each other and take turns saying one thing the other could do that would come across as demonstrating affection, which would make you feel loved. Go back and forth until you each know three or more things you can do that will come across to your partner as real affection.

It's not important that they make you feel that you're being affectionate. It is important that they make your partner feel that she's receiving affection from you.

For example, one guy used to try to show affection by buying his wife presents. She liked the presents but they didn't make her feel loved. Then they followed the above prescription. She said she'd feel he was really showing affection if, when they got into bed to make love, he'd let her talk for as long as she liked about whatever she'd like. The guy said, "What's affectionate about that?" She said, "What do you care as long as it makes me feel loved?" By showing affection in the way that really came across to her, he eliminated the sense that something was missing from their sex life.

## Sexual Sticking Point #3

*Do you get stuck here?:* "For a long time sex has gotten more and more routine, but we've run out of ways to spice up our sex life."

One of the most creative artists I know, a woman the whole world knows as a creative singer/songwriter, could never think of anything creative to do in bed. She wasn't good at math either. The point is that you can be generally wonderful without being a creative genius when it comes to sex.

Probably the biggest blindspot that keeps people stuck here is that they think that it's stereotypically kinky stuff that will add the spice. It rarely is. Let me ask you this: Were the best sexual experiences you had when you were a teenager or college kid kinky? Or was it something else that made them so arousing?

**Prescription.** Instead of trying to spice up your sex life, make it warmer. Think *sensual*, not kinky. (Remember, the word *sensual* means physically pleasurable and interesting.) If the weird things you'd tried had been the answer, you wouldn't still be struggling with this question. When sex is sensual, people say it feels less routine.

Here's what many people say are the best ways to make sex sensual:

### THE TOP TEN WAYS TO LUST UP YOUR LOVE LIFE

1. Give your partner a *full* body massage. Do *every* part of her body.

2. Sit on your sofa and neck like teenagers hoping that your parents won't barge in on you.

3. Teach your partner one thing about your sexuality you think your partner doesn't know but that you feel confident she can deal with.

4. Lick your partner down one side, from the neck to the back to the rear end to the feet, turn your partner over and lick her all the way up the front side.

5. Play sex slaves (but only if you each get a full turn). Make love and have one of you be in complete charge, deciding who does what to whom, for how long, everything. The next time you make love, the other is in complete charge.

6. Make a tape of music to slow dance to. You know what to do with it.

7. Have a "Let's see how long we can kiss on the mouth without either of us breaking it off" contest. Whoever stops the kiss . . . well, there are just no losers here.

8. Each of you write on separate pieces of paper three adventurous things you'd like your partner to do while you're in bed, one suggestion per slip. Pull them out of a hat and do them one at a time.

9. Make a gourmet platter of bite-sized food like rigatoni primavera or steak tips and mushrooms and feed it to each other.

10. Take a bath or shower together. Pretend you're both very dirty and in tremendous need of being washed head to toe by the other.

### Sexual Sticking Point #4

*Do you get stuck here?:* "Having sex is just too much work and you get too little for it."

I think it's time we all acknowledged something. Some of us don't like roller-coaster rides. Some of us don't like martinis. Some of us don't like Paris. And some of us don't like sex all that much, even when you throw in an orgasm.

If you think sex is just too much trouble, you may fall into this category. To make sure, go through all the "do you get stuck here?" items to see if it's not really something else that's your sticking point. But if you come to rest here, at just not being a big sex fan, here's some help.

**Prescription:** Accept yourself as you are and that your feeling about sex has nothing to do with how much you love your partner. The bottom line here is that your partner is going to want to have sex more often than you and is going to be more into it than you are. I'll tell you something surprising. In most cases, when one person admits to the other that she's just not that interested in sex but she's willing to have sex because she knows it's important to her partner, sex feels better. It was the needing to feign interest that created resentment and distance.

The key phrase here is "willing to have sex." If "willing to have sex" with your partner, even though he's a lot more into it, feels like a free act of generosity and is accompanied with a sense of pleasure at being able to give someone else pleasure, then this can work. But if you resent what it costs you to give your partner this gift of sex, well, then, you're not really all that willing.

It's like when my husband agrees to go to Bloomingdale's with me when I need some new outfits so I can get his opinion. I *know* that's not something he really wants to do. And if he's going to moan and sigh and act sullen the whole time, I'm better off if he stays home. But if he can manage to make the best of it and get the satisfaction that comes from making me happy, then it's a good experience for both of us.

The only place you might get stuck further is where your partner wants to have sex *a lot* more often than you. Here's how you solve this. You write down on a piece of paper the most times a month you'd be willing to have sex. Your partner writes down the least number of times per month he'd be willing to have sex. If you overlap, you've already solved this problem. If there's still a gap, split the difference.

No matter what, accept each other's differences and be affectionate.

## Sexual Sticking Point #5

*Do you get stuck here?:* "There's this thing I want my partner to do in bed but I can't ask for it."

Of course you can't ask for it. Your partner would totally freak out.

You get the point. Whatever it is you're dying to ask for will either make you look creepy or will seem insulting or will be such a big deal that you'll owe your partner a lot for doing it. And yet you really want it.

**Prescription:** First ask yourself how much you really want it. Sometimes we obsess about something "forbidden" in sex that's either not as important as you think it is or that would cause more trouble than it's worth.

One guy was burning to ask his wife to have another woman join them in bed. He actually worked himself up into a fury at the thought of how his wife would freak out if he just mentioned this to her. But when he thought it through more carefully he realized that his wife was just not going to have sex with another woman nor was she going to lie there and watch him having sex with another woman. And what's the point of having sex with your wife so another woman can watch? Some of the things you might be dying to ask for are things you're just going to have to let go of.

But if you still really want to ask for something, here's how to do it:

**1.** Ask your partner if he's willing to talk about trying new things in sex, things you've never talked about. Most people say *yes*.

**2.** Suggest that the two of you do the following. You'll each write down on a piece of paper three things, however wild or kinky or gross, that you'd like more of or that you'd like to try at least once. Agree to exchange: "I'll do one of yours if you do one of mine."

**3.** Do that, and see how it goes, even if your partner didn't choose the item you were secretly most hoping she'd choose. You're still getting one of the three things you wanted.

**4.** Talk about how you both feel about the two remaining items on each of your lists.

What you're trying to work toward is the idea of openness, acceptance, and exchange. Even if you don't get everything you want, if there's a sense that the two of you are open to some new things, and you can accept each other for wanting what you want (even if the other isn't willing to give it), and you show that you're willing to exchange favors, you'll stop feeling so stuck about this sticking point.

### *Sexual Sticking Point #6*

*Do you get stuck here?:* "There are things I've asked my partner to do in bed but he won't do them."

**Prescription:** You've got to find out why your partner won't do what you'd like. "That's gross" or "I just don't like it" aren't specific enough. The more you get down to brass tacks, the more good solutions emerge.

For example, some men refuse to perform cunnilingus. The couple has fights about this. Maybe the woman says, "Why don't you want to do it?" And the guy says, "Because I don't like it." He's embarrassed to *say* why he doesn't like it, and she's embarrassed to *ask* why.

But when people get specific about this, it turns out that 90 percent of men who don't want to perform cunnilingus are reluctant for one of two reasons.

First, the last time they tried, the woman hadn't washed carefully or had some kind of infection without realizing it. Once this is out in the open, many men will be willing to give it another try if the woman promises to wash carefully.

Second, these men are reluctant because the last time they tried performing cunnilingus they licked for forty-five minutes, their tongues fell off, they needed neck surgery, and the woman still hadn't reached orgasm. If the guy openly tells her his concern they can talk about changing positions or agree that he won't do it for more than a certain length of time.

The idea to remember is that people refuse to do something in sex for very specific reasons.

When you talk about these obstacles honestly and concretely most can be overcome.

We get so tangled up with each other that we forget how much we share. The way to feel you share more is this: You each describe three completely different ways you would like sex to be—three mini-sexual scenarios—as long as they're all different from one another. You might prefer one scenario to another, but they're all scenarios that would make you happy. Then you compare your three scenarios to your partner's three scenarios.

There's one question: Which scenario on your list is closest to which scenario on your partner's list? That's where you have a chance for a meeting of minds, and bodies.

## *Sexual Sticking Point #7*

*Do you get stuck here?:* "Sex is too mechanical, too perfunctory. There's no soul connection in our lovemaking."

First, let's put this sexual sticking point in context. It's not the same as needing more affection. And it's not the same as needing sex to be lustier, spicier, more varied. As I've heard people describe this need, the sense I get is that "our bodies are physically connected, but on the inside our hearts and souls are either absorbed in selfish bodily sensations or are drifting off to some place far away."

Part of the problem is that learning how to make love to each other is difficult. The more you know about how to turn each other on, the more details you have to attend to. So in a way your sexual learning distracts you from having a soul connection.

**Prescription.** To get back your soul connection, you need to do something that I know is hard for a lot of people. You need to get specific about what exactly you would do that would feel as if the two of you were having a soul connection. I know this is hard because a lot of people say, "If I could write out some little script for how to have a soul connection, I'd be making that mechanical and it wouldn't be a real soul connection."

These people are in the same trap that would-be poets fall into who say they're not going to write until inspiration strikes but then inspiration never does strike and they never produce any poems. *Real* poets—including the ones who seem most inspired, who seem to be speaking most from the depths of their souls—do whatever works to get themselves to sit down and produce poetry because they know that you can make deep experiences happen if you go about it in the right way.

So take another try at asking yourself what specifically would make you feel as though you were having a real soul connection as part of your lovemaking. If you're still drawing a blank, let me tell you two things that work for a lot of people. I bet they'll work for you.

**1. Make eye contact.** I've done an experiment with people who say that their lovemaking doesn't really feel intimate. I've told them, "The next time you make love don't do anything different. Just monitor how much eye contact you have, how much time you spend actually looking into each other's eyes." People are almost always amazed to report that they spent 34 minutes making love from the beginning of foreplay to the end of the afterglow without spending more than two minutes looking into each other's eyes. When I tell them to make a point next time of looking into each other's eyes as much as possible, they always report feeling more of a soul connection.

**2. Talk in a more personal way before and after making love.** This too is based on asking people to report what actually goes on during their lovemaking. What we've discovered is that people talk about petty, practical details of their lives, or they're mostly silent, but they don't talk in that personal, intimate, getting-to-know-you way that went on when they were first together. It's not that you have to bare your souls to each other. But if you're truly at home with each other, you can afford to come out of hiding and share a little bit of what you think about and how you feel about things.

Only *you* know what's going on inside you. But to help you be more personal, here are some openings that can prime the pump. Start with what I've written, fill in the blanks on your own:

### THE TOP TEN OPENERS TO START TALKING MORE PERSONALLY

**1. "You know what I've been hoping for recently? It's that . . ."**

**2. "These days I keep thinking about . . ."**

3. "I know it's a long way off, but do you ever think about what we'll do when we retire? Sometimes I think I'd like to . . ."

4. "There's something I used to like about myself that I don't like so much anymore. It's the way I . . ."

5. "For some reason I've been thinking about my childhood a lot recently. In particular I've been thinking about . . ."

6. "I had a dream last night. Do you want to hear about it?"

7. "Do you like the new music that's coming out? The last song I really liked was . . ."

8. "Do you remember the way we used to . . . ?"

9. "Do you think we spend too much time watching television? Should we think about doing something about it?"

10. "Let me tell you something I've never told you before."

Talking in a more personal way doesn't mean complaining and it doesn't mean bringing up problems. Before and after lovemaking the last thing you want to do is drop a bombshell. But by talking about any of the kinds of things I've suggested (or anything similar you'd like to add) you're offering a nakedness of your self to go along with the nakedness of your body. That's what makes people feel there's a soul connection in their lovemaking.

## Sexual Sticking Point #8

*Do you get stuck here?:* "We both want to have more sex more often but we never get around to it."

In case you're interested, *this is the sexual sticking point more people say applies to them than any other.* They often blame themselves for having insufficient desire, but that's not an accurate diagnosis. Did you ever have a day at the office so busy that you weren't able to get away for lunch? Of course you have. Did you ever start out on a weekend with a bunch of chores you wanted to get through and by Sunday night you realized most of them were still undone, even though you hadn't stopped being busy? Of course this has happened to you.

This is why real life is a potential love killer. The problem isn't insufficient desire. It's not even that sex is a low priority. What happens is that once the freight train of daily life pulls out of the depot so many tasks go along with it that by the time you've done everything you want to do and are relaxed from everything you've done, there's no time left for lovemaking.

Of course you could just leave this situation alone. You could just accept the reality of your lives, and decide there isn't going to be very much lovemaking. But for a lot of people this isn't an acceptable solution. If you can make room for so many other things in your life—why can't you make room for more lovemaking?

**Prescription.** Many people find that taking turns solves this problem for them. They weren't getting around to making love because no one was responsible for when they'd make love *the next time.* If it's your turn, you're the one responsible, and both of you know it. Lovemaking tends to happen sooner.

Here are some other solutions that work well, depending on your personality and circumstances.

Some couples look at the pattern of their lives and realize that there's one time every week that's actually best for them to make love, that's the time when they would make love if they could. So what they do is just designate that as their fixed, sacred weekly lovemaking appointment. It becomes almost a ritual. Thursday night or Sunday morning becomes the one time you can count on every week when you have to be there or be square. They usually come to find a great deal of comfort and satisfaction in structuring this for themselves.

For some couples a fixed time every week won't work. If that's your situation, it would make sense to use your appointment book to set up a "next time." But some couples are so afraid of looking like Yuppies that they'd rather not have sex than make an appointment to have sex. Well, if you really feel that way, fine. But all I can say is that most people report that sex by appointment is better than no sex.

One more solution, which requires some custom tailoring. Believe it or not, some couples never get around to making love in their busy lives because there's a misunderstanding about what they need for lovemaking to be a satisfying experience. One couple, for example, got in the habit of starting off lovemaking with leisurely wine drinking. Sharing wine together set the mood. But when real life set in, they discovered that there was time for sex but no time for wine and sex. It was as simple as that.

I'm not saying that a busy life means you're doomed to quickie sex. I am saying that unless you check out your expectations, you may be doomed to no sex. Accept the pressures on you as your reality and find a way to have more sex in the context of these pressures, rather than waiting for the pressures to go away.

## Sexual Sticking Point #9

*Do you get stuck here?:* "He comes too quickly and/or she takes too long to climax."

I know what you've tried already. If you're a man, you've tried to delay your orgasm. If you're a woman, you've worked at ways to be more aroused at the point where intercourse begins.

Let's not forget the real problem we're trying to solve here. Sexual depression is the love killer. From the point of view of sexual healing, unsynchronized orgasms never killed a relationship. Sexual depression has killed too many relationships.

Maybe your expectations are unrealistic. Let's work this through. First, do you need to have simultaneous orgasms to have a happy sex life? No, you don't. The big double-O is a white whale couples spend their lives chasing without asking themselves if they really need to catch it. But suppose you knew in advance that you'd never have simultaneous orgasms. Why would that have to make you miserable? And if it wouldn't make you miserable, why suffer in a vain attempt to get it?

Next, suppose you let go—*really* let go—of that simultaneous orgasm orientation that so many couples have. It might change everything about how you make love and about how you feel about making love. Here is an interesting discovery we made: Many couples who see that they're not going to be having simultaneous orgasms make the mistake of still orchestrating their entire lovemaking as if to set the table for something they know will never happen. And every time it doesn't happen—and that usually means the guy's had his orgasm but she hasn't had hers— they deal with her needs as if they were an afterthought, as if they were playing catch-up.

If that works—and by "works" I mean if that makes you feel close, satisfied, and comfortable—then this really isn't a sexual sticking point for you at all, unless you're still suffering from the expectation that it shouldn't be this way. But suppose that it doesn't feel right to you. Try this.

**Prescription.** This is a big pill to swallow. You're going to have to talk about how you make love. But you have to start by giving up on the idea that you'll have simultaneous orgasms. Now think about what that means. If you don't have to climax together, then you may not have to do many of the things you've been doing in the ways you've been doing them. Why not, for example, completely separate the time you have your orgasms, so that first one of you has an orgasm and then the other has an orgasm? That way, at least, you can take turns going first.

But give yourself a chance to accept your lovemaking the way it is. What if you didn't change anything *except* your hope of getting the big double-O? Would sex be so terrible?

## Sexual Sticking Point #10

*Do you get stuck here?:* "I just can't relax during sex; I'm always distracted, always thinking about other things; I'm just not there for it."

There are four reasons for this, and I'll give you a prescription for each:

**1.** There's so much on your mind because you really do have a lot on your mind.

**Prescription.** When real life has affected you to this extent, you have to take care of business or get away from business. For example, one woman never made love until she'd first jotted down items on a To-Do list. By putting things she needed to remember on paper she got them off her mind. One man realized that at night his mind was full, but in the morning it was empty. Making love in the morning was the answer.

**2.** There are things you're needing to talk to your partner about that may have nothing to do with sex. For many people the minute the first gentle notes of foreplay are sounded there's a letting down of barriers, perhaps for the first time that week. In other words, the minute you start making love you experience the need to talk.

**Prescription.** One solution is to talk. But a lot of people don't want to talk before making love. So another really good solution is to make sure you'll be able to talk afterward or some other time. Often, just knowing that there will be a time and place to talk removes the sense of distraction.

**3.** The minute you begin to relax, your mind fills with details of all sorts of things. Experienced meditators understand something that frustrates the novices. They understand that even under the best of circumstances the mind is constantly flooded with distractions. People who are deemed masters of meditation acknowledge that the process of emptying the mind is really the process of feeling your mind continually filling up as you try to empty it.

**Prescription.** Do what master meditators do. Don't get into a wrestling match with your thoughts. If they come of their own accord, they will leave of their own accord. Don't force yourself to be there in sex; relax your way into being there, even if it means accepting a headful of distractions. As one Zen master put it, "Don't be distracted by your distractions."

**4.** Your mind fills with ideas you have about sex, but you begin to obsess about them rather than asking for what you want.

**Prescription.** Give yourself permission to ask for what you want.

## Sexual Sticking Point #11

*Do you get stuck here?:* "It's hard to get aroused."

I find that people who complain about having trouble getting aroused fall into three different groups. I'll give you a different prescription for each.

**1.** One group is suffering from no more than unrealistic expectations. How long have you been in this relationship? How old are you? As time goes by, it often takes longer to be aroused. Not only that, but arousal that might've occurred just because you were lying in bed together now needs direct stimulation to happen.

**Prescription.** You may only need more appropriate expectations.

**2.** The second group is having trouble because they're going about getting aroused in the wrong way. For example, there was the woman who said she had trouble getting aroused even after her husband had spent fifteen minutes licking her clitoris. She thought that it "should" arouse her but she forgot that based on her real experience it had never aroused her.

**Prescription.** You've got to be honest and active about figuring out what really arouses you.

**3.** The third group is having trouble because they're suffering from sexual depression. They can't get aroused because they're too bummed out. "Why bother?" they say.

**Prescription.** Don't worry about arousal. Work on all the love killers here. Do all the prescriptions in this sexual healing chapter. Doing this work will arouse your sense of being effective at dealing with your problems. It will stimulate your sense that you have solvable problems. Sexual arousal will come all by itself.

# Love Builder #6:
## Special Satisfactions

Sheer animal lust really exists. Let's not minimize it. It's often what leads people to make love right here, right now. But it's not enough to serve as the foundation of lasting love. Pure sexual desire may play a role in bringing you together, but most people report that there are special satisfactions at the heart of lovemaking that are more important than simple sexual release. These special satisfactions are different for everyone. Often they can't even be put into words. But they're important for what you anticipate when you make love with your partner.

To illustrate, here's what Nate, the kind of guy who never

imagined in a million years that he'd end up on the pages of a relationship book, said:

> NATE: *"I always thought of myself as a real meat-and-potatoes guy. I loved my wife, and I was attracted to her, but I always thought that sex for me was about . . . you know, you're horny, you want to come. Sorry to be so blunt. But I've had two years to think about this since Marla died. And I never think, Gee, I wish I could be having sex with Marla now because I'm so horny. What I find myself really missing is the way she smelled and the way her skin felt. That was for me the treasure at the heart of our sexual experiences. That's what I'd give anything to get back now."*

The love builder that comes to our aid as we try to solve the problems in our sexual relationship is whatever special satisfactions there've been for us in our sexual relationship with our partner.

In spite of the problems you're having, there are good things too. It's the desire for these good things that makes sex special with your partner. We all have something that makes sex with our partner satisfying, just the way Nate had something.

It's these special satisfactions that make us feel at home in our sexual relationship. You've been focusing on what's missing in your sexual relationship, but you also need to focus on what you've been getting. Don't ever let your dissatisfactions destroy your satisfactions.

## A Look Ahead

It's a funny thing about sex. It should bring two people together, but one thing that happens when people fall into a state of sexual depression is that they start feeling they're just "too different."

It's time now to tackle this sense of being "too different."

# · 8 ·

# We Can Work It Out

· · · · · · · · · · · · · · · · · · · · · · · · · · · · · · · · · · · · · · · · · · · · · · · · · · · ·

LOVE KILLER #7:

## Difference Sickness

ISSUE:

Are you suffering from all the ways you're
different?

Isn't it wonderful to think about the ways the two of you are similar? Isn't it horrible to have a sense that you and the person you're sharing your life with are growing increasingly different, until there's such a huge gulf between you that your partner seems almost like an alien creature?

Emphasizing difference has become fashionable these days, particularly emphasizing male/female differences. But that plaintive cry of "We're just too different" for many people is the death rattle of a relationship. They think that "too different" *means* the relationship is doomed. *But they're wrong.*

Even though you may be feeling wounded by the *depth* of your differences and plagued by the endless *ways* you seem different, this love killer—if it's the one threatening your relationship—can be eliminated much more easily than you might think, once you understand what it really is.

Difference sickness is like a fungus. It breeds, and spreads, in darkness. Sunlight is its enemy. A sense of difference comes with all the love killers, but with difference sickness the feeling that the two of you are incompatible digs down into the very roots of your relationship. With difference sickness the battles we conduct with the people we love over our differences are battles we fight in darkness, no matter how hot our words are. You can and will learn how to use light to cure difference sickness, if we diagnose it as a disease that threatens your relationship.

## ○ *Dan and Jackie*

They were famous for being a great couple in college. What struck everyone who knew them was how they seemed to be on the same wavelength. They both liked Motown when everyone else was caught up in the rock-versus-disco battle. They liked funny movies, from Richard Pryor and Eddie Murphy to Mel Brooks and Woody Allen. They both played tennis. They both liked pizza but hated anchovies on pizza. They both hated politics but liked politicians who wanted to help people. They both looked forward to living in the country, growing a little garden, raising a couple of chickens. They both liked morning sex, with Jackie on top.

For all the things they had in common, there were huge differences between them, and their friends talked a lot about their differences, maybe as a way of reassuring themselves that in a world full of strangers you can still find someone to love. Dan was tall and Jackie was short. When it came to how they dressed, Dan was preppie, Jackie was hippie. Dan was a math major, a hard-numbers guy. Jackie was an art major and loved to paint watercolors. Dan was the son of conservative Catholics, Jackie the daughter of liberal Jews.

**Living with their differences.** For all the talk of how opposites attract, it was what they had in common that launched their relationship from college couplehood to marriage. At first even their differences seemed to be working for them. Dan the numbers guy went into finance, where he made a good enough living so that Jackie the artist wouldn't starve. Jackie loved art and nature so much that she'd go off alone for entire weekends to paint landscapes. They complained about missing each other, but Dan was working so hard that when Jackie wasn't there on the weekends it was easier for him to get his work done, and when he wasn't working, he could spend some time alone.

Then they had kids, they were busy and distracted, and . . . well, they have no idea how it happened but next thing they knew, when their youngest was ten, they were swamped by the sense that they had nothing in common.

I don't know where to begin in describing all their apparent differences. Jackie, missing religion while growing up, got more and more involved in developing her spiritual life. That meant she felt alienated from Dan, who'd had his fill of religion as a kid and was deeply suspicious of religiosity, which meant he felt alienated from Jackie.

There were little things, too. Dan needed to be organized. Artistic Jackie hated organization and unapologetically embraced the idea of being disorganized. That meant that doing anything together was a major ordeal and source of conflict, everything from getting to a Friday night movie on time to having friends over to deciding how to plan a summer.

Dan, the guy who liked comedy movies, still liked having fun. "Keep it light" was a phrase he found himself using more and more. Perhaps that was because artistic, spiritual Jackie, with few worldly accomplishments to allow her to feel she could relax, kept looking for deeper connections between them, more serious things to talk about. Sometimes Dan felt Jackie was almost torturing him with the serious issues she demanded he share with her, while to Jackie it seemed an act of pure deprivation and abandonment when Dan mocked her hunger for depth and kept trying to escape to surfaces.

## *The Sense of Your Differences*

There are hundreds of different kinds of music. There are dozens of different ways of listening to music. There are countless levels of understanding and appreciation of music. Given that, what are the odds that any two people will have the same taste in music? Slim.

That's the problem with difference. There are many potential differences that can arise between two people, but what's the real love killer? The most starry-eyed newlyweds can name ways in which they're different. Couples on the verge of divorce can still point to some ways in which they're similar.

I call Love Killer #7 difference sickness because the name highlights the ways difference kills love. It *works* like a sickness. There's a sense that it spreads and deepens, that it weakens you. You feel as if you're in the grip of forces you can't control and don't understand, and that you're drifting away from the world you're familiar with.

Things start out a little bad, but then your sense of your differences begins to seem worse. You begin to fight over them, and the more you fight, the greater they seem. Soon you realize that the person you thought you loved is someone so alien you're not even sure you want to bridge the differences.

This sounds familiar to most of us, including people who aren't suffering from difference sickness. But where do you draw the line between sickness and health? Where do you say, "So we're different, so what?" and where do you say, "These differences will kill our love if we don't do something about them"?

# Diagnostic #7:
# Are You Suffering from Difference Sickness?

Let's talk to the real experts, people like you who've struggled with the same kinds of differences you've struggled with in your relationship but who've gone a bit farther so that they can see how things turn out and what they wished they'd paid attention to when they were at your stage. When I asked them exactly where they started down the path of no return, here are the symptoms they mentioned. At the end of each one I'll ask you a diagnostic question to see whether that symptom points to difference sickness in your relationship.

## Lack of Acceptance

It's true that we all pick at each other about our differences and complain about them, but that's not a symptom of difference sickness. If you get into squabbles because one of you is a morning person and the other isn't, you may be able to end those squabbles by going back to basics. But lack of acceptance marks a real turning point. It's where eliminating difference becomes a *cause*. It's where you say to yourself, "My partner has got to change the way he's different or we can't be together."

Let's look at a difference a lot of couples are fighting over these days: "He just won't talk about how he feels," she says. "I can say how I feel about things but he can't, or won't."

I don't know if my parents were aware of this difference, but I know they didn't care. They accepted it. Many couples today are at war over a difference that meant nothing to our parents. We pick at each other and push on each other. For us this difference seems to boil down to the difference between being a complete healthy human being and being a defective, half-formed human being. "How can I be with someone who isn't in touch with his feelings?" she says. "How can I be with someone who's always trying to make me feel badly for not being in touch with my feelings?" he says.

Both people feel they're holding on to needs and principles too important to let go of. Acceptance across this difference feels impossible.

## DIAGNOSING LOVE KILLER #7

1. Do you feel there's something seriously wrong with your partner for being different from you, and does that difference make you worry about why you're in a relationship with someone like that?                    YES⎽⎽ NO⎽⎽

A *yes* answer means your relationship has come down with a case of difference sickness.

### *Heavy-duty Lifestyle Implications*

It's when they affect some important part of how you live that merely having differences can turn into difference sickness. Two people of completely different religious backgrounds get married, for example. They're not all that religious, so at first their difference doesn't matter. It has nothing to do with how they live. But then children come along. Some relationships are destroyed when children enter it because the couple realizes they will have to live with one religion or the other.

The difference between the two of you doesn't have to be as heavy-duty as a religious difference for it to have heavy-duty lifestyle implications.

### ○ *Madeline and Roger*

Every weekend was a battle. They wanted to be together, but Roger was exhausted after a pressure-filled week as a stockbroker, and all he wanted was to stay home and watch television. More important, he felt that being able to relax together was a vital part of their relationship. "Do you think I could relax with a stranger?" he said.

Madeline thought that doing nothing but relax together in

front of the television meant they were strangers. "People who really have a good thing going, people with some juice in their relationship, go out and do things together," she said. "They have friends. And they give energy to their friends and get energy from their friends."

The basic differences between them were slight. Roger was only a little more tired when Friday rolled around than Madeline. Madeline was only a little more sociable. But the lifestyle implications of these small differences were enormous.

. . . . . . . . . . . . . . . . . . . . . . . . . . . . . . . . . . . . . . . . . . . . . . . . . . . . . . . . . . . .

2. Is there a difference between you and your partner that has to do with any one of the following:

- how you live your life
- where you live
- how you spend your free time
- what your future will be like

Has it gotten to the point where for one of you to be happy, the other must be unhappy?  YES___  NO___

. . . . . . . . . . . . . . . . . . . . . . . . . . . . . . . . . . . . . . . . . . . . . . . . . . . . . . . . . . . .

A *yes* answer means your relationship has a case of difference sickness.

## Losing Ways to Connect

Here's a question almost no one asks. What's the point of having something in common with your partner? The answer: so you can connect. That's what we really want: connecting, feeling connected. Differences that don't affect the sense of connection usually don't matter. My mother-in-law was a passionate New Deal Democrat. My father-in-law was a Richard Nixon

Republican. What a huge difference. But they enjoyed arguing politics, and this difference gave them endless things to talk about. This difference connected them. No problem.

Now let's look at two couples for whom losing ways to connect is a problem. They're same-sex couples and their experiences will reveal that you don't need gender differences to understand the way differences affect relationships.

## ○ Derek and Arthur

In the past few years Derek and Arthur started sliding apart fast. They'd thought they had so much in common, then Arthur began dabbling in various forms of New Age spirituality. Before anyone realized what was going on, he was busy with drumming circles and Celestine Prophecy study groups. He had his own meditation trainer.

Well, there's nothing wrong with that. Unfortunately, around the same time, Derek was getting into computers. When the Web exploded, Derek's involvement exploded along with it. "I can't pry him away from that machine" was how Arthur put it to me.

If you've ever seen that stunt where people with sledgehammers demolish a piano, that's what Arthur and Derek were doing to their relationship with their different interests. They were destroying any sense of connection. They had no time to connect, and neither had any desire to connect with someone who was interested in what the other was interested in.

## ○ Rosemary and Elaine

Sometimes subtle or very specific differences can destroy the sense of connection. When Rosemary and Elaine got together they ignored the amount of time it took Elaine to reach orgasm. After all, differences in sexual styles are still differences. They both passionately believed that this was the kind of difference that shouldn't matter.

But Rosemary started getting impatient with how long it took them to make love. Elaine started getting passionate about her belief that sex should take a long time. To avoid fights they stopped making love, because the less often they made love, the less often they fought. The problem was that lovemaking had been an important way for them to connect and feel married to each other.

* * * * * * * * * * * * * * * * * * * * * * * * * * * * * * * * * * * * * * * * * * * * * * * * * *

3. When the two of you find yourselves alone together for any length of time, does it feel as if you've lost the ability to connect because of your differences?　　　YES＿＿　NO＿＿

* * * * * * * * * * * * * * * * * * * * * * * * * * * * * * * * * * * * * * * * * * * * * * * * * *

A *yes* answer means your relationship has a case of difference sickness.

## Sex War Addicts

I'm sure you're aware that there's a strain of difference sickness that's hitting a lot of people today. It might become less common in the future, the way it was less common fifty years ago, but right now a lot of people are being hurt by it. It's the popular belief that men and women are somehow wildly, radically different creatures from different planets who work in completely different ways, have completely different needs, and speak completely different languages.

People who fall victim to this love killer believe that men and women are poles apart, yin and yang, east and west, and never the twain shall meet. *These people are wrong.* From my experience as a couples therapist, whenever I see a couple making a big deal about his guy things and her woman things and how different they are, I see a couple sliding off the cliff toward a dead-end relationship.

Now get this. I never see *happy*, healthy heterosexual relationships in which the two people make a big deal of gender differences. They're aware of whatever differences they want to be aware of, but they just don't let gender difference run the show.

. . . . . . . . . . . . . . . . . . . . . . . . . . . . . . . . . . . . . . . . . . . . . . . . . . . . . .

4. Do you and your partner spend a lot of time pointing out or underlining ways you're different based on gender?

YES____ NO____

. . . . . . . . . . . . . . . . . . . . . . . . . . . . . . . . . . . . . . . . . . . . . . . . . . . . . .

A *yes* answer means your relationship has a case of difference sickness.

## A Mushrooming Sense of Difference

If you remember Dan and Jackie, you'll see that they're a good example of another way difference sickness takes hold. When you fall victim to the belief that you used to be the same and had a lot in common, but you've become different and the number of differences is increasing, concerning increasingly important areas, such feelings have a devastating impact on how happy you are in the relationship. Your sense of your differences mushrooms.

It's one thing to step off a curb and see a bus sitting there facing you; it's another thing to see that bus facing you and know it's headed toward you at sixty miles an hour. That's the emotional reality for couples facing a growing sense of their differences.

5. Do the two of you talk about how you "used to" have so much in common, and how you don't have much in common "anymore," and how the two of you are very different "now"?                    YES___ NO___

A *yes* answer means your relationship has come down with a case of difference sickness.

## Overwhelmed by Difference

You can die from a stab wound to the heart; you can also bleed to death from a million paper cuts. One way or another, they both can overwhelm you. It's the same with difference sickness.

Sometimes there's one single difference that works to kill your relationship. I remember one couple I worked with. You wouldn't think two people could be more similar. Same social class: upper. Same kind of education: boarding schools and Ivy League colleges. Same religion: Episcopalian. They liked all the same kinds of things. There was just one difference. She wanted to live the life of the rich upper classes—high-paying prestigious jobs, two houses, one at a fashionable place to summer. He was happily downwardly mobile and perfectly content to earn a modest living, so long as he had the time to pursue his many interests. In many ways the gulf separating me from the typical Borneo head hunter is smaller than the one between these two people.

But you don't need a huge difference to be overwhelmed by difference. It can be a number of very small things: When the weather gets cold, you fight about whether or not to leave a bedroom window open at night. As you cycle in and out of the kitchen in the morning, one of you keeps turning the radio to one station, the other keeps turning it to another. One of you comes home from work hungry, the other wants to lounge around and eat later. One of you wants to engage in conversation about what happened during the day, the other wants to talk about anything but.

You don't even have to be that far apart on any of these issues. But they can add up. It gets very easy to lose hope that you'll be able to connect.

. . . . . . . . . . . . . . . . . . . . . . . . . . . . . . . . . . . . . . . . . . . . . . . . . . . . . . . . . . . . . .

6. Are you more or less convinced that you and your partner are "just too different"? Signs that you're "just too different" might include constantly fighting about how to do things, fighting about little things, never being able to make decisions together, having the same huge fight over and over about the same issue you can never resolve.     YES___ NO___

. . . . . . . . . . . . . . . . . . . . . . . . . . . . . . . . . . . . . . . . . . . . . . . . . . . . . . . . . . . . . .

A *yes* answer means your relationship has come down with a case of difference sickness.

## Prescription #7: Put Your Differences to Rest

*You can cure your relationship of difference sickness surprisingly easily,* even if it has put your relationship in the love hospital.

The way you eliminate difference sickness is the way you clean up after a party or the way you clear off a cluttered desk. You're faced with a mess. You feel overwhelmed. But then you go through the mess *one item at a time*. You pick up each item and *you have a highly limited menu of options for what to do with that item*. For example, you pick up a dirty glass from the party. Plastic? In the recycling bin. Glass? In the dishwasher. You pick up a bowl of food. Worth saving? Head for the Tupperware. Gross? In the trash.

You get the point. A task stops being overwhelming and

starts being manageable when you deal with it item by item and you know exactly what to do with each item.

Well, guess what? This is exactly the approach couples turned to on their own for ending difference sickness. I didn't teach people this; they taught it to me. Here's what you do.

**1.** Make an appointment for a time when you'll have a couple of uninterrupted hours to work on completely resolving your differences. This prescription is the only one in this book that requires this much time.

**2.** When you get together write down a list of differences that have been a problem. Whatever differences were in your mind when you answered the six diagnostic questions in this chapter should appear on this list. So should any difference that rankles or causes trouble. Take turns writing down, once and for all, all the differences that bug you. Ways in which you're fundamentally different. Different desires and goals. Different approaches to problem solving or performing tasks. Any difference that makes one of you angry or sad should go on the list.

Let me tell you something. Maybe your list will number hundreds of pages. But the average couple suffering from difference sickness is surprised to find their list is usually less than a page.

**3.** Now I'm going to tell you how to deal with the items on your list one at a time. It turns out that people in your situation have discovered ten solutions that work for eliminating almost any difference. Think of these solutions as the ways you sort through the papers on a cluttered desk. Each solution is like a place you put that piece of paper. I'll give you a list of these solutions in a moment, with a brief explanation. Then:

- You'll take the first item on your list of differences.
- You'll look at your list of ten solutions.
- You'll go to the first solution.
- You'll say, "Can we eliminate this difference by using so-

lution number one?" (It's like picking up something when you're cleaning up after a party and saying, "Can we deal with this by putting it into the fridge?")

- If solution number one takes care of that difference, you'll write the solution next to that difference on your list.
- If solution number one doesn't take care of that difference, you'll go to the next solution to see if it will do the trick.
- You'll keep going through the solution list until you find the best solution for eliminating the first difference.
- You'll write down that solution next to that difference.
- Then you'll go to the next difference on your list and look for which of the ten solutions works for both of you to eliminate that difference.

I told you it was just like cleaning up after a party, one item at a time. Except *this* time you're cleaning up a big mess in your relationship.

Here are the solutions, the ten best ways to eliminate differences between lovers:

## THE TOP TEN WAYS TO ELIMINATE DESTRUCTIVE DIFFERENCES

**1. Can you put this difference aside with a coin toss?** For example, a couple had been fighting about how different they were when they talked: one liked interrupting, the other hated interrupting. They flipped a coin. No interrupting became the rule. Goodbye to a difference.

**2. Can you just let this difference go, ignore it, stop paying attention to it?** For example, one couple argued because one was spiritual and the other wasn't, and they kept trying to convert each other. Then they said why can't we just leave each other alone about this and let this difference go as something neither of us will be concerned with? The difference remained. They just didn't pay attention to it.

**3. Can you resolve the difference by going your separate ways with this issue?** For example, one couple couldn't work out their evenings. He wanted to eat the minute they got home from work. She wanted to relax and take care of herself and eat later. So they decided that during the week they wouldn't eat dinner together. Separate dining stopped the way this difference had been separating them.

**4. Can you resolve two differences at the same time by trading off with each other: you go one way with one difference, the other way with the other difference?** For example, one couple had been seeing their relationship slowly die because of differences over the pace of lovemaking (she wanted them to take much longer) and differences over what it meant to "be responsible" (he felt he shouldn't be held to a timetable about when he showed up, whether he called, when he got things done). They settled it by agreeing that they'd do things her way in the bedroom but the rest of the time she wouldn't bug him about being late or not doing things.

**5. Can you decide that you will resolve this difference in one person's favor but take as long as necessary to bridge your difference?** For example, one couple had been growing apart over the issue of his not sharing his feelings and her wanting him to. Their difference dissolved when they agreed that he would make it his long-term goal to learn how to share his feelings and would actually share his feelings more often. But instead of his having to immediately become someone who shared his feelings, they agreed that he would have a pace that felt comfortable to him, as long as she felt he was making some progress.

**6. Can you see that there's no real difference between you?** For example, one couple owned a trendy card shop together. They'd gotten to the point where she accused him of being lazy (because he always talked about quitting early, taking time off for lunch, etc.) and he accused her of being a workaholic (because she always wanted to get to work early and always thought of things for them to do in the store). But when they talked about their actual goals and what they truly cared about, they realized that he was just as committed and willing to work as she was. It was only his style that made her think he was lazy.

**7. Does one of you care a lot more about this difference than the other?** For example, one couple was going to break up over what religion to raise their children in. Neither one was very religious, but she was Catholic and he was Jewish and they'd gotten increasingly polarized. Then they remembered to use the Love Tool where each ranks his or her preference on a scale of one to ten. She said it was a nine for her to bring their children up Catholic; he said it was a ten for him that they be brought up Jewish. Why? Because of all the people in his family who had been killed in the Holocaust. If their kids weren't brought up Jewish, it would be just that many more lost Jews. She accepted that it was more important to him than to her and agreed to do it his way. (If it's a ten for both of you, use one of the other nine Top Ten Ways to Eliminate Differences.)

**8. Can you bring this difference to a wise, objective outsider to settle?** For example, one couple had had bitter fights for years over his tendency to spend money, her desire to save it. Which was the best thing to do, which was the right way to be a person? They decided to go to a financial planner. They canvassed their friends and found someone whom they both agreed sounded sensible. They agreed that whatever budget and plan this person set up for them, they would follow.

**9. Can you have your cake and eat it too?** There are many ways to do this. Taking turns in sex (or anything else) is one. You do things one person's way one time, the other person's way the other time. Another way is to do what you both want at the same time. One couple felt that their formal china represented who they were, but each wanted completely different china. They bought two sets. Some couples settle the problem of which religion to raise the children in by raising them in both religions.

**10. Can you find a completely different alternative beyond the two you and your partner are fighting over or can you split the difference?** For example, one couple fought over whether to live in the city or the country. They settled on the suburbs. Another couple had been fighting over whether she should be able to give him a lot of feedback, the way she wanted, or not give him feedback, the way he wanted. They came up with a third alternative: she'd write out the criticisms and suggestions she wanted to give him in a special notebook he kept on his desk that he agreed to read.

*I've never yet seen a difference—no matter how deep or passionately held—that some couple hasn't put to rest by one of these ten solutions.*

Let's put this prescription to the test.

## ○ *Amy and Nick*

Amy and Nick would have bitter fights almost every morning and evening. Rushing to get out of the house was stressful, particularly since Amy's boss or one of Nick's clients usually phoned almost every morning with some urgent problem. The evenings were just as bad, with both of them coming home late, tired, hungry, and with work still to do.

The important task they had to manage together was *how to get through these stressful hours*. The battleground was Amy's not being affectionate to Nick during these stressful hours. She'd never kiss Nick or touch his arm. She'd get upset if he tried to kiss her or even if he affectionately stroked her behind in passing.

There was a huge difference between them about how a couple should be during crunch time. Amy's image was that if you loved and supported each other then the only considerate, constructive thing to do was stay the hell out of each other's way. A little hug here and there was just superficial romance. The whole point about stress for Amy was that there were too many demands already, so demands for affection just added to her overloaded situation. If Nick loved her, he would just leave her alone.

Nick's image was that you deal with combat by rising above it, by pretending it's not going on around you. He had this image of himself walking nonchalantly across a battlefield, smoking a cigarette, ignoring the guns going off around him. Yes, we're under stress, Nick might've said, but we can still act like people with all the time and energy in the world.

Deep down there was a battle over whose vision would prevail. His vision: two people who show affection even when they're rushing like mad? Or her vision: two people who show they care by leaving each other alone?

That was the battle deep down, but they didn't know it. Here's a brief excerpt from one of their fights:

AMY: "You're always annoying me."

NICK: "No, I'm not. You find a kiss annoying? What's wrong with you?"

AMY: "I'm sick of your telling me there's something wrong with me. Who do you think you are? You are so completely wrapped up in yourself you don't even see me."

NICK: "I see that you act like a bitch."

This is the point at which you have to scrape Amy off the ceiling.

Here's how they used this prescription. They went through the list of the top ten ways to eliminate differences. Here's that list in capsule form:

**1.** Can you put this difference aside with a coin toss?

**2.** Can you just let this difference go, ignore it, stop paying attention to it?

**3.** Can you resolve this difference by going separate ways with this issue?

**4.** Can you resolve two differences at the same time by trading off with each other: you go one way with one difference, the other way with the other difference?

**5.** Can you decide that you will resolve this difference in one person's favor but take as long as necessary to bridge your difference?

**6.** Can you see that there's no real difference between you?

**7.** Does one of you care a lot more about this difference than the other?

**8.** Can you bring this difference to a wise, objective outsider to settle?

**9.** Can you have your cake and eat it too?

**10.** Can you find a completely different alternative beyond the two you and your partner are fighting over or can you split the difference?

It never matters how many solutions don't seem to work. You just have to find the one solution that does. If you were in their shoes you might have chosen a different solution. They chose number 5: Can you decide that you will resolve this difference in one person's favor but take as long as necessary to bridge your difference? Amy had this nagging sense that she should be the way Nick wanted her to be when it came to showing affection. She *felt* that they should leave each other alone, but she'd *like to be* the kind of person who could rush off to work and be affectionate at the same time.

They agreed she'd try to be the way he wanted her to be in

the future, as long as he accepted the way she was now. What had to happen was for her to make it easier over time for them to connect as they were rushing around. "Just let me know if you don't think we're making progress," she said.

They agreed that at first Nick would leave Amy alone but when it was time for him to leave the house, she would give him a big hug and kiss goodbye. Finally they could agree to do something specific to bridge what had seemed like a huge chasm. Instead of the fight being over Amy's not being affectionate or Nick's not caring, the solution focused on one simple path they could begin to follow and that would fit into their busy lives.

The differences that make relationships sick are most often paper tigers. For this couple, as for so many others, a solution like this was enough to make them hopeful that their differences were neither too deep nor too wide. Nick really didn't want for them to fill all their busy time with hugs and kisses. He just wanted to know that affection wasn't completely out of the question. And as stressed as she felt, Amy wasn't incapable of shifting gears. She just had needs and wanted to know that Nick recognized her needs.

With one solution they brought a love killer to its knees. And by arriving at this solution together they were able to stand up as people who were not made sick by their differences but were healthy in their essential compatibility.

# Love Builder #7:
# The Couple You Fell in Love With

When you fall in love, you actually fall in love with three things.

You fall in love with *the other person*, the way he looks and acts and smells and talks—all the things about him that seem wonderful.

You also fall in love with *yourself*, a special way you feel inside. Of course it's the way the other person makes you feel.

You feel smarter, wiser, better looking, more generous, more powerful, more interesting—all the things you want to feel about yourself.

And you fall in love with *a couple*, two people, you and your partner. You fall in love with the way these two people are together. Their style—cute or cool or cuddly. The kinds of things they do together. The ways they give each other space or stay close. The roles they play for each other in the future they have together. It's this last thing, the couple you fell in love with when you fell in love with your partner, that can serve as a love builder now.

The person you fell in love with also fell in love with a couple. But you probably didn't talk about it very much. A lot of it was unconscious. A lot of the things you did talk about were the things you found easiest to agree about. You'd never be one of those couples, for example, who sat in a restaurant together for a whole meal without exchanging a single word. You'd be really cool parents, but you'd never let your kids get away with some of the stuff you got away with.

*That couple the two of you fell in love with is still alive and well.* When a relationship is not too bad to stay in, when it's not too late to save it from the clutches of the love killers, that couple you fell in love with and wanted to be like is still very much a part of who you are now. You need to go back to your roots and remember the things that brought you together. Instead of talking about how different you are now, talk about how similar you were then.

What you'll find out is that many more similarities than you thought still exist. If you let yourselves, you'll find still more similarities.

And this process of finding similarities, starting with the couple you fell in love with, is one of the best ways to recover from difference sickness. Think of it like this. Suppose you bridged none of your differences but instead discovered many new ways you were similar. Your sense of being "too different" would fade. You can always use the ten best solutions for bridging differences, but let the couple you fell in love with help you find your similarities.

## A Look Ahead

For many couples, being able to "work things out" means just one thing: one of you is hurt, angry, and scared because of things the other has done in the past. If differences are a kind of wall between you, these issues from the past are a kind of wall trapping you in the past, preventing you from moving freely into your future. It's time to break that wall, if it in fact exists for you.

# Freeway of Love

............................................................

LOVE KILLER #8:

## Toxic Buildup from the Past

ISSUE:
Has your relationship gotten bogged down in
hurts and grievances from the past?

Northern Ireland. Bosnia. The Middle East. The Hatfields and the McCoys. Many marriages.

What all these have in common is that someone hurt someone else very badly in the past, and that the hurt has become a painful grievance in the present. Like any poison, you should be able to get rid of hurts from the past. If you can't, the toxins build up. First you feel lousy, often for a very long time, and then you die. It happens to the human body. It happens to countries.

And it happens to love. Here are some examples:

- **Joan.** The deal was that she would support him through law school and then he'd support her in whatever she wanted to do, but babies came along, money was tighter than they'd thought, and he ended up doing nothing for her. Ten years of her life are gone, and every day her anger over this spoils what is otherwise a loving relationship.

- **Sandy.** The day before the wedding, with all their plans set in concrete, she sat him down and told him that she was adopted, that she'd slept with eleven different men, including one of his best friends, and that she had diabetes. He could've lived with all of this if he'd known about it as soon as possible. But to tell him at the very last minute . . . his distrust wouldn't go away.

- **Karen.** Who knows what got into him, because he seemed like a really nice guy? But when she went through a difficult first pregnancy he was demanding and critical, when he wasn't just staying away. When she called him at work to tell him she was going into a fast-moving labor, he managed not to get to the hospital until after she'd given birth. How could she forgive this betrayal?

- **Mark.** Isn't a person entitled to be a little blue, a little pessimistic, from time to time? That's what she said, but her depression and negativity had spoiled many years of their time together, and the more he thought about the situation, the angrier he got.

Has it happened to *your* relationship? Not just that there are things you're angry about, but has your anger over all your hurts and disappointments reached the dangerous, destructive threshold of being a real love killer? You'll find out in a moment.

You'll also find out that you can feel extremely hopeful about eliminating this love killer if it does exist in your relationship. For all the ways it seems to dig in and refuse to go away, for all the damage it does, I've discovered ten ways to eliminate this love killer and eliminate the toxins that have built up in your relationship. And you'll find out what these solutions are in a moment, too. But first we should look at what it really means when we talk about toxic buildup.


## How to Pollute a Relationship

We get angry at the people we love or disappointed in them for all kinds of reasons. Toxic buildup is something special. For this disease to kick in, you need a chain of events.

**Step 1.** When someone does something that hurts the other person, the chain of events begins. Obviously, the prime example of an action that leads to toxic buildup is when someone cheats on his partner. But any time we do something that causes our partner a lot of pain, damages trust, or causes unnecessary problems, negative feelings that don't go away are created. They spoil the happiness and ease of the relationship, the way a bad stomachache can spoil a day in the park.

The event doesn't have to be one major "crime." In most cases, a lot of not-so-big "crimes" loosely organized around a central theme cause the hurt.

For example, taking most of the money the two of you have been saving and lending it to an irresponsible relative without asking is a major "crime." But having done a lot of little things that were selfish and irresponsible without consulting your partner can be just as hurtful.

When you add up the time you came home with an expensive new set of golf clubs you hadn't talked about, and the time you went off to buy a new car and came back with a much more expensive model than you'd agreed on, and the time you took an old friend on a fishing trip and paid his way!—well, your partner now has one huge indigestible cruller sitting in her stomach, but that doesn't mean it didn't take a lot of little bites to get it there.

**Step 2.** But toxic buildup doesn't begin only with someone doing something "bad." The other person has to *experience* it as being bad. Ten days after we met, my husband told me that he'd been seeing a woman who'd gone away for the summer and that they had planned to see if they wanted to be with each other when she got back. I don't think that what my husband did was so terrible. He'd had no commitment to that woman. And after all, when do you tell someone you're starting to get involved with about your previous entanglements?

But it hurt me. I'd thought that we had been perfectly open and honest with each other. I couldn't help but see this old girlfriend as a real threat. So it took me weeks to forgive my husband for not telling me sooner, and throughout those weeks this issue overshadowed our relationship. So it's not just the hurt but the reaction to the hurt that creates the pollution.

**Step 3.** But just because she hurts you, it doesn't mean you'll end up suffering from toxic buildup. Toxic buildup also requires some kind of stickiness that prevents this hurt from passing out of your relationship. After all, even if you get food poisoning—a little diarrhea and vomiting takes care of it. A day or so later you can be as good as new, as long as the poison passes out of your system.

The difference between this love killer and a single bad incident is that something prevents you from letting it go. Things stick for a reason. You'd be surprised what people can let go of when there's nothing to make it stick.

## ○ *Ruth and Ernie*

You'd think that a woman could never let go of the hurt and fear that would come from her husband hitting her. But one couple I interviewed, when prodded, remembered how they'd had a fight about fifteen years earlier about his giving some of their money to his alcoholic brother. Ruth still couldn't forgive Ernie for doing this. But in the course of a fight in which they'd said terrible things to each other, Ruth slapped Ernie across the face. And he slapped her back.

She instantly understood that she'd provoked him and that his slap was restrained, that he'd done everything possible to not use an ounce more force than she'd used on him. There was just something about the tit-for-tat quality of that exchange that left Ruth with no fear he'd ever do it again. And so Ernie's action injected no poison into the environment of their relationship.

This little story, in which there were no toxic consequences, helps us understand what's necessary for Step 3. In addition to Step 1, doing something bad, and Step 2, being hurt, you need any of the following reactions for the damage to stick:

- **Fear.** "This thing you did that hurt me . . . because you did it, and because nothing has changed, I can't see why you won't keep on doing it."
- **Confusion.** "It's not how much I was hurt, but the way you hurt me. It made me wonder who you are, because the man I know wouldn't do that."
- **Loss.** "When you did what you did I lost something very important to me that I really need, and I don't know how to get it back."

We experience a mixture of these three feelings when there's some hurt we can't let go of. Take the sense of betrayal we all feel when our partner cheats on us, the betrayal I certainly felt when my husband announced he'd gotten close to another woman. I felt fear: Was our marriage over? I felt confusion: Who was he, and who were we to each other? And I felt loss: Whatever specialness we had was gone.

But we can understand what makes the damage stick, which is good news. As you'll see when we get to the prescription (in case this love killer applies to you), eliminating toxic buildup is in large measure a process of dealing with whatever is making the toxins stick. It's as if there were a magnet holding them. You don't have to do anything about the toxins. You just have to deactivate the magnet and the toxins disappear by themselves. But I'm getting ahead of myself.

# Diagnostic #8:
# Have Hurts Piled Up to Pollute Your Relationship?

As you read this, you may be thinking that toxic buildup is killing your relationship. But don't be so sure. Just because you can't forget bad things that happened doesn't mean you're actually suffering from toxic buildup. That can only be determined by diagnosing whether toxic buildup is present.

The questions that will allow us to make a diagnosis are based on some very special relationships I've studied. These are relationships in which the same kind of hurt caused very different results. If the hurts were the same (for example, someone had had an affair in both cases), what signs pointed to the different outcomes?

Let me tell you about a couple who suffered through a few serious hurts. We can use this case to make the diagnostic questions clear.

## ◯ *Jill and Charlie*

He's forty, she's thirty-nine. They've been married for thirteen years, and they have an eight-year-old son. They came to see me because Charlie had just found out that shortly before their son was conceived Jill had gone on a business trip with her boss to Denver where she ran into (or looked up, depending on whose version you believed) the man she'd loved in college who'd dumped her without any explanation.

Among the many things that had upset Charlie was his fear that this man was his son's real father, although the paternity test he took proved that Charlie was the father. Jill was very sorry for what happened, made a convincing case that she hadn't planned it, and helped us believe that the reason she did it, once the opportunity presented itself, was to put to rest her occasional fantasy that this man had been the love of her life.

But there was misery, tension, and anger between Jill and Charlie that seemed to come from somewhere else besides Charlie's sense of betrayal. He was the seemingly aggrieved party. So why did Jill seem so bitter?

I asked her, and she said in a cold voice, "He pretends to be one thing, but he's really something else. Even with this anger and disappointment he's putting out, I don't know if I believe it. For all I know he's got something on me, finally, and he's delighted to have gotten it."

We've all heard of cases where someone lied about how much money he had or who he was to get someone to marry him. What Charlie did seemed more subtle, more minor, and there was a good chance that it was mostly unconscious. But it had the same effect. When they met Charlie had been out of dental school for a year. "I was just a secretary," Jill said. "Didn't he know that just being a dentist made him a really good catch, specially since he was handsome in a Geraldo Rivera kind of way?"

**"I don't know who you are."** Here was the issue for Jill. Since he had enough going for him as he was, why did he make this big effort to seem like he cared so much about all these important causes, and why did he talk about his art, his painting, as if under the dentist's smock beat the heart of a true artist? Within a year of their getting married it was clear that he was a guy who came home from work, watched sports on television, played golf on the weekend, and liked double dating with couples he could brag about to the other couples they double dated with.

To add insult to injury, Charlie had made a point of telling Jill when they were dating that as a dentist he'd make plenty of money and that if she wanted to be a stay-at-home wife that would be fine. The problem was that their income never quite kept pace with their debts and expenses. Theoretically Charlie was a successful medical professional, the way he was theoretically a whole bunch of things. In reality Jill had to keep on working to make ends meet. She liked working. She was proud of being an executive assistant to the CEO of a reputable commercial real estate development firm. But it was hard for Jill to forgive Charlie for making it sound as if she really had a choice.

It's clear that Jill and Charlie had circumstances they fought about that made them miserable. But was a real love killer at work?

To diagnose this I'm going to talk about something I call *the grievance*. This is more than just the stark deed (if it was just one deed) that launched the bitterness. It's the whole package of events, the fights you had over it, the unhappy memories you carry with you, and the feelings you have to live with that grow out of the initial hurt.

To diagnose toxic buildup, we first have to establish the preconditions for it. So the first question is separate from the others:

## DIAGNOSING LOVE KILLER #8

1. Is there some grievance or hurt or incident or situation from the past, based on something your partner did or didn't do, that you can't forget or forgive?        YES ＿＿ NO ＿＿

A *yes* answer to diagnostic question 1 means only that your relationship has the *precondition* for toxic buildup: some hurt from the past you're still holding on to. It doesn't mean that the hurt has reached the point of being a love killer.

Obviously, Charlie and Jill met the precondition. But just because you and your partner have had a lot of miserable fights about something doesn't mean that you meet the precondition. One couple had terrible fights for five years because she wanted to have a third child and he didn't. They might have every other love killer in this book, but they don't have this one unless, for example, she somehow tricked him into getting her pregnant, say by "forgetting" to take her birth control pills, and he was confronted by a fait accompli. Then he'd have a grievance.

If you do meet the precondition for toxic buildup, answer the following six questions. If you answer *yes* to *even one* of the following six diagnostic questions, your relationship has come down with a case of toxic buildup.

## DIAGNOSING LOVE KILLER #8 (continued)

2. Do you find that happy occasions keep getting spoiled because the topic of the grievance keeps intruding?   YES ＿＿ NO ＿＿

3. Do you obsess over the grievance?        YES ＿＿ NO ＿＿

4. If you should ever talk about anything even remotely connected to the grievance do you almost inevitably find yourselves embroiled in a fight?        YES ＿＿ NO ＿＿

5. Does every fight you get into about this grievance feel the same, as if you keep having the same fight over and over?
YES ＿＿ NO ＿＿

6. Does it seem as if the hurt and damage haven't diminished over time?        YES ＿＿ NO ＿＿

7. Are you powerfully convinced that if you had learned the lesson this grievance has taught you that you never would have married your partner?        YES ＿＿ NO ＿＿

Again, if you met the precondition by answering *yes* to question 1, and if you answered *yes* to even one of questions 2 through 7, then you guys have come down with a case of toxic buildup.

**Charlie's answers.** As far as Jill and Charlie are concerned, Charlie couldn't really answer yes to any question besides the first one. He was still angry at Jill for sleeping with her old boyfriend, but the issue was very much on the back burner for him. They fought about it for a month or two but it had happened a long time ago and Charlie believed Jill when she told him what it meant to her. It didn't stimulate the fear, confusion, and sense of loss that it would have had to stimulate for this to be a real love killer for him. And it wasn't just that Charlie hated confrontations. Late at night he didn't think about how this made everything different between them. Of course, it would have been a very different story if he'd found out their child wasn't his.

**Jill's answers.** But Jill answered *yes* to four of the six questions, besides the first one. She definitely found herself obsessing over the huge gap between who Charlie was and who he'd led her to think he was. Every time she met an interesting guy at work, it's not that she was attracted to him but she'd always think, "That's the kind of guy Charlie claimed to be." Jill was absolutely convinced that she wouldn't have married Charlie as she now knew he was, even though in their fights she told Charlie that he would have been quite a catch without any of his pretenses.

Perhaps worst of all, every time Charlie promised Jill something, every time Charlie talked about who he was and what he wanted (even if it was something innocuous such as saying he cared about his patients), Jill felt the full force of her grievance and found it almost irresistible to let Charlie know that she couldn't trust what he said about himself.

# Prescription #8:
# Getting Rid of Toxic Buildup

If you're scared that this love killer is hard to treat, don't be. But I do want you to be scared about what will happen if you don't treat it. If you do nothing, your relationship will be a scene of endless joy-destroying warfare. You'll get no satisfaction out of the things you do with your time. You'll blame each other for ruining your lives.

Now here's why you should be optimistic about getting rid of toxic buildup. Here's what you have working for you:

1. **You want to be in this relationship and make it feel good again.** People understand instinctively that holding on to grievances is what you do when you want to end a relationship. Letting go of grievances is what you do when you want to stay together. So wanting the relationship and wanting to let go of the grievance go hand in hand.

2. **You have the ability to focus on whatever it is that's making you hold on to your grievance, the emotional magnet that's making it stick.** Whether it's fear, confusion, or loss, addressing the fear, ending the confusion, or compensating for the loss can take the power away from the magnet.

3. **You have the ability to simply let go of your grievance.** You might need help doing this, but in fact people every day make a decision to stop holding on to a grievance. Sometimes the ability to let go doesn't even require a decision. It just requires time.

## Finding the Right Way Out

How actually do you use your abilities to get rid of a specific grievance? Look, I know you feel that the hurts you're carrying around that spoil your relationship cut very deeply, but I'd like to ask you for a moment to think of them like stains in fabric. Suppose our problem was "I spilled grape juice on a white linen tablecloth. How do I get rid of it?"

What would we do? We'd put out the call to see if there were people who'd faced the same stain and done something that worked to get rid of it. Then we'd try it ourselves just to make sure. What else would you do? Study the chemistry of grape juice? Experiment on your own with a million and one possible solutions? No. You find people who solved the problem and learn from them.

That's what we've done here: We searched to find out what works and then tried to put it all together in a form that's easy for you to use.

As I show you exactly what the prescription for eliminating toxic buildup is, step by step, I want to illustrate it with an actual case, because it helps to see it in action.

## ○ *Judy and Allen*

The hurts and grievances Judy and Allen had to deal with may or may not be identical to the ones you have to deal with, if you've diagnosed this love killer. But the most important thing when it comes to eliminating toxic buildup is to follow all the steps in the prescription. The procedure is the same for everyone.

For Judy and Allen, there were toxins on both sides, and as you'll see that's just as easy to work with as when only one person has a grievance. Judy is ten years younger than Allen. For the first several years of their relationship (they've been married for seventeen years) Allen was highly critical of Judy and constantly did what a lot of older men in relationships do: played the role of teacher. But his "teaching" took the form of confidence-destroying put-downs. Judy went on to become a very successful residential real estate agent and that muted a lot of

Allen's criticisms. But the old hurts still lingered and made Judy want to keep her distance from Allen.

But Allen had his own grievances. When they met, Allen had owned a tiny little lamp manufacturing business that was in desperate need of new capital. Only in the last few years did Allen find out that both Judy and her parents had a lot more money than they'd let on, money that could very easily have made a big difference in his business. He understood that investing in him was risky, and he understood that Judy didn't want to feel that he was marrying her for her money. But the sense of selfishness, separateness, and mistrust she conveyed by keeping silent about her money made Allen furious every time he thought about it, even though now his business was doing fine.

But they had one thing going for them. They understood that toxic buildup was a real love killer, that it could and would kill their relationship, and that they'd have to follow a prescription for eliminating toxic buildup if they wanted to save their marriage.

Here's are the steps of the prescription:

1. Make the decision to eliminate the toxins.

2. Commit to forgiveness.

3. Get what you need to let go.

4. Let go of the poisons.

5. Convalesce.

Now here's exactly what you have to do to follow this prescription.

**Step 1. Make the decision to eliminate the toxins.** For some people this is the easiest step. You just sit down together and say, "Look, toxic buildup is killing us. There'll be no *us* if we don't do something about it. I know we're both feeling righteous and defensive about everything that's gone on in the past and the ways we've been hurt, but as long as I know we'll both get our needs met, I'm willing to do what's necessary to eliminate the toxins. Are you?"

Make sure you both agree. Note the simple ingredients in this step:

- Acknowledge that your relationship has a potentially deadly disease.
- Acknowledge that this disease probably isn't going to cure itself.
- Understand that you both have needs that have to be addressed in the process of eliminating the toxins.
- Be willing to do what's necessary.

And what *is* necessary? The next four steps must take place over four weeks. Time and the healing of wounds have always gone together, and they go together here. The moment you've taken the first step, you can take the next step immediately. Then make sure to set aside time, preferably the same time every week, to get through the next four steps.

**Step 2. Commit to forgiveness.** *(Week #1 begins here.)* You're not actually forgiving each other at this point. You're not letting go yet. All you're doing is making a simple promise, and this is what you say:

*We have issues we have to work through, but I promise that as long as we work through these problems I will be the kind of person who can let go of the grievances I've been holding on to. I will be the kind of person who can forgive the ways I've been hurt. I'm tired of being someone who holds on to hurts and grievances.*

For those of you who are religious, you're doing nothing more than promising each other something that God promises: the possibility of forgiveness. No religion omits the insight that God has the capacity to forgive. Otherwise every fault would be a permanent trap and the universe couldn't be healed. In your own relationship, the universe of your love needs to be healable. No one should say forgiveness is impossible, except as a way of announcing that the relationship is beyond all help.

Allen and Judy had trouble with this step. Judy said, "I keep hoping I'll forget, but I don't know if I can forgive you for undermining my whole sense of self-confidence. How can I forgive you for trying to make me a nothing?"

Nothing can change the past. But our understanding of what was really going on in the past *can* change. Our sense of what's real in the present and possible in the future *can* change. You don't actually forgive anything in this step. You just have to commit to forgiveness if the remaining steps make it at all possible. You have to understand that there's a choice—either forgiveness or ending the relationship—and if you're not going to choose to end things the only choice left is to commit to forgiveness. Judy saw that her unwillingness to leave Allen meant she'd have to commit to forgiveness. And so she did.

That's all you do at this step. You walk away from this encounter with the sense that perhaps for the first time you now know that forgiveness is a real possibility.

**Step 3. Get what you need to let go.** *(Week #2 begins here.)* You're *still* not ready to forgive anyone yet. That can't happen until you identify what you need in the present. That means you have a lot of thinking to do.

Whatever hurts and grievances you've been holding on to, ask yourself the following three questions:

**1. What am I afraid of that keeps me holding on to my sense of hurt?** This situation applied to Allen. If Judy had kept things from him in the past, what was she keeping from him now? He was afraid there was something.

If you're afraid of something, you have to spend this week identifying exactly what you're afraid of. Usually what we're afraid of is that the other person will hurt us again. We feel there's something inside the other person that caused him to hurt us and that that thing inside him hasn't changed. That's why you have to figure out what would make you less afraid. You need some kind of evidence that whatever produced the hurts before isn't there now.

Here's what you have to be ready to say when the two of you get together: "It's been hard for me to let go of how hurt I've been because I'm afraid I'll get hurt again. I realize you can't prove that I'll never get hurt again. But I need something solid from you."

*And then you have to say what you need.* No one can do this for you. Only you can identify something specific that would lessen your fear. Here's an example. Allen was afraid Judy was hiding money from him. He asked Judy to show him all her accounts. Of course this didn't prove she wasn't still hiding money. But it helped. To take another example, a woman whose husband had had an affair with a subordinate asked him to fire her or transfer her.

But don't underestimate the possibility that what you need is simply for your partner to understand your position. That's what happened with my husband and me. I realized there wasn't much he could do to remove my fear that he wouldn't get involved with someone in the future. But he *could* understand what I was saying: that if anything like that happened again it would be all over for us. I *made* him understand that. Even though there was nothing specific he could do, I got what I needed to eliminate my fear.

So be ready to tell your partner what you need to eliminate your fear.

**2. What don't I understand about what happened, such as why it happened or what it means that it happened?** If you're confused as a result of having been hurt, you have to spend this week identifying exactly what's confusing you. When one person has had an affair, their partner often can't make sense of it. Wasn't he getting sex and love at home? Was he really wanting to put the marriage in jeopardy? If you need enlightenment about the meaning of what happened, this is the time to put your finger on exactly what you need to have clarified.

For instance, it may end your confusion to hear that the two of you were distant and angry with each other, that your partner was hungry for affection, and this other person was available. It doesn't mean that your partner is going to have sex with every available person. It just means that there was a whole set of circumstances that made sense of what happened.

All you're doing here is coming up with a fresh look at an old story. But don't grill your partner. If you do, he'll get evasive. Then you'll get more confused. The magnet holding on to your grievances will get more powerful.

Instead of grilling your partner say this: "Take some time to think about it if you need to, but I need to know the true story of why you did what you did so that I can get to the point of believing you won't do it again." That's right. You are explicitly giving your partner the opportunity to let himself off the hook. But that's real. That's what you actually want. If he can't make sense of what happened in a way that makes the whole thing less awful and less threatening, how are you going to let go of your hurt in the first place?

**3. What do I need to rebalance things?** As Judy thought about it, she realized that she really wasn't afraid of Allen undermining her confidence anymore. She had the confidence she needed. But the loss she'd experienced from years of feeling that she was stupid and ignorant made her feel that a real debt was owed her.

237

And if you're experiencing a sense of loss, you have to spend this week figuring out what could possibly compensate you. You must realize, as I'm sure you do, that you can never get back exactly what you lost. Allen couldn't give Judy back those years in her twenties and thirties when she desperately needed someone to help her feel good about herself. But you don't need to get back exactly what you lost to let go of your grievance. Most of the time all you need is something solid, something that feels like a real gesture.

So don't be afraid to ask for . . . well, a payoff. It's not that you're chiseling your way into getting some goodies. But what else could Allen do for Judy? By buying her something expensive that she wanted—in her case a natural pearl necklace—he was saying something important. Yes, he was saying, I did take something from you, and you do deserve repayment. Even though I can't give you back what I took from you, I can give you a sign showing you that I'd like to rebalance things between us.

This is a lot for you to think about: what it would take to eliminate your fear, confusion, and sense of loss. But you have to deactivate the magnet that's holding on to your grievance. In any case, when you come together in Week #2, this is when you say what you need to be able to let go.

A word of warning. I'm sure you understand that you'd be a damn fool to ask for something there's no way your partner could give you. Allen thought of asking Judy to "make" her parents reveal all of their assets, but she simply didn't have the power to do that. The woman who asked her husband to transfer the subordinate he'd been having an affair with could get away with that request partly because the affair had been so damaging, but partly because this subordinate was not a key employee and her husband had the power to make the organizational change.

When people really want to eliminate the toxins choking their relationship, they ask for what's obtainable and try to give what's asked for.

But don't get into a fight about it when you get together on Week #2. Ask for what you need. Talk about it. And if your partner can't say *yes* right away, give him until the following week to figure out what he can give.

I can't tell you how many of these cases I've seen where people had to identify what they needed to let go of a grievance, but everyone who accepted their partner's offer was glad he or she accepted it. And everyone who said that what his or her partner was willing to do was not enough, ended up regretting it.

**Step 4. Let go of the poisons.** *(Week #3 begins here.)* People who are serious about stopping smoking often make a little ceremony out of putting out their last cigarette and throwing away all the cigarettes they still have. It doesn't eliminate the urge to smoke. That takes time. But it serves as a defining moment of their pledge to stop smoking and reinforces their commitment to it.

That's what you're going to do in Week #3. You're going to go through a kind of ceremony in which you formally, ceremonially, snuff out your grievances and throw them away. What you're doing here is taking your last puff of grievance talk. We understand that it's still going to take time for your hurt to subside and the memories to fade. But ending the grievance talk, in combination with your previous week's work, will make it happen a lot faster.

Here's the ceremony you go through.

**1. You let loose one last explosion of anger and sorrow.** There's a way I want you to do it, because it works. Take five minutes *and no more* to let loose with everything you feel about the hurt that was done you. If your partner had an affair, tell him how it broke your heart (if that's true), how it made you want to kill him (if that's true), how it made you feel you'd never love anyone again. Whatever you feel, let it out now.

But make sure it's understood that you'll take no more than five minutes. Make sure you stop when the five minutes are up. I know that five minutes doesn't sound like much when it comes to unloading the entire contents of your heart. But I've been there countless times when patients have done this, and I've been through it a couple of times in my personal life. To listen to someone yell and scream and cry in your face for five minutes is an eternity. To do it can feel like an eternity. In any case, if you don't allow for the safety of a five minute limit your partner will just end up feeling dumped on.

**2. Your partner has to tell you what he's heard as you were expressing your feelings.** He's not supposed to apologize at this point or explain himself or anything except say something like, "I hear you say that because I slept with that woman you didn't want to live anymore."

When your partner says what he's heard, it will probably sound a little lame and anticlimactic to you, and he might leave out something very important in what you said. Don't worry about this. Calmly point out what he left out. Ignore the lameness of his summary. You felt devastated, and he said you were upset, that's enough.

**3. He says he's sorry.** There's one rule for this. Show genuine and complete remorse for the pain you caused. I once saw a relationship end in front of my eyes when the guy who was supposed to be apologizing for having an affair started off with, "I never meant to hurt you," and then spent the rest of the time unapologizing—listing all the things he *didn't* feel he had to be sorry for. Hello! That's not saying you're sorry.

You don't have to eat crap. You're not apologizing for who you are. But the fact that you were a big fat bubblehead who didn't have a clue what he was doing, or even thought he was doing the right thing, doesn't mean you have nothing to apologize for. Look, if you were in a store and accidentally stepped on someone's foot, you'd say you were sorry, and you'd probably mean it, at least a little. Well, here something you've done has caused enough pain to threaten your whole relationship. That's worse than running over someone's dog. You've got to show how really sorry you are.

This last step was a problem for Judy and Allen. Allen was willing to buy Judy the pearl necklace because he knew that what had happened had been a big deal for her. But what would he apologize for? Ruining her life? She had a good life. Hurting her? He'd been trying to help her by being so critical. Hadn't she said on their third date, "I could learn so much from you"?

"The pain," Judy said. "I want to hear you say you're sorry for the pain I went through. It's not complicated, Allen. I was in pain. You were involved. I want you to say you're sorry for your part in it."

Judy's words sank in, and then Allen's own words of sorrow started pouring out. The more he talked, the more he plumbed the depths of the real sorrow he felt. It's hard for people to say they're sorry, but when they let themselves go it hits them very hard how sorry they really feel. All that's necessary is to give yourselves a chance for this to happen.

That's what this encounter during Week #3 is all about. A last venting of pain. An acknowledgment of the pain. A last expression of sorrow.

You're not quite done. Now you have to bury the grievance. Here's how you do it. Take a piece of paper. The person who hurt his partner writes down, *in 25 words or less*, a statement of the pain he caused and how sorry he is for it. Then the person who was hurt writes down, *in 25 words or less*, a statement acknowledging the apology. You do this all on one piece of paper.

Now take this piece of paper and tuck it away somewhere in your living space. Put it in some book you never read. Put it in the back of your filing cabinet. Toss it on to the top shelf of a closet. It's as if you're putting it away from you, but not throwing it away. It's possible you'll never see it again. But you'll know you might see it. The point is that you've buried your grievance.

**Step 5. Convalesce.** *(Week #4 and beyond.)* Believe it or not, your work is done. The infection has been treated. The antibiotics have killed the germs. The bullet's been removed. But the hole it made is still there.

Now you have to acknowledge that your relationship needs time to convalesce. Acknowledge that it will take time for your memory of pain to disappear. Acknowledge that your grievance might come up again and it might still hurt.

*So what?* Sometimes we feel the twinge from old wounds. It doesn't mean we're still wounded. And it would be self-destructive to act as if we were. Both of you need to accept that you've buried your grievance.

There's an inevitable paradox involved with convalescence from toxic buildup. You want to forget. But you also want to prevent the same hurt from happening again. So you have to remember those hurts in order to forget those hurts. That's the paradox. But people do it all the time. Whenever Allen started getting critical, Judy would say something like, "That's the kind of thing that hurt so much those first years. I've let go of that grievance. But I just don't want any new grievances. So don't be critical of me now."

It's a judgment call. You could always accuse someone who says something like what Judy said of trying to parade old wounds, just the way you could accuse Allen of trying to open old wounds. But it's really not that complicated. Specific toxins built up. You need to prevent them from building up again. Saying something like, "That's what hurt me in the past," helps heal old wounds and prevent new ones.

## An End to Love Pollution

What I've just done is help you build a machine. That's what the prescription for eliminating toxic buildup is—a machine that can chug through the environment of your relationship and eliminate toxins wherever they've built up. And if we look inside that machine, the heart of it is a mechanism for forgiveness. Think of it like a carpet shampoo machine. It's a bit of a big deal to shampoo your carpet. But if the carpet's dirty enough, you've got to do it.

# Love Builder #8: Wanting to Be Together

The love builder here is very basic, and we've touched on it already. You want to have a relationship with each other. And you can't do that if you're married to your grievance. It's like when there's a polluted lake. If there's a tiny amount of pollution that doesn't bother anyone, you ignore it. But if the pollution makes you sick—and the diagnostics here are designed to get at whether toxins have built up to the point of making your love sick—then you either end the pollution or stay out of the lake. If that lake is your love, you've got to end the pollution. And now you know how to do it.

Now you can do what people do in healthy relationships. If one of you gets upset, you can tell your partner how you feel and he can listen. Your partner gets feedback about what makes you upset. You feel supported and cheered up. There's nothing to cause blame and disappointment to back up and spill out into your emotional space. You're free.

## A Look Ahead

Craziness. That's what toxic buildup is about, in a way. The craziness that goes on between people and the hurts it causes and the ways those hurts linger and the need to heal those hurts.

Now it's time to look at a different kind of craziness. The kind that resides inside a person. The kind that can make someone keep on doing things that make it hard for you to love him.

# · 10 ·

# Crazy

· · · · · · · · · · · · · · · · · · · · · · · · · · · · · · · · · · · · · · · · · · · · · · · · · · · · · · · · · · · · · · · · · · · · · · · · · · · · · ·

## LOVE KILLER #9:
## Problem People

### ISSUE:
Do you or your partner have a personal problem
that's preventing your relationship from
being healthy?

### *Sometimes It Is the Other Person's Fault*

Vivian was one of the first people I interviewed for this book. "Where do you go to get ten years of your life back?" she asked me within moments after I asked her to tell me the story of her relationship. "Is there some office where you tell them how ten years of your life were stolen from you and they give it back to you?"

You'll meet Vivian in a moment and hear more of her story. But behind her words of frustration is one chilling fact. She spent ten years working on her relationship with her husband, thinking that their problems had something to do with "their" patterns, "their" couples skills. But her husband Walter had real problems of his own, which affected their relationship but were essentially separate from it. They'd tried to solve "their" problems, when in fact a more accurate diagnosis would have zeroed in on the destructive impact of *his* problems on their relationship.

I can't tell you how many people asked me, "If we're so smart, why is love so hard?" in one form or another. And when I asked them what they in particular found so hard to understand, they'd reveal the terrible frustration that comes from a problem that the other person in the relationship had. *"We're* not happy because *he's* got this problem" is what they told me.

But they were ashamed to admit it. A high proportion of the couples who considered themselves responsible had already had some form of couples therapy. And the two messages they'd gotten from this work were that, first of all, you shouldn't blame the other person if you want to fix the relationship, and, second, the other person's problems were very likely a result of factors in the relationship.

## The Help We Need

Just think about where this leaves you if you're on the receiving end of it. You know in your heart that your partner's problem is sabotaging your relationship. But you think you're not supposed to blame your partner, so you ignore the problem, and that's devastating for most relationships.

The couple you're about to meet shows how one person's problems can masquerade as a relationship problem. You'll find out in a moment what that person's problem was. But I want to make something quite clear. This couple's story focuses on only one of the many different psychological and emotional problems that threaten the health of relationships.

## ◯ *Vivian and Walter*

This couple was saved from having to get a divorce after eighteen years of marriage, but it was close. Eight years into the marriage it was clear to both of them that something was wrong.

It was the old story of a couple who couldn't talk without fighting, but it's interesting what their fights were about. Vivian would complain about something Walter hadn't done, or a way he hadn't come through for her. Think about a car that always gets flat tires. That's how Walter was. He was always deflating somehow, going soft and weak in a way that prevented him from coming through for her.

It was usually little things, but they had a big impact. Vivian often traveled on business, but Walter never offered to pick her up at the airport. Once Vivian made a really big deal about this. The next time she came home, Walter picked her up at the airport, but he just stood there like a cigar store Indian without even a hug or a smile.

When Vivian would complain about this kind of thing, Walter would deny that anything had happened, or he'd say that Vivian was making a big deal out of nothing. Just to make Walter hear how unhappy she was, Vivian would raise the decibel level by talking about how Walter was never there for her, how he had nothing to give. The more misery Vivian expressed, the more likely it was that Walter would tell her to leave if she was so unhappy. Then Vivian would be sorry she'd said anything.

They thought that having kids would make them feel more like a family. Walter was a high school assistant principal and liked kids. Maybe he'd come into his own. But the only thing that changed in their relationship was that the demands of real-life stresses and pressures that come with a new baby made things even worse. Walter's never wanting to do anything, never having anything to give, became a bigger issue than ever.

So they went into couples therapy, where they stayed for ten years, changing therapists twice. They kept feeling their therapists were failing them. Vivian kept feeling like a failure herself. But no one wanted to blame Walter.

**Hidden depression.** Throughout the entire time they were together, Vivian couldn't shake the sense that there was something wrong with Walter. Now she knows she was right. It was Walter's boss, the school principal, who sensed something that Walter and Vivian couldn't see. There were too many conversations he'd had with Walter where Walter's main response was to wonder what the point of doing anything was or to sigh that he had nothing to offer.

A better diagnostician than their therapists, the principal insisted that Walter sign up for a depression-treatment program. Within eight months the change was dramatic. Walter had been one of many people whose depression takes the form of depriving you of energy, leaving you with little to give. He hadn't so much felt sad as low. It had been a "why bother" kind of depression. So the effect of the treatment wasn't so much that Walter was cheered up, it's that he was just up period. He had something to give and he wanted to give it.

**Bailing out.** But years and years of Walter's having been a problem person had almost capsized their relationship. His depression had kept Vivian so busy bailing out their little boat of love that none of her needs had gotten met. She couldn't count the number of friends who'd told her, "If you're not getting anything out of this marriage, you should leave him." She almost did.

In the end, though, Walter and Vivian were lucky. Hard data is difficult to come by, but I'm now convinced that even if everyone in the world had a Ph.D. in couples therapy, countless relationships would still be destroyed by this love killer alone. Yes, these relationships have been destroyed, but not because there was a relationship problem.

But you deserve to feel hopeful about this, because hope is realistic. If your partner has problems it does not *in itself* mean that you'll be better off leaving the relationship. If your partner can *acknowledge* that he's got a problem and is *willing to try* to deal with it, then there's a good chance your relationship is viable.

But only if you take this love killer seriously. If you don't, it can be a deadly love killer. Part of the danger comes from how sinister the effects of their problems are, how termitelike they chew into the foundation of your love. Part of the danger is that psychological problems are hard to detect, particularly when they are subtle or develop slowly or when you see the other person every day and the problem behaviors keep getting mixed up with normal-seeming behaviors. Even cowgirls get the blues, but how do you know when they're really depressed? How do you know when there is some other problem?

That's what we're going to tackle here. By the end of this chapter you'll learn how to diagnose the presence of Love Killer #9 by learning how to detect the possible presence of serious psychological problems. I realize that psychiatric diagnosis is difficult even for master clinicians. But you *can* learn how to detect when it might be a good idea to obtain a professional's opinion about whether a diagnosable disorder is present.

### Real Help for Real Problems

We can go one step further, and we will. It's not enough to *say* that someone has problems. You also need good ideas for how to prevent those problems from causing daily mischief in your relationship.

Let's face it, we've all got psychological quirks and flaws. Whether your partner is suffering from depression or just happens to be a little bummed out today, whether your partner is suffering from a chronic, debilitating social phobia or just happens to be really nervous about a talk he has to give, or whatever the case might be, you're going to be called on—the way you've already been called on—to function as a kind of live-in amateur therapist. Every time you say something like "for Christ's sake snap out of it," you're functioning like a therapist. So why not do a good job of it?

I know. I know. You're *not* a therapist. You don't *want* to be your partner's therapist. And you don't have time to learn how to be a therapist. And if your partner has real problems, it's not even healthy for you to be his therapist. *But* what do you do when he's blue or nervous or starts drinking too much at a party or starts expressing ideas you know are distorted?

I'll show you what to do when we get to the prescription. You wouldn't dream of sitting around your house utterly clueless about what to do if someone cut a finger or bumped a head. We all know enough first aid to get by. Well I'll teach you basic things you can do if your partner starts exhibiting "symptoms" so that you can at least prevent things from getting worse and maybe even make them a little better. Everyone should know how to do basic psychological first aid.

And in the process you'll know how to make your relationship and your life feel a lot better. You'll know how to eliminate this love killer.


## ○ *Hilary*

For the first three years of her marriage, Hilary was proud of having such a hard-working, highly respected investigator for the D.A.'s office as her husband. And if Clark was a little possessive, a little jealous—well, *very* possessive and jealous—part of her felt good about that, too. He cared.

After all, don't we all believe that someone who's a little overinvolved, a little overcontrolling, is someone who cares?

Eight years later they were in deep trouble. They went to a couples therapist, and here's the problem they complained about: "We fight all the time. We never agree about anything. Hilary's closed, hidden, evasive. She keeps stopping us from being intimate. Clark has a short fuse and sometimes he's a bully. It's no fun being together anymore." The therapist worked on their communication as if Hilary and Clark were just another one of those *we can't communicate* couples. Things just got worse.

When Hilary came to me for individual therapy she was thoroughly miserable. She kept talking about some "barrier" between her and Clark. But I just couldn't quite grasp what that barrier was at first. Then I asked her, "What do you and Clark fight *about?*"

The more Hilary talked, the more two words came into focus: *suspicion* and *accusation*. Clark was always suspecting Hilary of something, always accusing her of something. He was always talking about *what Hilary was up to*. I began to smell paranoia. Clark, I thought, might be one of those thousands and thousands of people who do well at their jobs, but who have some nonpsychotic form of paranoid disorder. He wasn't actually hearing voices, but he was figuring out things on his own. And Clark's problem was causing problems for both Hilary and their relationship.

# Diagnostic #9:
# Is Your Partner a Problem Person?

The problems Hilary had with Clark and that Vivian had with Walter show just how hard it can be to believe that your partner is a problem person. A lot of psychiatric problems don't show up until after you've fallen in love with someone and had a couple of children together. A lot of psychiatric problems are extremely hard to diagnose. Lots of serious problems are easy to write off as "moodiness," or "sensitivity," or "being imaginative."

So how in the world can you tell if this love killer is stalking you? You're not a licensed clinician, so how can you diagnose whether your partner has some kind of psychiatric disorder?

I'll show you how. You just have to answer a few questions, but you've got to do this, because it's by screening for problem partners that you diagnose the presence of this love killer in your relationship.

## Problem Partner Screening Quiz

You're not going to use the following questions to make a clinical diagnosis. You'll just use them as a kind of screen for the *possibility* that some kind of psychopathology might be present. If so, your partner needs to be checked out by a professional to determine if in fact he or she *really* has a problem.

## DIAGNOSING LOVE KILLER #9

Answer each of these eleven questions with a simple *yes* or *no*:

1. Has your partner gotten so blue or moody or upset that both his patterns and his personality seem significantly downshifted, does he generally seem to be carrying around a gloomy cloud, or does he complain a lot about being discouraged and that things aren't worthwhile? Have these things been going on for more than a month? In other words, *is your partner glooming up his life?*

2. Are you afraid your partner is an alcoholic? Does it seem to you that he drinks too much, too often? Has his drinking been causing problems?

3. Does your partner act as though without her constant vigilance things are always threatening to spin out of control; does she always fight to have things done her way; does she always seem angry and frustrated with the people around her for having their own styles and needs? Does your partner's need for control consistently damage her relationships?

4. Does your partner have mood shifts that seem to coincide

with his taking or not taking any drugs, or does he seem to need drugs to maintain his mood?

5. Does your partner have "weird" beliefs that *either* affect her ability to function on the job *or* interfere with her relationships? (I'm not talking about unpopular opinions here but an obsession with beliefs that are not only unusual but clearly odd.)

6. We all make mistakes and have bad luck, but does your partner seem to have much more than his share of episodes where he fails or screws up or acts out or messes up?

7. Is your partner unusually fearful of things most people don't find scary, and do her fears have a significant impact on her ability to function? Are your partner's phobias hurting her life?

8. Is there some activity or pattern your partner seems out of control with, so that he either takes it to extremes or can't stop doing it even when it interferes with his life? Is your partner so compulsive or obsessive that he doesn't function well?

9. Does your partner get involved in activities that are clearly illegal? Do the things your partner does scare you?

10. Does your partner have a pattern of wide, deep mood swings seemingly unrelated to events that generally make people happy or unhappy, where she spends weeks, even months in a glum, depressed, low-energy state followed at some interval by a weirdly high-energy, scarily exuberant period in which she pushes all out to pursue some grandiose scheme? Is your partner on a scary rollercoaster of moods?

11. Comparing your partner to people you know personally of the same gender and of a similar age and background, do the things that bother you about him make him very different from these other people?

A *yes* answer to any of these eleven questions is a clear sign that your partner *may* have a diagnosable psychiatric condition that's responsible for the problems in your relationship.

But that doesn't mean he or she *does* have a diagnosable psychiatric condition. Pay particular attention to question eleven, and remember that when you're evaluating people you have to compare apples to apples, and that means comparing women to women, retired businessmen to retired businessmen, and so on. Let's never forget the lesson we can learn from Bill:

BILL: *"If this were the old days, I might've tried to get my wife locked up. The thing is I thought that with her PMS she was suffering from some kind of psychotic manic depression or something. Just think of my background, though. I had no sisters, my mother had a hysterectomy, and my parents would never have talked about this stuff anyway. I never had a relationship in college, then there was the army, then I fell in love with Marti. The point is that I'd been with a lot of women but I'd never really lived with a woman. Okay, so then here's Marti going through PMS, and she gets bitchy and weepy and goes off on me all the time, and it's like she's crazy, and it makes me crazy so when the whole thing's over and she's fine again I'm upset and frankly scared shitless. Two weeks later, when I finally stop being upset and I feel comfortable enough to get close to Marti, bang!, the PMS starts all over again. Now here's the part that kills me. We lived through this for seven years, and I'd pretty much written Marti and our whole marriage off, when I finally got around to talking about it to my brother and he blew my mind. He said, 'Sandy [his wife] is worse.' Well, I checked that out. I mean I was desperate. I even asked two women at the office that I've known for a long time and we can sort of say anything to each other. All that pain. And it all changed when I realized that Marti wasn't crazy."*

Bottom line—if you said *yes* to any of the eleven questions, comparing your partner to other people in the same category as your partner, then Love Killer #9 has the potential to destroy your relationship. It doesn't have to. There's plenty you can do to prevent it. But if you do nothing, you might as well kiss your relationship goodbye.

By the way, *you* don't get a free pass here. The diagnostic questions apply to you too. You have to answer them for yourself as well. And if you answer *yes* for yourself, then you too have to follow the prescription. Your relationship is just as much under threat if you're the problem person as it would be if your partner were. You can't say, "Well, it's me, I'll just keep it under control." Can you control arthritis or diabetes by sheer willpower alone? Of course not. It's the same with problem people, you included.

If this love killer is present, you have to take this prescription.

# Prescription #9:
# Putting the Problems Behind You

You can sum up this prescription easily. You have to deal with two different things. You have to deal with the impact the problem has on your relationship. And you have to deal with the person who has the problem.

Let's take these one at a time.

### *Facing the Problem*

What would you do if you're a woman and you found a lump in your breast? You'd go to the doctor to have it checked out, right? What would you do if you're a man and you found a lump on one of your testicles? Ditto.

You'd do that because we've come to understand that these kinds of lumps are one good way to screen for the possibility of cancer. In fact, most lumps aren't cancer. Most lumps aren't even a sign of something for which you need treatment. But the lump marks a line in the sand between *forget about it* and *get this checked out.*

That's exactly how the Problem Partner Screening Quiz works. A *yes* answer to any one question in it is like finding a lump in your body.

But if you don't handle it well, you could make things worse. Don't bully or threaten. Since making your partner feel small is Love Killer #2, as you now know, don't label your partner as sick or crazy.

Instead, tell your partner you're very worried about him and your future together. Ask him if he would, *for your sake*, go to a licensed mental health clinician to be evaluated. He'll probably say no at first, but persist. Tell him about the specific question you answered that made you think he has a problem. Tell him that unless the *behavior* that made you answer *yes* changes you're going to keep on insisting he be evaluated.

If he still refuses to see a therapist, make an appointment to see the therapist yourself. Say that you want help determining whether your partner has a real problem and then describe all the behavior and symptoms you're concerned about. Make sure that the therapist is willing to seriously consider the possibility that your partner has a problem.

**Good news.** I have a good feeling as I'm telling you this, and that's good news for you. Most diagnosable psychological problems can be treated successfully today. Painful destructive patterns that you thought would never change can clear up in weeks or months. But that's not the best news.

The best news is that if a problem person is killing your love, then your partner's problems are the main, perhaps the only, obstacle between what you have now and the relationship you used to have and can have again.

Think about Walter and Vivian. All their anger and tension was an offshoot of problems caused by Walter's depression. Just the way going for a walk on a beautiful day can be spoiled by a pebble in your shoe and everything can be wonderful again if you just take that pebble out, many relationships can be fine again once you take the problems out of the problem people.

And remember Hilary's problem with Clark? That story also had a happy ending. Clark had a diagnosable psychiatric problem, but he certainly wasn't out of touch with reality. Hilary got together with Clark's brother, a lawyer whom Clark trusted, and they confronted Clark with his problem. Their message was stark: If he wouldn't consult a psychiatrist he'd better consult a divorce lawyer. He chose the shrink, and his problem got better. And that means *their* problems got better. He still had the tendency to get suspicious, but Hilary could call him on it and he'd realize that it was just his paranoia talking.

What this means for you is that you don't have to waste time fixing things in your relationship that probably aren't broken. It's always helpful to do Essential Maintenance, but you have good reason to expect that when your partner's problems get better, things in your relationship will get better too.

### Dealing with the Problem Person

The goals for dealing with a problem person are surprisingly simple. One goal is to listen. The second goal is to prevent bad things from happening. The third goal is to help your partner feel better. And I'll let you in on a secret. Ninety percent of reaching these goals comes from nothing more than avoiding mistakes. And I'm going to show you exactly what to do so you will avoid these mistakes.

But let me make something perfectly clear. There's no substitute for professional help for a diagnosable disorder.

You've probably had the experience of starting a new job and having someone warn you about a colleague and tell you how to handle him so you don't get on his wrong side. Think of the suggestions that follow like that.

Here in alphabetical order are the eleven most common kinds

of problems that problem people bring into our relationships, and here's how to deal with them:

**1. Anger.** Everyone gets pissed off and blows off steam from time to time. We all know that when someone we love does this the best thing to do is listen and sympathize and avoid provoking an argument, unless you want your partner to get more pissed off. But sometimes the other person's anger seems so intense or irrational and unfairly directed at us that we feel attacked, which makes it hard for us to respond intelligently.

**What to say.** An angry person is going to be ranting and raving. So first you say, "*Stop for a minute!*" And you keep saying Stop for a minute! until she shuts up. Then say, "If all you want to do is blow off steam, let me know and I'll listen for as long as I can. But if you're saying things you want me to respond to, I'd like to listen and to respond but I just can't until you calm down a bit." By making her choose between letting off steam and communicating intelligently, you're putting her in a situation where if she wants to seem reasonable, she's got to come across as less angry.

Other good things to say, if you want to avoid making things worse, are "I hear how upset you are," "Whatever the problem is, we can solve it," "How can I help you with this?" or "What are you asking me for?"

**Troubleshooting.** First, people don't turn on a dime. Expect a delay between your saying the right thing and their anger subsiding. Second, recognize that sometimes people just want to dump on you. Take it if you want to, or if you can't take it, say you're willing to listen but not to be yelled at. Third, don't take it personally and don't get swept up in a big, angry scene by countering any accusations. Fourth, don't tell the other person not to be angry.

**2. Being upset.** It's not the same as being angry. Anger is more focused, more clearly labeled. Being upset is a more generalized state of anger, fear, grief, helplessness. Think of the person who's upset as being knocked for a loop, thrown for a loss.

**What to say.** "I know this is hard for you. Talk to me about what's bothering you." This acknowledges that something's gone wrong and opens the door for your partner to talk about it. Then ask specific, factual, easy-to-answer questions. These will focus the other person and calm him down. For example, I once got a call at one o'clock in the morning from a woman whose husband had just hit her. She was hysterical. I listened but I also asked questions like, "What room are you in? What time is it exactly? What are you wearing? Where is he now?" You get the idea. The more I listened and asked specific questions, the less upset she got and the more she could focus on what she needed to do to take care of herself, which is all any upset person needs.

**Troubleshooting.** Just as with anger, don't tell the other person not to be upset. If it goes on for too long, you can say, "It's hard for me to hear you being so upset." You can actually ask for a break, five minutes or an hour, that will make it easier for you to be there for your partner. The person who's upset is likely to accuse you of "not understanding" or of "being no help." Deal with the first accusation by saying, "Help me understand." Deal with the second by saying, "Tell me what to do."

Remember that when someone's upset, he's talking about his feelings. This is not the time to debate who did what or who said what or who should do what or who's going to do what. Focus on listening and understanding *while* your partner's upset, then make sure you make an appointment for *afterward* to talk about what you're going to do to make things better.

**3. Control freaks.** There are two kinds of control freaks. One is someone who insists that things be done a certain way. The other is someone who insists on doing everything himself. One is in your hair, the other pushes you away. Either way, what makes them so hard to deal with is their conviction that there's some objective standard of a "right way" to do things that they understand and you don't.

**What to say.** "Look, I may not do things your way, and I may not do things the best way, but there's nothing wrong with the way I do things. When you insist on telling me how to do this it makes me tense and angry, and it's going to ruin our relationship. Is trying to get me to do things your way worth ruining our relationship? I know you're a fair person: let's decide who's in charge of this, and then whoever is in charge will be in charge."

**Troubleshooting.** The problem for some control freaks is that it *is* worth ruining everything to try to have you do things their way. If you start feeling that your partner is out of control with being in control, you've got to take charge by making it clear that the alternatives are getting help or getting out.

**4. Depression.** It's easier to deal with depression if you understand it. Compare depression to mourning. They're similar in that they're both about feeling bad because you've lost something and don't know how to get it back. Maybe you lost your job, maybe you lost your dog, maybe you lost a reason to feel good about yourself, maybe you lost your sense of a future. Maybe the loss is big, maybe small. Maybe actual, maybe imagined. The key to dealing with depression is the same as dealing with loss: mourn and move on. When you have a partner who's experiencing depression you have to help him mourn and move on.

**What to say.** First help your partner express her sadness. Say, "If you'd like to talk about it, I'm willing to listen." If she doesn't want to talk about it encourage her, but don't say, "Talk about it because you'll feel better." Instead say, "I'd really like to hear what you have to say.'' Listen to your partner express her sense of loss without minimizing it or trying to make it better.

At some point help your partner move on by gently asking how long she thinks she'll need to be sad about this. Ask how you can help during this period. But at some point you must express your own feeling: "I need you to get out of this. I'm willing to help you do whatever's necessary to accept whatever it is you're depressed about, or to pick yourself up and find a new way to get it.''

**Troubleshooting.** Depression destroys relationships by going on for too long. Whether it's clinical depression or everyday blues, you have to set a deadline that you can live with. Ideally this deadline is based on how long your partner has said she'll need before she's ready to start moving on. But if your partner, for example, is depressed because she's "wasted her life," well, it's okay to mourn the ways we've wasted our lives but it's not okay to waste our lives mourning the ways we've wasted our lives.

So when it's time to "move on," every comment you make to your partner should be something like, "I know this is hard for you, but what are you planning to do next and how can I help? It's not acceptable for either of us to continue without doing anything about your depression."

**5. Fear.** The polite word for this is anxiety. The kind that really applies here is the kind that interferes with our lives. If your partner is afraid of snakes, that's no problem unless he's a herpetologist. But problems ranging from fear of flying to fear of leaving the house can be crippling. Another form this problem takes is when your partner becomes someone who constantly expresses fear about anything and everything that comes up in your lives.

**What to say.** Just the way depression is about loss, anxiety is about not being in control, and that can be incredibly stressful.

When your partner's afraid, you can reduce the fear by helping him feel more in control. Say something like, "Right now you're overwhelmed. Let's take this a piece at a time. What's one thing you're afraid of, and how can we deal with it?" For example, if your partner says he's afraid of flying, ask him to tell you about one particular part of it he's afraid of. Talk about ways to deal with that part of it. With fear, breaking things down into manageable bits is always helpful.

Another way you can help with feeling out of control is offer the kind of understanding that makes people feel more in control. This will depend on the specific fear. For example, "I got a book from the library about airplanes and what keeps them in the sky," or "This group you're going to be talking to—all they want is someone to tell them some things they don't know about [whatever the topic], and you know a lot about it." Remember: it's not reassurance that's helpful, but specific information that makes for a greater sense of control. And don't forget to ask: "What would help you feel less afraid?"

**Troubleshooting.** Your partner will talk to you about how painful and powerful the grip of fear is. Don't try to talk him out of his fear or dismiss it. Explain that a lot of people are afraid of things but they do them anyway. Fear only becomes a problem when people become incapacitated by it. If your partner complains about fear but isn't seriously incapacitated, offer to help. If his incapacitation is serious or grows, make sure he gets professional help.

**6. "I can't help it."** Problem people often do things that hurt themselves or others. When you point out what they're doing and say stop, they say, "But, I can't help it." Whether the problem is compulsive gambling or chronic lateness, overeating or underperforming, irritability or irresponsibility, they will constantly produce reasons why things have to be the way they are. Every time you come up with an idea, they'll say, "Yes, but . . ."

If you start feeling helpless, that's when you know they're winning.

**What to say.** "You may not want to help it or you may not know how to help it, but you can do something about it. Someone knows how to get you to stop, probably people just like you who've learned how to stop, and if you don't want to stop for your own sake, you'd better want to learn how to stop for the sake of our relationship." Then tell your partner where to go for help.

**Troubleshooting.** People with problem behaviors can be a real puzzlement. Some change quickly, some seem stuck and then change, and some keep seeming on the verge of making improvement but never change. The point is you can get trapped into waiting for a bus that never comes. The way out is to set specific goals and specific deadlines for meeting those goals. Your goals don't have to be about making improvement. They can be about getting help. But realistic goals and deadlines will prevent your problem person's "I can't help it behavior" from killing your relationship.

**7. Indecision.** It's not cute. It ruins lives. People who can't decide what to do with their money or their careers or who can't make the simplest decisions about the children or about how to fix something in the house can leave real misery behind them. By being afraid of making a mistake, they make nothing but mistakes.

**What to say.** "You don't have to decide everything. You just have to decide what to do *next* about this issue. There are some good options. We'll never know what's best, but here they are. Pick one and don't look back."

**Troubleshooting.** People suffering from indecision are always waiting for more information they'll never get. They're haunted by fear of making a mistake. By helping them decide their way through things one small step at a time—"You don't have to decide whether to get that knee operation, you just have to decide which doctor you're going to listen to"—their decisions are smaller, as are the mistakes they're risking.

**8. Neediness.** These are people who make it clear that because they have so little to give they can't do what other people can do, and so they need you to take care of them. They're always more tired than you are when they come home from work. They can't hear your problems because their own problems are so devastating. They can't do some chore because it's too hard, too stressful, too demanding with all they have on their plate. Their needs always trump your needs.

**What to say.** About 65 percent of the time, neediness is just a bad habit; 25 percent of the time it's a sign of a problem that needs medical attention; 10 percent of the time it's a sinister form of destructive manipulation and malingering by a person who's too sick to be helped by you.

What you say has to be driven by your need to know that your partner isn't in this evil 10 percent. "It's just not fair that you do so little, or that you can't do this thing. I can't believe you'd be so unfair as to avoid doing it. If you don't think I'm being fair, let's talk about it. But I want you to start doing your fair share." By putting the focus on fairness, you'll motivate the 90 percent of people who don't want you to suffer from their neediness, and you'll find out if your partner's in the 10 percent who just doesn't care if you suffer.

**Troubleshooting.** Helping someone who's been putting out neediness can sometimes feel like helping a reluctant child get off to school. The problem is that needy people make it so hard for you to change them that it's actually easier to just keep on meeting their needs. And that's why you have to make it clear that you're willing to keep fighting and putting out the extra effort to get them to stop being needy, so you can ultimately put out less effort.

For example, the partner who complains about being so tired after work that he can't do his fair share, will in the short run make you feel as if you have a choice between doing all the work and not fighting and doing all the work and maintaining a running battle. If you can't outlast this person, he will win. To outlast him, you have to take your own needs seriously, plus acknowledge your resentment over his neediness, which will ultimately destroy your relationship if the two of you don't balance things out.

**9. Not taking the problem seriously.** I've never seen anyone who didn't duck when he was caught in gunfire, so there's no such thing as a person who can't take problems seriously. There are some people who don't see how serious a problem is, and often this is the fault, partially, of their partners. You and I complain and yell, but then we forgive and we forget, and on an occasion or two we even reward our partners for their problem behaviors, so the message "You must take this seriously" doesn't quite get through.

**What to say.** First you have to decide what your partner would do if he took his problem seriously. Then you have to insist that he do this, make it clear why it's important that he deal with the problem, and let him know what you'll do if he doesn't deal with it. Then you have to repeat this without fail *every single day*. People take bullets seriously because bullets don't fool around. You have to make it overwhelmingly clear that you're not fooling around.

**Troubleshooting.** The trouble you have to watch out for is your tendency to get sick of struggling and pushing. But your persistence will be the active ingredient in making your partner take seriously the problems that threaten to destroy your relationship.

**10. Suicidal thoughts.** One of the worst things in the world that can happen to someone occurs when a partner kills himself. To prevent this, if your partner is thinking about ending it all, you've got to make it easy for her to tell you. And that means responding to what she says in a way that doesn't make her sorry she opened her mouth.

**What to say.** Your job is to try to assess the risk. It's surprisingly common for people to think of dying occasionally or even talk vaguely about it. On the other hand, people who talk about wanting to die or being better off dead *do* kill themselves more often than people who don't say these things. The people who talk about it *are* the people who do it.

So if you hear something that sounds like "suicide talk" say, "Are you having thoughts about killing yourself?" A *yes* answer means that *immediate professional intervention is necessary.* If your partner says *no*, ask, "Are you thinking you'd be better off dead?" If your partner says *yes*, ask how long this has been going on and ask if she's thought of doing something about it. If it's been going on for a long time or if she's thinking of acting on her suicidal thoughts, *immediate professional intervention is necessary.*

If the answer is still *no*, ask your partner to make you a solemn promise to tell you about any gloomy thoughts she might be having and make her promise to tell you if she ever thinks about actually killing herself.

**Troubleshooting.** Sometimes after we experience a personal disaster—a house burns down, we lose a job, a lot of money gets lost in a bad investment—we feel that life isn't worth living anymore. This is a normal grief response. People who feel this way in response to some real loss deserve to be listened to, not locked in a padded cell. Your job is to make sure your partner can express normal grief without *your* overlooking situations where someone you love is starting to take seriously her feeling that she wants to die.

You've got to perform an incredibly difficult balancing act.

You must make it easy for your partner to feel she can share gloomy thoughts with you without causing an uproar. But if what you're dealing with is not "gloomy thoughts" but a serious risk of suicide, *you must treat this as a life-or-death medical emergency.* That means taking your partner to the hospital emergency room. If she won't go, call an ambulance and tell the people that you're dealing with an actively suicidal person.

You can tell whether the risk is substantial if you can see that your partner has moved *from* talking vaguely about how "life isn't worth living" *to* showing you evidence of a serious and specific intent. Evidence like this might include buying a gun or saving up pills, formulating a plan, giving away her belongings, saying goodbye to the important people in her life. If your partner acts as if she's taking her own suicide seriously, you have to take it seriously.

**11. Weirdness.** Here's a rough-and-ready way to tell if someone's probably unbalanced. Trust your own instincts and give the other person a chance to persuade you of how nonweird his behavior is. If, after he's explained what's going on, you still think he's got a serious problem, then there's a good chance he does.

One man, for example, got fired and stayed in bed for a week. His wife, after three days, asked him if he was losing his mind. He said, "Look, I'm hurt and I'm tired and I'm going to stay in bed for a week and then I'm going to get up and look for a job." She figured, "Well, I guess if he really does that it's not so weird. I can wait a couple more days." Sure as shooting, the following Monday he got up, got dressed, and began looking for a job. You've got to do the same kind of thing this woman did: you've got to check out how much real weirdness is going on.

**What to say.** You need to ask questions to make sure your partner knows what he's doing and is taking care of business. Frankly, there are plenty of people who have really weird ideas but they manage their lives fine and interact perfectly normally, and I don't see anything wrong with that. That's what you have to find out. Ask questions like, "What does this mean for [whatever you're most concerned about]?" or "What are you planning to do about this?" or "What difference is this going to make in our lives?"

Outlandish promises or promises that don't get delivered are not good answers. Trust yourself. If your partner doesn't act as if he knows what he's doing, and he couldn't convince your father that he knows what he's doing, trust that your partner is as odd as he seems and needs help. Getting that help must be a top priority.

**Troubleshooting.** There's trouble when you come to the conclusion that your partner's weirdness is going to be a problem for you and your lives together, whether the weirdness is represented by a crazy investment scheme, a strange dependence on some guru, or the sudden desire to wear aluminum-foil hats.

There are two possibilities. In a surprising number of cases the person isn't aware of how weird he's being. That's why you can't pussyfoot around. You and everyone you know and trust have to drive home to him that his behavior is disturbing. In a surprising number of cases, when people are confronted with how weird they're behaving, they just cut it out.

But if that doesn't work, you go to the second possibility. You must consult a qualified mental health professional, and perhaps also a lawyer if financial or career issues are at stake. *You're* weird if you don't take serious measures to deal with your partner's weirdness. It won't go away by itself.

# Love Builder #9:
# Troubled Minds Can Come with True Hearts

Even a problem person with a troubled mind can have a true heart. If she loves you and cares about you, she can work hard to solve the problem that's threatening to kill your love.

What's very good news for us is that if part of us gets sick, the rest of us can stay healthy. If you get the flu, you might feel sick all over but only one part of you is sick. All your basic organs might still be in perfect shape. A little stressed and inconvenienced perhaps, but perfectly healthy.

This is important because it works the same way with our hearts and minds. Just because your partner has a psychological problem doesn't mean her love is false or crazy. It doesn't mean that other parts of her mental and emotional equipment are flawed. It doesn't mean she can't communicate effectively or let you into her heart or make a real commitment to you. It doesn't mean she wants to hurt you.

The part of the person who's making you miserable and hurting the relationship may be completely unconnected to the part of the person who cares about you and wants a good relationship.

No one loses when you face this love killer. It's true that in a small number of cases the problem wins. That's sad, and it means the relationship can't work, but everyone who's been down that difficult road says it's far, far better to accept an unviable relationship for what it is than to hang around and let the problem destroy you along with the relationship. But in most cases, the person's problem is solved more easily than you'd thought and you get the experience of how wonderful your relationship is when your partner's problem is no longer sabotaging it.

## *A Look Ahead*

Did you ever get sick and have to stay in bed only to discover that by the time the disease was cured you were too weak to get up? That's a situation where it's not the disease but the convalescence that's causing the trouble. Something similar happens in relationships. That's what we'll look at now.

# 11

# The Promise of a New Day

. . . . . . . . . . . . . . . . . . . . . . . . . . . . . . . . . . . . . . . . . . . . . . . . .

## LOVE KILLER #10:
### The Low-Expectations Trap

ISSUE:
How do you get back your energy for each other
and for your relationship?

You're almost completely out of the woods. But let's take stock for a moment. If you've gotten this far, you have a lot going for you. Just think of what it means that you're here.

Perhaps you've discovered that none of the preceding love killers are threatening your relationship. That means you've gotten a clean bill of health so far. It doesn't mean that everything is perfect, but it does mean that your relationship is basically healthy. There's nothing going on so far that has the potential to kill it. If you keep remembering to do what you've been doing, and if you particularly remember to keep up with Essential Love Maintenance, you can continue to have a healthy relationship.

But if you've been diagnosed with a particular relationship disease, I hope that you've already started taking the prescription that will cure it. If so, things are starting to get better for you, and your relationship is beginning to get back to full health.

It means, for example, that you're not putting each other down and making each other feel small. You're talking to each other like human beings again and feeling closer to each other. You've worked out your sense that you're just too different from each other. You've eliminated all the hurt from the past that might have been polluting your relationship. You're having sex again, or more sex and better sex. You've lost that choking sense that you just can't get your needs met. The hassles and pressures of real life aren't threatening your relationship anymore—instead you're finding a way to have a relationship in spite of all the other demands that are placed on you.

Bottom line: you're nicer to each other, closer, less angry. And that's important to accept. Making progress is good, but you also have to let the progress you've made sink in.

## You Can't Love If You Can't Give

People in relationships often reach the point where they stop having energy for each other. And that, all by itself, kills relationships. *How* not having energy for each other threatens love, and how to get your energy *back*, is the issue here.

Let me introduce a couple who fell into this situation.

### ○ Kevin and Rita

For Kevin and Rita, the honeymoon lasted until their first child was born. When they met (both were in their late twenties) Kevin had just taken over his family's small furniture-manufacturing business. Rita was a designer who'd submitted drawings for a new line of headboards and other bedroom furniture. From the beginning, Rita understood the degree to which Kevin was wrapped up in the business, but she was eager to be part of his life.

And then reality struck. With the new baby Rita suddenly

had nothing to give Kevin. She was not only busier than ever, but her whole emotional focus completely shifted from Kevin to their baby. And Kevin didn't help. He responded petulantly, acting selfish and spoiled. He behaved so unattractively that Rita withdrew even further. Always interested in sex, Kevin had an affair. Most women hit the ceiling when they discover that their husband has been having an affair. Rita was relieved.

As bad as things were, what Kevin and Rita didn't realize was that they were only one step away from relationship health. But what's really going on here?

## From Partial Mending to Complete Mending

You fall off a horse and break your leg. Your leg mends. But you're afraid to get back on the horse. In fact, from now on you stay away from horses.

The same thing happens when relationships get bruised. It can happen in a very small way. You have a fight with your partner and say terrible things to each other. Then you make up. You both say you're sorry. You both say something nice to each other. You both say you want things to be good again.

But the truth is that you were hurt, and that means you're still afraid and still angry. So to be on the safe side you distance yourselves from each other. You talk less. You give less. You're less intimate.

Let's get inside the minds and hearts of two people who've been going through a hard time and are suffering from a bruised relationship. Here are the steps they go through, inside themselves, as they experience the full impact of their problems:

**1. When you're hurt you make distance so you can feel safe.** John: "You're mean to me, critical, hostile, so I avoid you. I have to keep making distance until I'm so far away that there's nothing for you to criticize except my distance."

**2. When one of you makes distance, all the forces are in place for the other to make distance.** Jane: "Because you've moved so far away, I stop making good things happen. So you start thinking of ways to get your needs met elsewhere. And then you become even more remote and unavailable. So I see even less reason to make good things happen."

**3. When two people are distant they have no basis for connecting.** John: "The last time we tried to talk, we found we had nothing to say to each other. And that feels awful. Let's avoid talking to each other, because that way we won't have to experience having nothing to say to each other."

**4. When there's no basis for connecting, there's no energy for rebuilding.** Jane: "I don't give to you because you don't give to me. And vice versa." John: "Because you've destroyed my trust, I'll destroy yours." Jane: "Because you've hurt me, I'll hurt you." John: "Because you don't care, I won't care." Jane: "Because I feel you pull away from me, I feel depressed. Because I'm depressed, you'll pull away even more."

No one actually *says* things like this. But if you could hook up people in a bruised relationship to an EKG for love, this is the printout you'd get. A message of hurt, distance, negativity, and fear of getting hurt.

This pattern happens everywhere in our relationships. For example, it happens in sex. Here's how one person put it.

ZOE: *"Looking back, I'm not sure how great sex ever was between us—what do I have to compare it to? It always felt a little perfunctory. But we did it. And now we don't. We arrange our lives so that we can avoid making love. Because every time we make love we have to face the ways we're not talking to each other. We have to experience how hurt we are at the other's coldness and distance. When we make love it's like visiting a park you used to like to go to with your dog but the dog died, and now when you visit the park all you feel is what's missing."*

Like the person who fell off the horse, you feel vulnerable. It may be that many things are better between you. But just to be on the safe side, you decide to take care of yourself a little more. Don't expect so much, you say to yourself. You won't get hurt that way.

It feels 100 percent like taking care of yourself. But if you don't understand what's going on and don't see what to do about it, you could be at risk—one step away from a clean bill of health—of falling victim to the last love killer.

## Broken Promises, Broken Hearts

The whole time I was growing up, my stepfather had a friend who was always promising me wonderful things. Every six months or so he'd show up for dinner and in the course of the evening make a big deal about how he was going to take me to the circus or on a boat ride or to the theater or to somewhere that would be calculated to make my head spin with the anticipation of delight.

I think he was just trying to get on my mother's good side. But in any case, he never kept a single one of his promises. It wasn't long before I got the point. After a few years in which every promise was followed by disappointment, this guy completely lost the ability to fill me with anticipation. He'd promise some new adventure and I'd respond with "Whatever . . ."

I was an endlessly chatty, bouncy, happy, fearless, loving child, like most children. But I had no energy whatsoever for him. As far as our relationship was concerned, he'd thrown me into a situation where I expected nothing from him, and I was willing to give nothing to him.

I call this the *low-expectations trap*. It's a trap because:

- as you expect less, you put out less
- as you put out less, you get less
- as you get less, you expect less (which brings you full circle)

Of course this man didn't really matter in my life. But how do you think marriages end? The death of the marriage is a direct result of the way low expectations lead you to give up. How do you know if you're in danger?

# Diagnostic #10:
# Has Your Relationship Fallen Victim to the Low-Expectations Trap?

## DIAGNOSING LOVE KILLER #10

To diagnose the low-expectations trap, ask yourself which, if any, of the following ten questions more or less describes your situation:

1. "When I think of doing something with my partner we might enjoy, I quickly end up feeling, why bother?"

    This pretty much describes me ____
    This doesn't really describe me ____

2. "The pattern in our relationship is that whenever we're hurt or disappointed or annoyed, one of us pulls back, and there's been a lot of that recently."

    This pretty much describes me ____
    This doesn't really describe me ____

3. "We do very little together, and the little we do is mostly routine."

This pretty much describes me ____
This doesn't really describe me ____

4. "Because of the way my partner has been, I have no desire to reach out to him until he makes the first move."

This pretty much describes me ____
This doesn't really describe me ____

5. "I'm incredibly bored by our lives together."

This pretty much describes me ____
This doesn't really describe me ____

6. "Neither of us has much to give the relationship."

This pretty much describes me ____
This doesn't really describe me ____

7. "I've learned that I'm best off when I expect very little from this relationship."

This pretty much describes me ____
This doesn't really describe me ____

8. "I've given up hoping that I'm ever going to know what's really going on with my partner."

This pretty much describes me ____
This doesn't really describe me ____

9. "I think I'm completely invisible to my partner."

This pretty much describes me ____
This doesn't really describe me ____

10. "After all that's happened, it's hard for us to respect each other."

This pretty much describes me ____
This doesn't really describe me ____

If you said that *two or more* of these statements "pretty much describes me," then you've come down with a case of Love Killer #10, Low-Expectations Trap.

Don't worry. I've actually got good news for you. If you've gotten this far, hopefully the other love killers aren't a factor anymore. Love Killer #10 is really just part of convalescence. It could still prove fatal for your relationship. But curing this disease is just a matter of getting back on your feet.

Suppose you got sick, so sick that you were forced to stay in bed for a couple of weeks. Eventually the disease itself left your body. But then you were so weak that it was hard for you to get up, and the longer you put off getting up the weaker you got. There's only one way out. You've got to get up, you've got to get up, you've got to get up in the morning.

But where? And how?

That's where your custom-tailored prescription comes in.

# Prescription #10:
# Getting Out of the Low-Expectations Trap by Renewing Your Vows

When someone breaks his promises to you, you give up on that person. When two people break their promises to each other, they give up on each other. You can solve this problem by running this process backward. When people have given up on each other, find out what promises they've broken and give them ways to start keeping those promises again. That's how you eliminate this love killer: by renewing your vows.

And that's what we'll do now. You'll get out of the low-expectations trap by renewing the real vows you once made to each other and once proved you could keep. We've already talked about what those vows are, at the beginning of this book. That's when I told you about love's three promises:

1. the promise to be honest with each other

2. the promise to respect each other

3. the promise to maintain your passion

Actually there's more to it than this. Within each of these three promises are a whole series of smaller promises, just as if when I promise to help you move I'm really promising to show up when you need me, to put out some effort for you, to stay out of your way, to let you boss me around, to stay until the job is done. You keep the big promises in life or in love by keeping the smaller ones.

So let's look inside each of love's three promises a little more closely. There's both drama and hope inside these promises. The drama comes from the gap between what you felt you were promised and where you are now. The hope comes from a belief that whatever your love gave you once your love can give you again.

### Eliminating Love Killer #10

Here's how to eliminate this love killer. We'll go through all the promises. For each one, I'll ask you if you feel that you or your partner hasn't been fulfilling your expectations. Then I'll give you specific suggestions for how to give to each other what you've been withholding. That's all you need to eliminate this love killer. If you know *exactly* where you've fallen down, you'll know how to get back on your feet.

### The Promise of Honesty

Do you remember what you said about your partner when you were first in love? "I feel I can tell him anything." "We talk about things I've never talked about to anyone else before." "She says things to me I've never been able to listen to from anyone else, but when *she* says them it is somehow okay." "We talk for hours, about everything. I don't think there is anything we don't get into."

These are the kinds of things people talk about as they describe one of the most important parts of falling in love. Reaching a new level of honesty. Feeling hope for a future filled with more honesty than they'd ever thought possible.

You might think this is an unnecessary question, but why do we care so much about honesty? It's because honesty feels like a lifetime free pass to the Disney World of our desires and all the rides to boot.

Honesty seems to make everything possible. Check it out. Here are the things you've told me you've promised each other when you promised to be honest. And if you feel you haven't been delivering on these promises, here's what to do to get back on track.

**Safety.** Most people look back with anger and sadness at how many lies there were in their previous relationship. It just wasn't a safe place for honesty. You were afraid to tell the truth because you got into trouble every time you did. Your partner lied.

Or else his "honesty" was just a form of cruelty. Imagine being in a relationship where you never got physically naked or where sex was always painful. That's what it's like in those relationships we're glad we got out of: it wasn't safe to be honest. And *that's* why honesty is so important to us. Honesty makes us feel safe.

*Has lack of safety made you withdraw hope and energy from your relationship? If so, here's what you can do.*

You may very well have the occasional meeting about safety on the job. Well, have a meeting about safety in your relationship. Here's how you set it up. Say, "We should talk about what each of us needs to feel safe in this relationship."

Then before you meet you each make a list of three things you need to feel safer with each other. Take the time to think about exactly, precisely, and specifically what your partner could do to make you feel safer in the relationship. To get your juices flowing here are the top ten things people named at their own safety meetings that made them feel safer in a relationship:

## THE TOP TEN THINGS PEOPLE NEED IN ORDER TO FEEL SAFE

1. "Please don't ever criticize my body or anything about my body."

2. "If you need something in this relationship, tell me now or don't ever tell me about it because I never want to hear that there was something you needed that I didn't give you."

3. "If I tell you I feel insecure about something don't throw it up to me later as some weakness I've got."

4. "Don't ever get involved with anyone else, and when I say 'involved' I mean emotionally, physically, any way."

5. "Don't say you're going to do something and then not do it. I'd rather you say nothing than make a promise you didn't keep."

6. "If something goes wrong in your life, I don't ever want to hear that you blame me for it."

7. "If I ever ask you a question, answer me. I don't care if you say you don't know. I don't care if your answer isn't what I've been hoping for. As long as you don't evade answering."

8. "Don't ever call me stupid or anything degrading."

**9. "If you find yourself in trouble, I want to hear it from you and I want to hear it early on."**

**10. "Don't ever go along with something as if it were okay and then later tell me it wasn't okay. I never want to hear years later that you hated something that I thought you didn't mind."**

What *you* need to feel safe might be different, of course. Whatever you need, make a solemn promise to each other that however else you might screw up you just won't do these things—whatever they are in your case—that make you feel unsafe.

A lot of the things you'll be telling each other will be new information and that takes a while to digest. The very thing you asked your partner not to do so that you can feel safe might be exactly what he does the next day. It's important that you give each other a grace period that you use as an opportunity to say things like, "That's what I was talking about when I told you what makes me feel unsafe."

**Intimacy.** When we're honest we tell each other what we've done and how we feel. But it's not honest to tell only things that are just like what everyone else says or that you'd be proud to brag about. That's not honesty, that's a puff piece. And you don't feel close to people when all they share is the kind of thing they'd easily share in public.

But when you're honest in love you say things you wouldn't want to share with anyone else. And that's exactly what it means to be close to your lover. It means revealing things you wouldn't tell a buddy from work. And you feel close to your lover when he reveals those kinds of things to you. There's a level and depth of honesty that shouts how special you are to each other. For most of us intimacy is impossible without honesty. And *that's* why honesty is so important to us.

*Has lack of intimacy made you withdraw hope and energy from your relationship? If so, here's what you can do.*

The chapter on Love Killer #4, The Chain of Silence, was all about intimacy. Just follow the prescriptions in that chapter, even if you weren't diagnosed as having that particular love killer.

You can also ask your partner, "What's one thing we could do now that would make you feel we're closer?" Then do that thing. Then (and only then) ask your partner, "Would you like to hear one thing that would make me feel closer to you?" He'll say *yes*. Tell him what it is and ask him to do it. If he seems reluctant, say, "How can I make it easier for you to do it?"

**Openness.** Freedom and hiding are poles apart. Honesty in a relationship is what happens when you're open with each other. There's a sense of freedom and spaciousness. When you feel you can be open with your partner it's like the feeling of being in your own house and being able to do what you want, not being in your boss's or in-laws' house where you've got to monitor everything you do because you're surrounded by rules and the possibility of making mistakes.

With openness there's a tremendous relief from stress. But when you can't be honest, then you're in hiding. And hiding is a fearful thing. When you have to hide the truth, you feel small and disgusting. You're never free from worry. *That's* why honesty is so important to us.

*Has lack of openness made you withdraw hope and energy from your relationship? If so, here's what you can do.*

Did you know that you can get completely naked in the middle of a busy department store? You can. There's a room for it. It's called the changing room. You go to a special place to get naked.

That's how you have more openness in your relationship. You have a special place for it. It's not a physical place really. It's more a matter of hanging out a sign over what you're saying. Instead of just blurting out something like, "We never have fun anymore." You say, "May I be open with you? You don't have to do anything about it. I just need to feel I can say what's on my mind."

When your partner says *yes*, then you say, "We never have fun anymore." If he starts to argue with you or gets defensive, just say, "This isn't about our agreeing. It's not about our changing things. It's just about our being open. All you have to do is say, 'I hear you.'"

Bottom line: Use the word *openness* to create a space where you do things for the sake of being open. Here's a Special Love Tool you can use that will help you create more openness. I call it *talking like best friends*. Frankly, *why* this tool works is a mystery to me. Most of us feel we should be best friends with our partners. But whenever *not feeling open* appears as a problem, this tool seems to work like magic.

• **When to use it.** We constantly give out little verbal cues that openness is a problem. Things like, "I just don't want to talk about it," or "If you don't understand, I can't explain it to you." Whenever you feel the other is refusing to walk down the path of openness, try talking like best friends.

• **How to use it.** It couldn't be easier. Just *say*, "Let's pretend we're best friends." Then talk to your partner as if she actually were your best friend. Make sure your partner talks to you as if you actually were her best friend. If you're at all confused about this, remind yourselves of how best friends talk to each other: they listen, they agree, they sympathize, they take your side, they ask questions, they encourage. You "win" at this if your conversation at all resembles the way best friends talk with each other.

• **Making it work.** A problem that sometimes comes up is that you might talk to your best friend very differently from the way your partner does. Here's how you deal with this. When one of you is having trouble being open, the other acts like that person's best friend. So if your partner, for example, says something like,

"I just don't feel comfortable talking about it," you could say, "Well, let's pretend I'm [the name of your partner's best friend]."

**Honesty opens the door.** So you see why honesty is such a big deal. But it does far more than give you safety, intimacy, and openness. It also opens the door to the other promises: respect and passion. If you can't be honest, how can you demonstrate your respect? And if you're not honest, passion is just a charade.

### The Promise of Respect

Respect is a collection of things like fruit in a fruit basket. The things that make up respect are all different but related. To see what this family resemblance is, here are some things I was told by men and women who I know were *not* respected by their partners.

- "I felt invisible, like I was nothing."
- "The whole time I've been in this relationship I've had this crazy sense that all I have to do is tell him that I want something and then I feel sure I won't get it."
- "I tell her something and then it's always about how *she feels* about what I've said. She responds to me but she's not listening and her response is never about what I've said."
- "Oh my God, the constant criticism. The put-downs were bad enough but what felt worse was when he'd try to be 'patient' and try to 'teach' me the right way to do something. He wasn't just saying I was an idiot, he was demonstrating it."

*That's* what it's like when the promise of respect is broken.

*When there is a lot of respect, you don't hear people say,
"Boy do I feel respected." You hear people say,
"I feel loved."*

...........................................

Nothing creates the feeling of love faster or more strongly than respect. Let's lay out just what those ingredients are.

**Feeling seen.** The word *respect* comes from a Latin word meaning *to look again.* When you respect someone you don't just glance at her or overlook her or fail to notice her. Instead, you look at her and your attention is seized and then you look at her again. The opposite of *feeling respected* is *feeling invisible.*

Invisibility is a big problem in relationships. At the beginning we fall in love because we "catch each other's eye." But what happens later on is that the pressures of daily life make us self-absorbed. To see your partner means you'll have to pay attention, then stop and feel, and finally act. That's why we behave as though beggars were invisible. But to act as if we don't see is to send a message that "You're nothing."

*Has not feeling seen made you withdraw hope and energy from your relationship? If so, here's what you can do.*

The tragedy here is that we almost always *are* seen more than we *feel* seen. In other words, the problem here is with our tongues, not our eyes.

You can solve it very straightforwardly. Say to your partner, "I need to feel seen. How can we be close if I feel invisible? But it's no big deal. Just tell me how you think I feel about things. For example, how do you think I feel about my job?"

Then wait for your partner's answer. Don't jump all over it if it's wrong. Praise the answer for any shred of correctness it has. Then tell him what's more true for you. But don't let it be like a test in school. This is not an opportunity for you to say, "You don't see me." It's an opportunity for you to say, "Here's what I'd like you to see about me."

Then go through any other parts of your life where you'd like to feel more seen. "How do you think I feel about our sex life?" "How do you think I feel about growing older?" "How do you think I feel about your mother?"

Then do the same exercise in reverse. Make sure your partner has a chance to ask you how you think she feels about different parts of her life where she feels invisible.

A major word of caution here. You're an idiot if you go through this exercise in feeling seen and use it as an opportunity to drop the hammer on your partner, either by criticizing him or by opening up some huge can of worms. This is about getting to know each other better. It's not about complaining about each other. This is an opportunity to show there's much more to you than unmet needs.

**Feeling cared for.** One of the easiest ways to show that you disrespect someone is to see that he needs something and do nothing about it. Respect that's more than words actually demonstrates that your partner is important to you.

And that means *doing* something to meet the other person's needs. I don't mean respect in the sense of deferring to someone because he's a big shot. Instead, I mean the kind of respect a mother shows her baby. When someone matters to you, you say, "I not only see what you need, but because of how I feel about you, I care about meeting your need."

*Has not feeling cared for made you withdraw hope and energy from your relationship? If so, here's what you can do.*

I always think of this as the Domino's Pizza promise: we deliver. It has to do with the difference between words and deeds, between saying you care and showing you care. If this promise is unmet, you've fallen into the low-expectations trap because your partner has said he's going to do things he hasn't done.

And that's how you get out of it. Identify *one thing* your partner has said he was going to do for you that he hasn't been doing. Then say to him, "Honey, I've been feeling that you don't care about me because you said you were going to do . . . and you haven't done it. Our relationship desperately needs for you to do this. If you show you care about me by doing this, here's what I'll do . . ."

Do the same thing in reverse. Make sure your partner mentions one thing you said you were going to do that you haven't been doing.

There's no relationship in the world where there aren't a whole bunch of things both people said they were going to do that they forgot about doing. But Rome wasn't rebuilt in a day. You regain your sense of caring one renewed promise at a time.

**Feeling special.** I'm sure you've heard the expression "No man is a hero to his valet." How do you manage to feel someone's wonderful when you've seen her struggling to get into or out of her jeans? Another expression is "familiarity breeds contempt." But think about what a huge distance this is from the way you and your partner felt when you were making love's three promises to each other. I know that you told your friends stories about some way in which your future partner was special or wonderful. Unless your partner holds on to the sense that somewhere, somehow you are a big deal, if only to him, you will feel he's broken his promise to respect you.

*Has not feeling special made you withdraw hope and energy from your relationship? If so, here's what you can do.*

This problem has come up so often with so many couples that I've had plenty of opportunities to find the best way for dealing with it. It's actually very simple. As always, you acknowledge to each other that you've got a problem, in this case, not feeling special. Then you each list Ten Things You Could Do to Make Me Feel Special.

Obviously, you write down whatever would do the trick for you. But as I always say, be specific. Don't say, "Make something nice happen once in a while." Say instead, "Take me out for dinner once a week." Don't say, "Treat me special in bed."

Instead say, "When we make love spend more time kissing me and telling me that you love me."

Then exchange lists. Here's what you do with them. Use them to surprise each other. But add the following wrinkle. The first person every week, starting every Monday, who does something from the lists to make the other feel special gets something done for her that she really likes in return, like a foot massage while you're watching TV or breakfast in bed.

**When respect is the answer.** It's breathtaking, what we've just gone through. After all, not feeling respected is a *huge* issue in many relationships. It's amazing to realize that all the pain and stormy seas we go through over the issue of respect are about feeling seen, feeling cared for, feeling special. To feel respected by our partners, all we need is for them to show us that we're not invisible to them, that what they see when they look at us matters so much to them that they're willing to do something about it, and that what they see is worth taking notice of. And I've just shown you how to make this happen.

### The Promise of Passion

When I think of the promise of passion between two people who are in love, I have very specific images in mind and they have little to do with sex. I think about incidents from almost everyone's childhood when you're sitting around at loose ends and your best friend shows up out of nowhere with some idea for something to do, which makes you incredibly happy to be with your friend and do that thing. That's passion.

I remember when I was in high school, my best friend would phone and I'd be so excited about talking to her and about what we had to say to each other that I'd lock myself in the darkness of a closet so that no one would intrude. That's passion.

I remember as a little girl in the country one summer feeling so excited I couldn't sleep at the thought of my best friend coming over first thing the next morning to go blueberry picking with me. That's passion.

With real passion you're filled with the kind of longing that can't be mechanically satisfied. Passion is not like what you feel when you haven't had a bite to eat all day and you're starving for dinner and you'd be happy to eat the first thing that's put in front of you. Real passion is like the creative impulse you feel when someone you care about is coming to dinner and you're dying to prepare something special.

The promise of passion we make when we fall in love certainly has to do with desire and satisfaction. But it has just as much to do with fun and adventure and the pleasure of the other person's company.

When our relationship gets sick, passion is the first promise of love to get broken. If your passion was real once, it can be real again. The passion that was yours is not some mountain you have to climb again. It's still within reach. It's only buried under a pile of distractions and frustrations.

To appreciate how much territory passion covers, let's look at the kinds of things people say are signs that passion is still in their lives:

**Sex.** A man and woman I'd been working with were sitting in my office. She was complaining, like so many people, about lifelessness in their relationship. "Then there's sex. You don't want me. You just want *it*."

"No," he said, "I want *it* with *you*."

You could immediately see that his words mollified her. But she went on, "Okay. If that's how you really feel, that's fine, but why can't you do something to show me that your desire has something to do with me and not just it?"

This conversation shows something of the vital but problematic role that sex plays in passion. Sex is unmistakably an outward and visible sign of passion. But it's got to be personal. The love killers destroy that sense that sex is personal before they destroy the desire for sex itself.

*Has not feeling that sex is personal made you withdraw hope and energy from your relationship? If so, here's what you can do.*

There's a certain restaurant I go to frequently we'll call The Purple Parrot. They had a reputation for taking a special personal interest in their customers. But when I first started going there I didn't see it. They were always very nice to me, but it was the general kind of niceness you expect from a good restaurant even if it's your first visit.

Then at some point I must've passed some kind of threshold where they felt they "knew" me. Suddenly things were a little different. It's not just that they remembered my name. But they remembered dishes I liked and the way I liked certain dishes prepared. They'd offer to make things for me that weren't on the menu.

By their behavior they showed the difference between being nice and being personal. Being personal is about you as a unique individual. You show a personal interest by doing something that makes a gesture toward that individual's uniqueness.

That's how you overcome the feeling that sex is impersonal and so dig your way out of the low-expectations trap. There are things your partner likes in sex that make her feel special—that you *know* her.

If you don't know what these special things are, ask. Say something like, "I know I should know this already, but what do you especially like when we make love? What could I do when we make love so that you'd know I was making love to *you* and not just anybody?"

Listen to the answer. Make sure you do it. It also wouldn't hurt to follow the prescriptions in the Sexual Healing chapter.

**Affection.** Cold has to pass through warm before it gets to hot. We think of passion as hot, but warmth is the secret weapon of people who know how to stoke passion in their relationships: a man who takes his wife's hand at a moment not prescribed by habit, a woman who kisses her husband on the cheek when he wasn't expecting it. Little things like that.

But nothing is more damaged by the grit and pressure of everyday life than simple gestures of affection that cost almost nothing. How can something so easy to do disappear so fast? This mystery reveals something of the deadly power of real life. But it also reveals how close we are to the possibility of rebuilding love, once we remember how little affection costs.

*Has lack of affection made you withdraw hope and energy from your relationship? If so, here's what you can do.*

The thousands of people I've talked to tell me that affection boils down to three main things.

- saying something nice
- doing something nice
- being physical with your partner in a nice way

So if lack of affection is a problem, save yourself from Love Killer #10 by doing all these things.

*Saying something nice* is simple. It's 50 percent compliments. It's 50 percent expressions of love. You're beautiful. I love you. Any time you compliment or express love, you're saying something nice. Say anything that feels real and comes from your heart.

Here's how to tell if you're doing enough of this:

Never ever let a single encounter or conversation with your partner go by without saying something nice.

A constant diet of that vaguely negative neutrality that most couples fall into destroys passion. Always add something nice— a compliment or an expression of love—before you walk away or hang up the phone.

*Doing something nice* is a matter of little gestures. Things like picking up something for your partner on your way home from work. Doing some little chore without being asked. Not saying *no* when your partner suggests something you've said *no* to in the past. You can go to the bookstore and buy whole books full of nice little things to do for someone you love. But you're smart. I'm sure you already know what to do. Do it.

*Being physical with your partner in a nice way* is just an elaborate way of saying that you should touch your partner, kiss him in a place you don't usually kiss him (a lot of women rarely kiss their partners on the cheek or on the neck; a lot of men rarely kiss their partners on the arm or on the back), hug him, stroke him, engage in all kinds of nonsexual physical affection.

It's best if you acknowledge that you're trying to be more affectionate with each other. Have a contest. Say, "A week from today we'll get together and see if we can agree on who's been more affectionate. Whoever wins gets a special treat." It's impossible to lose this contest. And it's a wonderful way to break through the coldness and distance that's such a hallmark of the low-expectations trap.

**Interest.** "Hi honey. How was your day?" If a couple's been married for forty years, they have ten thousand opportunities to speak this line of dialogue. And each opportunity is a time to demonstrate passion. It might seem as though there's nothing more mundane than asking someone how his or her day went.

But the connection between showing interest and genuine passion goes back to the days when real love was born in your relationship. Remember? There had to have been moments when your partner was fascinated, even excited, by things you were telling him about yourself. To feel that someone was truly interested in you—that's passion of the most personal kind.

*Has lack of interest made you withdraw hope and energy from your relationship? If so, here's what you can do.*

This is where you want to end up. You want to get to the place where you *no longer* say, "We're just not interested in each other." To do this you've got to work both sides of the street. You have to *show more interest* and *be more interesting*. Let's take these one at a time.

*Showing more interest* is the easiest thing in the world. Just listen to any interviewer on television. All you do to show interest is

- listen
- ask questions
- ask follow-up questions
- join in with some comment of your own

Make sure you literally do all four things at least once a day when your partner's talking. It doesn't take any more time than showing no interest. Most people, believe it or not, feel they're interesting to their partners when they get this *interest response* just once a day. And they feel they've gotten the interest response when their partners do these four things.

I bet you were afraid that *being more interesting* was going to be hard. You're wrong. It's easy. You don't have to do anything. You just have to remember to *avoid* doing a few things. That's right. If you simply avoid doing the following things, people will think you're interesting. Even the person you've lived with for five or forty years will think you're more interesting.

So, to be more interesting here are the top ten things to avoid:

## THE TOP TEN EASY WAYS TO BE MORE INTERESTING

**1. Don't complain.** I admit that complaining is fascinating for the person doing it. But it's almost always uninteresting to the person hearing it. In any social gathering the people who seem most interesting are the ones who do the least complaining. Don't be confused by the way some very entertaining people can manage to turn complaining into a form of high amusement. If you're not a professional late-night talk-show guest, don't complain.

**2. Don't take a long time saying things.** Again we get confused because we think that fascinating people have a lot to say. But if there are two people and they have the same information to convey, the one who does it in the fewest words will seem more interesting.

**3. Don't have grievances your partner doesn't have.** We've all got grievances. "Those bastards . . ." "The way the others in the office . . ." "The ways those Liberals/Conservatives in the media . . ." "Everyone's getting rich but me . . ." "The way things used to be so much better . . ." If your partner shares your grievance, then it's interesting. If your partner does not, it's not interesting. That's the rule. I didn't make this rule. I'm just reporting it. (This rule—your partner won't be interested in your grievances if he doesn't share them—is hard for me person-ally. My husband doesn't have any grievances. So anything I find annoying makes me uninteresting to him. But for you this means the two of you have an opportunity to get closer. Shared griev-ances make for a greater sense of compatibility.)

**4. Don't talk about yourself.** I know—this one's really hard. Why, just the other day I found myself . . . whoops. You see the problem. It's hard not to talk about yourself. But let me suggest an alternative. Talk about your partner. Just remember *don't complain* and you'll seem fascinating. In any case, talk about anything but yourself as much as possible.

**5. Don't talk about the same things all the time.** I know we all get fascinated and obsessed and absorbed by certain topics—like the endless ways your boss has proven he's a jerk. Okay. Your boss is a jerk. You talked about that once. Just make sure that the *next thing you talk about* is not your boss. If you can just avoid repeating topics, you'll do fine with this.

**6. Don't talk about things your partner is not interested in.** Now this may be hard because you may not be interested in the things your partner is interested in. Fine. But all I can say is that you will seem a lot more interesting every time you talk about things that touch on your partner's interest. Even better, learn something about what your partner is interested in.

**7. Don't talk about things that aren't interesting.** I don't want to sound like an ad for *Time* magazine, but if you want to make yourself more interesting, know what people are talking about that's new, that's controversial, that has an impact on people's lives.

**8. Don't say the same old things.** You're driving home from work. There's some topic everyone's been talking about, the way everyone was talking about the O.J. trial. Try to say something that everyone hasn't already said a million times. Even if you only come up with something new one time out of ten, you'll seem that much more interesting. Say something surprising to the person you love. (Here's a way to get around #4: if you can think of something new to say about yourself, then go right ahead.)

**9. Don't forget to have things to look forward to.** New things are always interesting. The more new things in your life, the more you'll be interesting to each other.

**10. Don't forget to ask questions.** Any question that's a sincere attempt to get information or learn something new—and not an attempt to play gotcha—will make you seem more interesting.

I don't want to make this sound like too much of a hurdle. Let's not forget how real life can be a love killer—one way is that it makes it hard for us to have the energy to be interesting. But if you remember these don'ts and add them to your life bit by bit and make small changes, then you'll go far toward digging yourself out of the low-expectations trap.

**Aliveness.** "There was just no spark left." This phrase may accompany more breakups than any other. The couple still had sex. There were still occasional demonstrations of affection. Sometimes they missed each other. And often there were parts of each other's lives they found interesting.

But do you remember when you were a kid hanging out with your friends? Do you remember the sense that almost anything could happen, the way the slightest spark could set you off into some adventure? And wasn't there a sense of *possible fireworks* when you and your partner were first together?

The good news is that if your relationship is not dead, it's alive. Just the way a bad cold makes you feel like death warmed over, the love killers can make your relationship *feel* dead. But if it's not dead, eliminating the love killers will bring back the aliveness.

*Has lack of aliveness made you withdraw hope and energy from your relationship? If so, here's what you can do.*

Aliveness is the Moby Dick that turns us all into Ahabs. For many of us it's an all-consuming obsession. We'll pay any price to feel more alive. But I hope you won't be shocked when I tell you that feeling more alive with your partner is a lot simpler than looking for Moby Dick.

To feel more alive with your partner there are only two things that work:

- Do something youthful.
- Do something new or different.

Either way, you'll get that feeling of aliveness you're looking for.

*Doing something youthful*, though, usually means something specific. It means doing something *you* did when you were younger. It's really not so much a matter of age. Even people in their twenties can settle into being like an old married couple very easily.

But do you remember what it was like when you were first together? Even people who meet and fall in love in their fifties or sixties act youthful as part of the process of falling in love. You go dancing. You argue politics. You spontaneously stop the car and take a walk at a place where you see something beautiful or interesting. You buy a puppy.

So each of you write down your five happiest memories from when you were first together. Most of those memories will be of things you did that made you feel youthful then and will make you feel youthful now if you do them again.

*To feel alive you also need to do things that are new and different.* That's where you run into a problem the longer you've been with your partner. Let's illustrate with sex. Sex tends to get routine over time. But that's often because you've tried a lot of new things, thrown away everything you didn't like, and settled in with what works for you. And that's why "new and different" equates for many of us to "probably going to be a disaster."

Let me solve that problem for you. People don't feel alive because they're protected from disaster. They feel alive because they do things that are new or different *even though* those things sometimes turn out to be a disaster.

So don't take your eye off the prize: more aliveness. Agree with your partner that *you will do one thing that's new or different every week or every month, whichever feels best to both of you.* Then take turns coming up with the new or different thing. I know you're busy. I know you're under a lot of pressure at work. But doing something new or different doesn't have to be a gigantic innovation or a time-consuming project. It might involve nothing more than thinking up a different topic for the two of you to talk about when you're driving home from work. It might involve staying home on a Saturday night instead of going out. What's most important is the sense that you're more open to change than to wanting things not to change.

But don't forget to score yourself properly. You *win* points for doing something new and different. You lose *no* points if it turns out to be a disaster. All you lose if it doesn't work is the sense that this is something you want to keep on doing.

You can do something very small. You know how book discussion groups are very popular these days. Well, every once in a while my husband and I will get two copies of a book and talk about it while we're reading it at the same time. Each new book is something new and different for us. I'll tell you something. Simply adding something new to our lives made us feel more alive.

You see, it's easier to feel more alive than you'd thought. I'm sure you can find ways that are much less boring than what works for me. Based on what a lot of people reported, here are some of the best ideas for adding something to your lives together.

## THE TOP TEN FAVORITE NEW AND DIFFERENT THINGS TO DO

**1. Learn something new together—Chinese cooking, Spanish, ballroom dancing, anything you'll be able to do together.**

**2. Take up a new sport.**

**3. Read aloud new books or your favorite books to each other.**

**4. Develop an interest in something new that you can talk about, like the stock market or what's going on in the news.**

**5. Talk to each other about what you want to get out of life and make plans to help each other get it.**

**6. Every once in a while, talk to each other as if you were strangers. Ask questions about everything. Assume nothing. Learn about each other.**

**7. Next weekend go somewhere you've never gone before.**

**8. Join a new organization, such as a church, civic, or cultural group.**

**9. Tell each other a secret you've never revealed before.**

**10. Go to the animal shelter and bring home a new pet.**

**When passion is the answer.** I don't know if you realize it, but you and I have just performed a kind of miracle. Passion has always seemed so deep and mysterious. It's made many of us feel helpless about sensing that our passion has ebbed and not knowing what to do about it. But look at what we've just seen. Fulfilling the promise of passion, which is important if we're going to prevent our relationship from falling victim to the low-expectations trap, is something that's not out of our immediate control. You can do something about it. Now you know what other people have found actually works to keep the wellspring of passion flowing freely.

# Love Builder #10:
# The Sense of Fulfillment

You know, they've done a lot of psychological experiments in which they give people rewards. And people always report more satisfaction when they get a reward they were anticipating than when they win a prize that comes completely out of the blue. That's how the material in this chapter works to get you out of the low-expectations trap. You don't end the coldness and distance that's threatening you by pulling a rabbit out of a hat. You simply deliver on the promises you made when you were first together, most of which you've already proven you can deliver on.

Nothing is as satisfying as a promise fulfilled. Take these two people.

## ⟩ *Dorothy and John*

One of the happiest married couples I know took forty years to keep a promise they'd made to each other. Dorothy and John married when they were both in their late twenties. John had come out of the navy and had just passed his CPA exam and Dorothy was a nurse. Like most people of their generation they just wanted to love each other, have a family, lead a normal life. But they also had a dream. One day, they dreamed, probably when they retired, they'd get a boat big enough to live on and spend their days sailing up and down the eastern coast of the United States. Happy boat bums.

They promised each other they'd try to make that dream come true. John was a small-town accountant who never made big bucks. And what with bringing up three kids and putting them through college, not that much money rolled in and most of it rolled out again. But they kept working toward their dream, and by God some time after their fortieth anniversary they were able to sell their house and have enough money to buy and maintain a forty-foot cabin cruiser with all the comforts of home.

They took me out on their boat one beautiful Sunday afternoon for a cruise around Boston Harbor. John and Dorothy both talked about how much they liked their lives now, but what kept coming through was the enormous satisfaction that comes with saying you're going to do something and then doing it. They weren't just two retirees who found themselves on a boat. They were two retirees who'd promised themselves that boat and worked toward it and made their promise come true.

The satisfaction that gave them was palpable.

But you don't need a boat to accomplish this. Just unpack the honesty, respect, and passion you promised each other when you first fell in love and that you delivered on so many times throughout your relationship. Unpack these promises as the prescriptions in this chapter have shown you how, and not only will your love be healthy again but it will feel healthy.

# 12

# Our Love Is Here to Stay

· · · · · · · · · · · · · · · · · · · · · · · · · · · · · · · · · · · · · · · · · · · · · · · · · · · · · · · · · · · · · · · · ·

## Tying It All Together

I want to congratulate you for caring about love and believing in your relationship. For caring and believing so much that you're willing to do something about it.

We live in an age of disconnect, where the easiest thing to do and the thing that far too many people do far too readily, is to give up and move on when things get hard. And when it comes to relationships, I'm not just talking about giving up in the sense of walking out on your partner.

I'm talking about a far more prevalent, far more insidious form of disconnect. Where you give up *inside*. You hang around, but you stop participating. You become like the person who gets dragged along to a party and finds he doesn't really like any of the people there and wanders around the place until he finds an out-of-the-way room with a television in it. He's not really gone, but he's not really there either.

I want to congratulate you because that's not good enough for you.

You understand that your life, as it is right now, is as if God gave you one shot at one party between now and death, and if the party isn't all you'd like it to be, your only shot at happiness is to commit to the party and work at making it the best it can be.

. . . . . . . . . . . . . . . . . . . . . . . . . . . . . . . . . . . . . . . . . . . .

The reason you've joined me on this journey we've just made together is that you haven't known quite what to do with your commitment. That's all. You want love in your life. You know that a life of love with your partner is possible. You just haven't known why you've been having problems or how to solve them.

### *Zeroing In*

Your sense of commitment had led you to believe that working on your relationship was the answer, as if mere sweat equity would break down the barriers to love. But part of you knew there was something wrong with the idea of wasting your precious energy and commitment by dispersing it over the entire field of love.

You were smart enough to suspect that in love, as in medicine and as in many other areas of life, symptoms may be overwhelming but they can only be eliminated if you zero in on the precise single disease that's causing those symptoms. And now, as you know, you were right.

So where do you go from here? How do you take the love and commitment and intelligence that's brought you this far and combine it with the hard-won lessons this book has drawn from the lives of thousands of men and women? How do you do this and make sure you really do eliminate the love killers in your life and keep your relationship free of these killers from now on? Let me guide you on the journey that lies ahead.

## *Focus*

It's very common for someone to get to this point and be afraid that he's fallen victim to every single one of the love killers he's read about. It's called medical student's disease because so many medical students read a medical book and are afraid they have all the diseases in that book. My favorite example of this is the young man taking a course in gynecological oncology who worked himself up into believing he had breast cancer. Yes, male breast cancer is possible, but it's highly unusual.

If you believe that more than one love killer is threatening your relationship, here's what to do.

First, remember that the diagnostics are in the order they're in for a reason. It's the order determined by which love killer is most common, produces the widest array of symptoms, and is easiest to treat. That's why, for example, Letting Essential Maintenance Slide is Love Killer #1. Where else could I put it? Not only do more people fall victim to this love killer than any other, but in many cases the symptoms that lead you to think that you have *every* love killer disappear when you eliminate *this* love killer.

So one thing you can do if you're convinced you have a few love killers threatening you is *focus on eliminating the first one you were diagnosed with and forget the rest for now*. So if, for example, you believe you've fallen victim to Love Killers #2, #4, #5, #7, and #8, *just* do the prescriptions for Love Killer #2, because that's the first you were diagnosed with, and put the rest aside.

Here's what you may find, because this happens to a lot of people. By eliminating the first love killer you were diagnosed with, things change when you answer again the diagnostic questions for the other love killers. By eliminating one love killer you very likely will eliminate those things that would cause you to be diagnosed with other love killers.

So focus. Deal with one love killer at a time, in the order they appear in this book. But before you go on to eliminate the next one, answer the diagnostic questions again: it may be gone already.

## When You Feel Like You Have an Emergency

There are times in life when you just have to use your judgment. If more than one love killer seems to be threatening you, then you may feel that you're suffering more from one of them than the others. More than one may apply to you, but one feels like a bigger problem than the others. If that's the case, deal with the love killer that feels like the biggest or most immediate threat. Trust yourself. If, for example, you're powerfully struggling with some problem your partner has, go right to love killer #9, Problem Partners.

The key is focus. It's *very important* that you only deal with one love killer at a time. That way you get your biggest bang for the buck.

## Making Progress

Your commitment to love, and to excellence in love, deserves to be rewarded. That means you deserve to see how you're making progress. What's the point of identifying a problem if you can't reach a point where you can say you've solved the problem?

Here are the answers to common questions about making progress:

**"How do I know if I'm making progress?"** You can use the diagnostics to help you here. If you're following the prescription for eliminating a particular love killer, answer the diagnostic questions for that love killer once a month. Your answers each time you ask yourself the questions will show you how much progress you're making. If you keep following the prescription, at some point when you ask yourself the diagnostic questions, you'll find you've gotten a clean bill of health. Your answers to that set of questions will be evidence that the particular love killer no longer applies to you. You're cured.

**"How do I know if I'm making *enough* progress?"** You're making *enough* progress if you're making progress *period*. I'm not being flip. Love operates by its own set of rules. And in the world of love moving forward is all that matters. In my work with couples, moving forward, *at whatever pace*, is a sign that cure is just around the corner. If you're making progress at all, you're making progress fast enough. You've already got the commitment—just hang in there. One day, before you know it, you'll answer the diagnostic questions one more time and find the killer's been eliminated.

**"What do I do if I'm not making *any* progress?"** What? You're not making any progress? Why that's impossible!

Actually, it *is* very unlikely. Fortunately, it's easily explained. In cases I've seen where people fail to make progress eliminating a particular love killer, they'd also failed to see that *they were suffering from a love killer that came before it in the book.* They didn't make any progress eliminating toxic buildup, for example, because they'd failed to realize they were suffering from the impact of everyday living on love.

So if you feel that you're not making any progress at all, answer the diagnostic questions for the previous love killers and work at eliminating the first one that applies to you.

And what if you can't make any progress with love killer #1? The only people (and they're extremely rare) who couldn't make progress eliminating love killer #1 were people who'd already made the decision to leave the relationship.

## Couple's Self-Esteem

I know you love your partner. It's time for you to fall in love with your relationship again.

My husband had a very mild heart attack a few years ago. His cardiologist said something very wise after treatment began. He said, "The most important thing now is that you *don't* think of yourself as a heart patient." He made it clear that my husband had to take his medication, but beyond following the prescription, it was absolutely essential that he not think there was anything wrong with him.

The worst thing that could've happened would've been that he'd thought he was incapable of a normal life. There were people in the nineteenth century in his situation who just went to bed and stayed there for the rest of their lives. Charles Darwin and Elizabeth Barrett Browning were two famous examples.

Feeling badly about yourselves as a couple if you've been diagnosed with a love killer is the same kind of thing. It can go on to poison you by giving you and your partner a terrible case of couple's low self-esteem.

You know how an individual who feels really badly about herself stays home beating herself up instead of going out and making her life better? Well, in the same way, a couple who believe that they have more problems than they should will feel badly about themselves as a couple and will huddle on opposite sides of their "cave of misery." You can start feeling about yourselves in your relationship like that kid you knew in summer camp who thought he did nothing well and never pulled out of a hangdog and gloomy sense of himself.

Well, don't do it. You're too smart for that.


## Why You Should Decide to Feel Good About Yourselves

There are two special reasons why you should never fall into couple's low self-esteem, why your love really is too good to feel so bad, why you should believe that you have everything you need to be one of the great couples:

**1. Life is short.** Your intelligence and commitment to love are signs that you already appreciate this point. Let me just underline it. Rainy Sundays and boring meetings can seem to go on forever, but the older we get the more the years fly by. We don't have much time to start with, but the time we do have is running out fast.

So what are you going to do? Are you going to spend it feeling bad about where you are? Are you going to spend it complaining?

Or are you going to focus on eliminating the love killer that's threatening you?

**2. It's not your fault that your relationship got sick.** If you fell victim to a love killer don't think that there's sand in your foundations. I think of these love killers like this: lovers are like primitive people living in a village in the middle of a jungle. All around them are snakes and lions and other dangerous wild animals. And at the very heart of the village is a water supply that can easily become tainted. The villagers are not weak people. The villagers just live in what is essentially a bad neighborhood.

Everyone in love lives in a bad neighborhood. The culprits are the real-life forces that stress us out, make us forget Essential Love Maintenance, pollute our lives, and lead to all the other love killers. In 90 percent of the cases, when people fall victim to a love killer, it's because they've gotten so busy and so distracted and so harassed and so anxious from all their other responsibilities that their relationship fell victim to what was essentially a public health hazard.

Here's what it means that your relationship fell ill through no fault of your own. There's nothing essentially wrong with your relationship for you to feel bad about. You just have to follow the prescription for the particular love killer that you've been diagnosed with. Your relationship can be healthy again. And it can be one of the best. You deserve it.

# P. S.: Let Me Hear From You

. . . . . . . . . . . . . . . . . . . . . . . . . . . . . . . . . . . . . . . . . . . . . . . . . . . . . . . . . . . . . . . . . . . . . .

I need you. I write the books you ask me to write. And every solution I've come up with has been based on what you've told me actually works for real people in the midst of real life. So I need to know what you think about what I've written here, what you liked, what you didn't like, what you think could be better. Beyond that, I need to know what you're struggling with in your relationship and your life right now. I want to make sure that my next book, and all the ones after it, give you exactly what you need.

Most of all, I need, and we all need, to know what answers you've found to solve specific problems in your life. Whatever problems you may still be struggling with, there are other problems you've solved brilliantly and beautifully, and you've solved them on your own. Just think of how many other people could benefit from the solutions you've come up with.

You can e-mail me, and your words will get to me immediately. My e-mail address is mirakirsh@aol.com. So let me hear from you. I'll make sure others benefit from the valuable lessons it's cost you so much to learn.

# Index